Europe, America and the World Economy

Edited by
LOUKAS TSOUKALIS

Basil Blackwell
for the
College of Europe

© College of Europe, 1986

First published 1986 for the College of Europe by
Basil Blackwell Ltd
108 Cowley Road, Oxford OX4 1JF, UK

Basil Blackwell Inc.
432 Park Avenue South, Suite 1505,
New York, NY 10016, USA

87-1469

British Library Cataloguing in Publication Data

Europe, America and the world economy.
1. Europe—Foreign economic relations—
United States   2. United States—Foreign
economic relations—Europe
I. Tsoukalis, Loukas   II. College of Europe
337.4073   H1532.5
ISBN 0-631-14322-X

Library of Congress Cataloging-in-Publication Data
Main entry under title:

Europe, America, and the world economy.

Includes index.
1. United States—Foreign economic relations—
Europe—Addresses, essays, lectures.   2. Europe—
Foreign economic relations—United States—Addresses,
essays, lectures.   3. International economic
relations—Addresses, essays, lectures.
I. Tsoukalis, Loukas.   II. Collège d'Europe (Bruges,
Belgium)
HF1456.5.E8E88   1986   337.4073   85-15104
ISBN 0-631-14322-X

Typeset by DMB (Typesetting).
Printed in Great Britain by
The Bath Press, Avon.

Contents

Contributors

Michel Aglietta Professor of Economics, University of Paris X – Nanterre; Scientific Counsellor, Centre d'Etudes Prospectives et d'Informations Internationales (CEPII).

Frank Benyon Member of the Legal Service of the Commission of the European Communities.

Gary Bertsch Professor, University of Georgia; Fulbright Professor, University of Lancaster (1984–5).

Stanley Black Professor of Economics, University of North Carolina.

Miriam Camps Writer; formerly Senior Fellow, Council on Foreign Relations, New York.

Benjamin Cohen Professor, Fletcher School of Law and Diplomacy, Tufts University; Senior Visiting Fellow, Council on Foreign Relations, New York.

Robert Crandall Senior Fellow, The Brookings Institution, Washington, DC.

Paul De Grauwe Professor of Economics, Centre for Economic Studies, Catholic University of Leuven; Professor, College of Europe.

Paul Demaret Professor of Law, University of Liège; Director of Legal Studies, College of Europe.

Wolfgang Hager Professorial Fellow, European University Institute, Florence; Professor, College of Europe.

William Hogan Professor of Economics and Director, Industrial Economics Research Institute, Fordham University.

Henk Jager Professor of International Economics, University of Amsterdam.

D. Gale Johnson Professor of Economics, University of Chicago.

Tim Josling Professor, Food Research Institute, Stanford University.

Paul Luyten Deputy Director-General, Directorate-General for External Relations, Commission of the European Communities.

Ronald McKinnon Professor of Economics, Stanford University.

Patrick Messerlin Professor of Economics, Fondation Nationale des Sciences Politiques (Service d'Etude de l'Activité Economique), Paris; University of Lille.

Tommaso Padoa-Schioppa   Director-General, Bank of Italy, Rome.

Jacques Pelkmans   Professor of Economics, European Institute of Public Administration, Maastricht.

Michel Petit   Professor, Ecole Nationale Supérieure des Sciences Agronomiques Appliquées, Dijon; Professor, College of Europe.

John Pinder   Senior Fellow, Policy Studies Institute, London; Professor, College of Europe.

Douglas Rosenthal   Partner, Sutherland, Asbill & Brennan, Washington DC; former Chief of the Foreign Commerce Section, Antitrust Division, US Department of Justice.

Pascal Salin   Professor of Economics, University of Paris – Dauphine.

Jean-Claude Scholsem   Professor of Law, University of Liège.

Jonathan Story   Associate Professor, INSEAD, Fontainebleau.

Susan Strange   Professor of International Relations, London School of Economics and Political Science.

Niels Thygesen   Professor of Economics, University of Copenhagen; Senior Research Fellow, Centre for European Policy Studies, Brussels.

Loukas Tsoukalis   University Lecturer and Fellow of St Antony's College, Oxford; Director of Economic Studies, College of Europe.

Roland Vaubel   Professor of Economics, University of Mannheim.

Frank Wolter   Counsellor, Economic Research and Analysis Unit, GATT Secretariat, Geneva.

Preface

This volume arose out of a conference organized and held at the College of Europe in Bruges in September 1984. Its chapters are revised versions of the papers presented at the conference, and the short comments following each chapter are written by those who acted as discussants for the papers.

The book focuses on some of the most important economic issues which have arisen in the context of Euro-American relations in recent years. Its main purpose is to identify the nature and causes of conflict in different spheres of economic activity and to assess the conditions upon which improved relations between the United States and Western Europe may rest. On the other hand, it is inevitable, and indeed highly desirable, that any discussion of Euro-American relations is placed in a multilateral context and examined against the background of an increasingly integrated world economy. In view of the relative weight and the role played by both sides, the prospects for international economic co-operation, as well as the prospects for a return to high growth rates for the world economy as a whole, very much depend on the convergence of interests and policies on the two sides of the Atlantic.

There is, however, an additional reason for focusing on the bilateral relation, which goes beyond economics. Membership of the Atlantic Alliance remains the pivotal axis around which the foreign policies of Western European and American governments turn. In the real world, economics and politics interact closely with each other, despite the continuous efforts of many academics to draw artificial lines between them. In fact, what can be more political than the issuing of money or the setting of conditions under which international trade takes place? Clearly, a deterioration of economic relations between the United States and Western Europe would necessarily filter through to the political level, and vice versa.

When I was invited by the Rector of the College of Europe early in 1984 to propose a theme for the annual conference organized by the College, the subject of Euro-American economic relations was for me an obvious choice. Having just come back to Europe from a six-month

stay in Washington, DC, where, in my diplomatic capacity, I had tried
to contribute in the context of my country's presidency of the Community towards better-coordinated EC policies *vis-à-vis* the United
States, I was only too aware of the complexity and the importance of
the issues at stake. All the subjects dealt with in this volume figured
prominently on the agenda of our regular meetings in Washington,
which I had been asked to chair. I can now say that had I carried with
me on my arrival in Washington the knowledge which I acquired by
preparing the Bruges conference and this volume, I would have surely
done a better job. I hope that this book may contribute to a better
understanding of the main issues covered by policy-makers on both
sides of the Atlantic as well as by students of international relations and
international economics.

In the introduction, Loukas Tsoukalis traces some common threads
between different economic issues in Euro-American relations. Robert
Crandall and Tim Josling examine steel and agriculture as representative problem-sectors, while Jacques Pelkmans discusses some wider
trade issues in the context of a possible reform of GATT. Paul Demaret
deals with the extraterritorial dimension of national or Community
laws and policies, especially in the areas of antitrust, taxation and the
transfer of technology. This is a subject which straddles the areas of
law, politics and economics. Niels Thygesen examines the experience
with floating exchange rates and their effect on the autonomy of national
monetary policies, while Ronald McKinnon puts forward his proposal
for international monetary coordination. In the last chapter, Susan
Strange discusses the links between politics, trade and money. Each
chapter is followed by a short critical-comment section written by
leading experts from both sides of the Atlantic.

As editor of this volume and organizer of the Bruges conference, I
should like to thank the Commission of the European Communities,
the German Marshall Fund of the United States and the US Mission to
the European Communities for their contributions, financial and
otherwise, towards the organization of the conference. Special thanks
are due to the Rector of the College of Europe, Professor Jerzy Lukas-
zewski, for his constant support and advice. I am also greatly indebted
to members of the teaching and administrative staff of the College of
Europe for their invaluable help at the various stages of the preparation
of this volume. I can only mention a few names: Rosemie Arnout,
Maria Brindlmayer, Nicole Claeys and Jimmy Jamar. The contribution
of Robert Strauss to the organization of the Bruges conference deserves
to be singled out. I am also grateful to Heather Weeks for her excellent
work in editing the book. Last but not least, thanks are due to all the
contributors and the participants at the Bruges conference for having
made this book possible.

Loukas Tsoukalis

1

Euro-American Relations and Global Economic Interdependence

LOUKAS TSOUKALIS

The early part of this decade has been anything but uneventful in terms of world economic developments. A very deep economic recession, which raised the rate of unemployment in many Western industrialized countries to double-digit figures, was followed by a recovery which, at least in its first phase, remained remarkably lopsided. This lopsidedness was accompanied, probably unavoidably, in view of the short memories and the narrow time-horizons that characterize many economic and financial observers, by much talk about the inherent strength and vitality of the US economy, which was usually contrasted with the rigidities and the lack of dynamism of its European counterparts. A new term was even invented to describe the economic disease from which Western European economies were apparently suffering – 'Euro-sclerosis'. Gone clearly were the days (not so far back) when everybody was pointing to the gradual shift in the economic balance of power between the two sides of the Atlantic in favour of Europe.

These were also the years which saw interest rates reach record heights in both nominal and real terms, and which saw the exchange rates of major currencies fluctuate wildly and usually in little relation to the good old 'economic fundamentals'. The early 1980s also saw a major international debt crisis, which shook the very foundations of the world financial system.

Euro-American economic relations have been characterized during this period by serious disagreements, which sometimes turned into open conflict. Although conflict may be inevitable where economic interaction is very close, it is probably fair to say that there has been a clear deterioration in bilateral economic relations which seems to have gone hand in hand with a marked decline in international economic co-operation. The term 'uncoupling' quickly passed from the military into the economic vocabulary, and threats of trade wars and retaliatory action have been all too frequently used by both sides.

There is a general question which immediately arises, namely, whether the economic developments of recent years should be considered as exogenously determined, or whether instead much of the responsibility lies with policy decisions taken at the national level or even with those which have failed to be taken at the international level. In this respect, the role played by the United States and Western Europe would be absolutely decisive, given their preponderant position in the world economy. A second question, which partly overlaps with the first, is whether the intensified strain in bilateral relations and the general decline in international economic co-operation should be explained mainly in terms of the particular economic and political conjuncture, or whether they should be seen rather as a reflection of underlying long-term trends in the international economic system. Is it a conflict of short-term interests or the result of fundamental differences in the perceptions and the policies pursued on the two sides of the Atlantic? Tentative answers to these questions would contribute to a better assessment of the prospects for the world economy and also identify the conditions upon which improved bilateral or even multilateral relations may rest.

PROTECTIONISM, ADJUSTMENT AND MACROECONOMICS

The 1980s have witnessed the spread of trade protectionist measures, which are usually of the non-tariff kind and taken outside the legal framework of the General Agreement on Tariffs and Trade (GATT). Although the alarm expressed in many quarters, and especially by the trade specialists in Geneva, is not much substantiated by figures for the past few years referring to world trade as a whole, there is clearly cause for concern, especially given the mounting pressures for further protection in various countries and most notably the United States.

Friction in bilateral trade relations between the United States and the European Community has been concentrated in a few sectors, and especially in agriculture and steel. Although trade friction has sometimes reached dangerous levels, the action that has followed it has been, until now, relatively limited. This is particularly true when compared with the trade measures taken by both sides against third parties such as Japan and some of the newly industrializing countries.

Agriculture is an old problem, which dates back to the setting up of the Common Agricultural Policy (CAP) by the six original members of the EC. As Europe gradually moved beyond the original objective of a high degree of self-sufficiency in food to become, in recent years, an important exporter of various agricultural products, including cereals, the emphasis on the American side has shifted somewhat away from the question of access to European markets to that of subsidized EC exports to third markets. The growing dependence of American farmers on exports, coupled with what was seen as increasingly offensive behaviour on the part of the Europeans and tight world markets, brought about another, and more dangerous, phase of the 'ploughshares war between Europe and America', as one observer has so colourfully described it.[1]

The macroeconomic environment has exacerbated the sectoral problems. High interest rates and the persistent overvaluation of the dollar have added much to the plight of American farmers, and thus have also contributed to the need perceived by the Reagan Administration to try to deliver something tangible on the international front. It is rather ironic that the US Administration should have succeeded through its domestic economic policies and their effect on the exchange rate of the dollar in giving a longer lease of life to the CAP in its present form.

The agricultural sector has a long history of government intervention, which is not likely to vanish overnight, despite the efforts of the Reagan Administration. Given this political reality, the problem is not whether or how to achieve free trade in agriculture; it is instead how to reconcile the high degree of trade interdependence already reached in the sector with domestic policies which have an effect on other countries and which are usually considered as unnegotiable by the governments concerned.

A considerable difference appears to exist in terms of the approach adopted by the Americans and the Europeans with respect to the agricultural sector, although this difference is probably exaggerated by the rhetoric used by the two sides. The former talk about 'free and fair trade' and draw a distinction between export subsidies and other forms of government intervention in the domestic market. The latter refer to social and political considerations behind their agricultural policy, use terms such as economic security and self-sufficiency, and declare themselves ready to participate in a joint management of agricultural trade.

On the other hand, international rules are inadequate and vague. Agriculture has always been on the margin of GATT, mainly at the insistence of the Americans back in the 1950s. Domestic policies are prohibited territory. According to the code negotiated in the Tokyo Round, export subsidies should not be used as a means of obtaining

'more than an equitable share of world export trade.' But what constitutes an 'equitable share', a multi-million ECU question which
various GATT panels have found so difficult to answer?

In view of the situation which has prevailed in agricultural markets
in recent years, the political power of agricultural lobbies on both sides
of the Atlantic and the inadequacy of international rules, the contain-
ment of the conflict may be a tribute to the restraint shown by the
governments concerned. The realization that a war of export subsidies
would be a dangerous, costly and self-defeating exercise for both sides,
and fears about the escalation of the conflict into other sectors have undoubtedly had an important moderating influence.

Steel is a relatively more recent problem in Euro-American relations.
However, the bilateral conflict is only one aspect of a more general
problem. Since 1974, the steel sector has suffered from a sharp fall in
demand on both sides of the Atlantic, which was partly due to the
recession, following the first and then the second oil shock, and partly
due to a long-term downward trend in the steel content of total output
in Western industrialized countries. The problems of domestic steel
producers have been compounded by the rapidly changing pattern of
world production and trade in steel away from Western Europe and
North America, and towards Japan, Eastern Europe and, more recently,
some of the newly industrializing countries in South-East Asia and
Latin America. The result has been a large amount of surplus capacity,
and hence the need for adjustment: The competitiveness of US steel
producers, already very poor, has deteriorated further as a result of the
large overvaluation of the dollar.

Adjustment is always painful for those directly involved, and therefore resistance to it is usually quite strong, especially in pluralist demo-
cracies with strong trade unions and job-security legislation. Moreover,
in view of the capital-intensive nature of the steel industry, adjustment
to structural changes in demand is bound to be a long-term process.

On both sides of the Atlantic, governments have tried to influence
the process of adjustment. But the methods used have been quite different. In Europe, direct government intervention, including nationalization of firms running big financial losses, increased considerably, as
did the amount of money spent on loans for investment and restructuring, various forms of subsidies, and compensation and retraining of
redundant workers. Steel has become a test-case of EC collective
management of industrial adjustment, which is indeed a novel experiment in co-operation among sovereign countries. On the other hand,
government intervention in the United States has taken almost exclusively the form of import controls affecting the exports of EC countries
(which are themselves also guilty of similar practices) and other producers. The result has been a barrage of mutual accusations of 'Ameri-

can protectionism' and 'European unfair trading', and a continuous danger of further escalation of the conflict. The vagueness of GATT rules regarding the use of domestic subsidies and the right of importing countries to countervail has helped to perpetuate the feeling of self-righteousness on both sides.

Steel is not unique, nor is the difference in the approach adopted by governments so untypical. In the last ten years or so, there has been an increasing number of sectors where the combination of a prolonged economic recession, the internationalization of trade and production, and the continuous shifts in comparative advantage have brought about the need for large-scale and rapid adjustment. Governments have intervened in the process, as a result of social and political pressures, and often also for legitimate economic reasons. The instruments used have varied from country to country, depending on history, institutions, ideology and the social and political balance of power. GATT has been unable to cope with developments, and the result has been a proliferation of bilateral deals between countries and the *de facto* withdrawal of whole sectors. One prominent example is cars, but there are also many others.

In more general terms, we have been witnessing the strains arising from high and constantly growing trade interdependence (and, even more, the internationalization of production in many sectors) among mixed economies, where both the mix and the social and political priorities differ considerably. The problem has been compounded by periods of stagnating world demand and misalignment of the major currencies. An important source of strain can be found in the contradiction between the growing openness of national economies and the major role and responsibilities of governments in the economic sphere. More recently, the rediscovery of 'the magic of the market-place', with the 'Reagan-effect' also spreading gradually all over Western Europe, has brought about a partial reversal of a trend of growing government intervention in the economy which had continued for many years. Nevertheless, the proclamation of the death of the mixed economy appears to be rather premature, especially in Western Europe, where the roots are very deep indeed.

Preliminary talks have been taking place to prepare the ground for a new round of international trade negotiations. In conformity with tradition, the initiative has come from the United States, where the Reagan Administration has been trying to fend off mounting pressures for the introduction of new protectionist measures. Thus, the 'bicycle theory' has been resurrected yet again. The emphasis is on the liberalization of trade in agriculture, services and high technology. All three sectors have one important characteristic in common, namely, that the protection of national producers is mainly the result of complex domestic policies and not of specific measures applied at the border. This makes protection less transparent and much more difficult to negotiate in an international forum. There are also important characteristics specific to each sector, which are likely to make the process of liberalization both slow and arduous. There is the political importance of agricultural lobbies, the complexity and often highly discretionary nature of government intervention in the services sector, and the issues of security and national sovereignty in the area of high technology.

The Europeans have been approaching this new GATT round with much hesitation. They are clearly not enamoured with the agenda proposed by the Americans, but at the same time they are unable to come up with any serious initiatives themselves. The hesitation shown by the Europeans goes much beyond the question of liberalization in individual sectors. It is partly a reflection of different domestic priorities, the strength of the mixed economy and the more political approach adopted by the Europeans with respect to international trade. It has been argued that 'through the continuous effort to balance the economic, political and social costs associated with industrial adjustment . . . European governments have developed a sensitivity to the political aspects of any trade dispute and a suspicion of finite legal solutions';[2] and strict international rules, one might add. This contrasts with the legalistic approach adopted by the United States, itself a reflection of the American system. This difference in approach is important, although neither side has been very consistent when it comes to specific cases. European reservations about a new trade round are, however, also a reflection of a fundamental lack of confidence in the competitiveness and capacity for adjustment of European economies, which is in turn a product of the experience of recent years. Although the symptoms and the gravity of the disease have been grossly exaggerated, Euro-sclerosis has been clearly present in the minds of policymakers.

Trade friction in Euro-American relations and the apparent weakening of the liberal international trading order goes beyond short-term problems in a few individual sectors; nor can it be explained entirely in terms of an adverse macroeconomic environment. The roots of the problems encountered in recent years go much deeper. They are related to increasingly international economic processes, the persistence of national political realities and the distribution of the costs of adjustment. The problems will not disappear by treating all forms of government intervention as non-tariff barriers that ultimately have to be eliminated. Such an approach would not lead very far. However, an effective management of trade interdependence would require that national policies be brought under increasingly close international scrutiny. It would require a strong international trade policy organization, partly along the lines of the stillborn International Trade Organization (ITO) of the 1940s, more precise international rules, and effective dispute-settlement procedures. It would also require continuous consultations and negotiations among member countries. But there seems to be little prospect of a movement in this direction in the foreseeable future. We have not yet acquired a sufficiently high degree of political awareness of the issues involved, not to mention the political will to tackle them effectively.

BENIGN NEGLECT AND ASYMMETRIES IN THE INTERNATIONAL MONETARY SYSTEM

Irrespective of whether a formal link is established between a new GATT round and monetary reform, a political issue which certainly has elements of *déjà vu* in it, any discussion of trade issues cannot ignore the monetary framework or the general macroeconomic environment. In fact, it can be argued that in recent years by far the most serious threat to the liberal trading system has come from the persistent overvaluation of the dollar, coupled with high interest rates and the adjustment programmes imposed on many heavily-indebted developing countries.

International monetary relations in the 1970s were marked by the abandonment of fixed exchange rates and the partial privatization of the creation of international liquidity through the important role played by commercial banks in balance of payments financing. Both developments represented a clear shift to the market and, to a large extent, a negation of the post-war idea of a collectively managed monetary system with tight official control over financial markets. This was partly an inevitable outcome of the increasing complexity of international monetary relations and the growing liberalization of trade and capital movements. But it was also the result of the inability of the major countries to agree among themselves about new forms of collective management, which would take those changes into account. In fact, many countries saw important advantages in the new 'system', mainly in the form of increased national monetary autonomy. The partial dismantling of the Bretton Woods edifice also reflected the collapse of the post-war ideological consensus, based on the Keynesian paradigm. The new 'system', as it gradually emerged, partly by design and partly by default, was as much a reflection of economic reality as it was of a new international political environment characterized by a wide divergence of perceived interests and policies as well as growing nationalism. The new economic orthodoxy, under the general label of monetarism, provided an intellectual justification for the main changes in the system.

The experience with floating exchange rates to date falls far short of expectations. First of all, floating rates have been highly volatile, and 'overshooting' has been a regular phenomenon. In addition, the period of floating has been characterized by serious and persistent misalignment between the major currencies. If there may be some doubts about the negative effects of short-term volatility, the consequences of persistent misalignment of exchange rates should be less controversial, although even more difficult to quantify. Such misalignment is associated with additional adjustment costs in the tradable-goods sector and should also lead to a reduction of productive investment in this sector, as well as to a more inefficient allocation of resources. On the other hand, long periods of overvaluation of currencies have been in the past closely associated with strong protectionist pressures, and this is clearly true of the United States in the last few years.

In practice, floating exchange rates have not provided governments with an all-powerful and painless medicine for balance of payments adjustment. The J-curve effect, low elasticities, labour-market rigidities and floating itself have turned the exchange rate into a less effective instrument than had been generally expected. Nor have floating rates eliminated or even significantly reduced the need to hold foreign reserves. And this is for the simple reason that most governments have never practised clean floating, nor have they believed in the absolute wisdom of the market.

Expectations about increased autonomy of national monetary policy had been the main factor behind the adoption of floating exchange rates in the early 1970s. Have these expectations been fulfilled? Floating rates have indeed allowed governments greater flexibility in the conduct of domestic economic policies than the previous system of fixed parities. But the difference seems to be a question of degree rather than kind. Floating rates have not and could not provide governments with a convenient escape from the policy dilemmas arising from external shocks or from the constraints imposed on national autonomy by international trade and financial interdependence. Many governments soon abandoned the idea of an independent monetary policy and adopted some form of exchange-rate target. The importance of the exchange rate in the determination of national price levels and the international competitiveness of national producers have been the crucial factors behind the concern shown by governments for the exchange rate, especially in countries with relatively open economies. Moreover, if it is true that the observed instability in the income velocity of money is associated with shifts in currency portfolios, which would make sense in a world of high capital mobility, then national money-supply targets lose much of their meaning.

European criticism of US policies of benign neglect, associated during most of the 1970s with a declining dollar, were succeeded by repeated complaints about the meteoric rise of the US currency. This was mainly attributed to high interest rates, the latter seen in turn essentially as a product of the policy-mix adopted by the Reagan Administration. European appeals for international economic co-operation were usually a diplomatic camouflage for calls, addressed to Washington, for a change in domestic US policies leading to a reduction in the fiscal deficit and a less strict monetary policy. The American response was, on the other hand, based on the 'own house in order' argument as being clearly superior to this vague and impractical notion of international economic co-operation. A comparison was drawn, often with some delight, between the strength of US economic growth and the fragility of the economic recovery in Western Europe. This was considered to be the main factor behind market confidence in the dollar, rather than the level of interest rates which, anyway, was not necessarily related to the budget deficit.

There are a number of misguided perceptions and objective differences of interest behind this apparent dialogue of the deaf, which lasted for some years. Initially, the Europeans had clearly underestimated their own margin for manoeuvre and the scope for 'uncoupling' their interest rates and their economies in general from the United States. This 'uncoupling' did gradually take place, and it has become very evident since 1983, when substantial interest-rate differentials became apparent between the two sides of the Atlantic, as the countries of the European Monetary System (EMS) tried to resist much of the upward pressure on interest rates emanating from the United States. This was achieved at the cost of a significant depreciation of their currencies vis-à-vis the dollar. Here again, European policy-makers seem to have exaggerated in their public statements the costs associated with the dollar depreciation of their currencies.

First of all, this collective depreciation did not lead to much imported inflation, as had been originally feared, both because intra-European trade represents a large percentage of the overall external trade of European countries and also because the dollar appreciation has coincided with falling commodity prices in dollar terms, the two being not unrelated. Moreover, the significant appreciation of the dollar against European currencies, coupled with high economic growth in the United States, has been largely responsible for the partially export-led growth which European economies experienced after 1983. However, this should be set against the costs associated with higher interest rates in Europe than would have existed without this particular policy-mix in the United States, and the loss of productive investment resulting from

European capital outflows. In fact, those costs have surely been much greater for many of the heavily-indebted countries of the Third World.

On the other hand, the Reagan Administration had clearly over-estimated the ability of the US economy to overcome a constantly growing import leakage resulting from the overvaluation of the dollar, and also the ability of the political system to resist the protectionist pressures associated with it. There is, undoubtedly, a 'closed-economy' syndrome from which much of the American political establishment is suffering and which is increasingly divorced from reality. Many US policy-makers have also apparently been carried away by the initial success of the supply-side experiment, aided by a strong fiscal stimulus, and mesmerized by their own rhetoric about 'the magic of the market-place'. They have also tended to ignore for the most part international linkages and the effects of US economic policies on other countries. For example, the extent and the timing of the international debt crisis of the early 1980s and the burden of adjustment imposed on many developing countries cannot be dissociated from economic decisions taken in Washington, DC. This does not, however, absolve commercial banks, strongly encouraged by Western governments, from much of the res-ponsibility for the unconditional lending to various countries in the aftermath of the first oil shock.

There are, however, also some structural differences which lie behind the divergence in attitudes over exchange rates and monetary policy between the Americans, on the one hand, and the countries of the EMS, on the other. For the Europeans, the openness of their econ-omies and the rigidity of their labour markets considerably reduce the attraction of floating rates. This is especially true when EC economies behave as separate units and not as a unified bloc. For the Americans, on the other hand, the international role of the dollar reduces the short-term cost of exchange-rate fluctuations and, coupled with the size and depth of domestic financial markets, it gives US Administrations a margin for manoeuvre which no other government enjoys. All this results in the large asymmetries which still exist in the international monetary system, asymmetries which have probably been accentuated since the abandonment of the gold-dollar standard. Money is very dif-ferent from trade in terms of the relative balance of power between the United States and Western Europe, and much of the difference can be attributed to the lack of financial unity of the Europeans. This is indeed the main factor behind the persistence of the asymmetry between the two sides of the Atlantic.

In a period in which the fight against inflation has been the main priority for most Western governments, appreciation of the national currency was extremely advantageous. This is more like a zero-sum game with winners and losers, and it has been an important factor in the Euro-American dispute over exchange rates in recent years. More-over, appeals for international economic co-operation usually come from those who feel weak and vulnerable. This is exactly the position in which the Europeans found themselves in the first half of the 1980s. While the US economy was booming, the dollar was strong, and dom-estic protectionist pressures were under control, the Reagan Adminis-tration clearly saw little interest in heeding those appeals.

In an attempt to reduce the excessive volatility and misalignment, which have characterized the period of floating, various proposals have been put forward for the setting up of 'target zones' for the exchange rates of the major currencies. At least in the initial experimental stages, the emphasis would be on relatively wide bands of fluctuation and flex-ibility.

In practice, any exchange-rate arrangement would require the par-ticipation of the United States, the EMS countries as a bloc, and Japan. It would, therefore, be strictly a matter for a small group of industrialized countries. This should, *ceteris paribus*, increase the chances of agreement and effective co-operation in a context in which specific rules can only be of limited use. Such an arrangement would require that all parties concerned adopt exchange-rate targets. This should be translated into a responsibility to intervene in exchange markets in order to smooth out short-term fluctuations and, even more important, to coordinate their monetary and fiscal policies. This co-ordination could take either an explicit or an implicit form, as for ex-ample suggested by McKinnon (see chapter 7 below), through the adoption of an exchange-rate target in the conduct of monetary policy. In this respect, the IMF should also play an important role; hence the need to give more substance to the surveillance function entrusted to the Fund.

The above would mark a radical departure from the pattern estab-lished during the last decade. Apart from any doubts that may exist about the theoretical basis or the practical feasibility of specific pro-posals, the crucial question is whether the countries concerned would be prepared to accept the responsibilities and constraints involved. The joint management of exchange rates would necessitate a shift in American attitudes, which would be much more dramatic than any-thing required from the Europeans or the Japanese. With no major international currency of their own and with more open and highly in-terpendent economies, the Western Europeans have, albeit slowly and reluctantly, accepted the constraints on national monetary autonomy. This has been the foundation stone of the EMS. On the other hand, the United States has never really accepted an external constraint on the conduct of its economic policies. A change in US official atti-tudes may come about gradually through the growing openness of the US economy. This change could be precipitated by a depreciation of the dollar. Fears about the inflationary impact of such a depreciation, perhaps coupled with some anxiety about the international role of the dollar (what would be, for instance, the effect on US attitudes of an OPEC decision to start quoting oil prices in SDRs or ECUs?), could act as an incentive for the American Administration to rediscover the virtues of intervention and international co-operation in the macro-economic field. Appeals for international coordinated action could also follow a slowdown of the US economy.

In the foreseeable future, probably the best we can hope for is the avoidance of major incompatibilities in the macroeconomic policies pursued by the large Western industrialized countries and the acceptance, even in principle, of the need for some degree of collective management of international financial interdependence. The main developments in the international monetary system in the 1970s were to a great extent a negation of this need. There are already signs that the pendulum has started moving in the opposite direction. Certainly, the problems of the international monetary system go beyond the management of exchange rates. There are other important questions such as the adequacy of official liquidity for countries without access to bank credit, the equity and effectiveness of the IMF adjustment programmes, and the long-term viability of the approach adopted so far to the problem of accumulated sovereign debt. The attitudes of the United States and Western Europe will be absolutely crucial in determining the way in which those questions will be tackled in the future.

The lack of any serious progress in terms of international co-operation could eventually act as a strong incentive for further financial integration at the regional level as a means of reducing Europe's disproportionate financial dependence on the United States. One crucial step in this direction would be the strengthening of the international role of the ECU for both commercial and financial transactions. The creation of a real multiple-currency standard, which would also involve a greater role for the yen, might act as a catalyst for closer and more effective co-operation among the Americans, the Europeans and the Japanese. Greater symmetry would make international economic-policy coordination more attractive to the Americans and less one-sided to the others.

EXTRATERRITORIALITY AND FOREIGN POLICY DIVERGENCE

In recent years, the issue of extraterritoriality has emerged out of its legal shell into the political limelight. The issue itself, which refers to attempts by nation-states to apply their laws and implement their policies beyond their own frontiers, provides a very good illustration of the close links between international economics, domestic legal and political processes, and foreign policy.

As regards economic legislation, the issue of extraterritoriality has been traditionally associated with antitrust laws. Here, extra-territoriality seems to be deeply ingrained in US legal practice. The so-called effects doctrine permits US courts to hold foreign persons or companies liable for actions which may be legal in their home countries, where such actions have an intended adverse effect in the United States. The definition of intent has often been far-reaching. This has been a regular source of conflict with foreign governments which, on the other hand, have not always been innocent of similar practices. The number of instances of extraterritorial application of national antitrust laws leading to conflict at the intergovernmental level seems to be constantly on the increase.

The issue of extraterritoriality has also appeared in other areas as regards Euro-American relations. One subject which became the target of strong criticism by European and other countries, coupled with intensive lobbying in the United States and the occasional threat of retaliation, is the so-called system of unitary taxation applied by several US states. Here, US fiscal federalism was extended beyond the borders of the federation. On the European side, the proposed Vredeling directive concerned with the disclosure of company information to employees would extend EC jurisdiction over foreign-based companies with subsidiaries in Europe. However, in view of the strong opposition by European and foreign industrialists, and the lack of enthusiasm exhibited by some EC governments, the Vredeling directive is not likely to be adopted, if at all, in anything but a very diluted form.

Extraterritoriality seems to have spread in recent years, partly as a response to the growing integration of the world economy and the inadequacy of international rules or agreements in areas such as anti-trust, foreign investment and taxation. The result has been growing unilateralism, which unavoidably leads to imitation and sometimes retaliation. If this is the only way in which national governments can be brought to recognize the need for international rules, negotiation and compromise, it is surely a costly and inefficient way. The fact that most cases of extraterritoriality have originated in the United States must surely be related to the division of power in a federal system and the rather insular legal and political traditions of the country.

However, if extraterritoriality has reached the newspaper headlines, it is because of the Soviet gas pipeline dispute and the 1982 US embargo. Behind the dispute there lay differences of views between the Americans and the Europeans regarding East–West relations, and East –West trade in particular, as well as the use of trade as an instrument

of foreign policy. The extraterritorial dimension arose when the US
Administration decided to make use of provisions of the 1979 Export
Administration Act to impose a unilateral US embargo on export of
equipment, which was extended to US subsidiaries abroad and foreign
firms using US technology and equipment. This was naturally deeply
resented by the European allies, and the dispute was finally resolved
by the withdrawal of the embargo and an agreement to tighten controls
over the export of sensitive high technology to the Soviet Union and
Eastern Europe.

Important differences in foreign policy often do spill over into the
economic sphere. However, the decision to establish a close link
between politics and trade, and then to try to impose it on others by
giving an extraterritorial dimension to national laws is a sure way of
provoking strong reactions abroad. The 1982 US embargo was clearly
an ill-considered act of unilateralism which was deeply offensive to the
European countries.

Since the lifting of the US embargo, the subject of transfer of
technology and East–West trade has slipped back to the specialized columns of the quality press, probably waiting for the next opportunity to
reappear on the front page. The problem has certainly not gone away.
The United States, and especially the Pentagon, have reportedly been
trying in a consistent fashion to impose on other Western countries
their own very restrictive view of East–West trade by extending substantially the list of controlled commodities. They have been seeking to
do this through direct pressure on individual countries and through
Cocom (the Coordinating Committee on Multilateral Export Controls),
which is based in the US Embassy in Paris and consists of representatives of the major Western countries. Political pressures have been
coupled with threats to make use of the extraterritorial provisions of the
Export Administration Act.

According to one observer-participant from the private sector 'the
US Government goes to extraordinary. lengths to seek to impose its
security considerations on other nations'.[3] Others have suspected the
United States of trying to protect its own technological lead through
ever-tighter control of export licensing. Thus, there is a high risk of
another flare-up in the future. What is at stake is not only trade with
Eastern countries, but also intra-Western trade and investment, as well as
questions of foreign policy, defence and national sovereignty in general.

PULLING LOOSE THREADS TOGETHER

The deep economic recession that followed the second oil shock, following as it did several years of relatively low economic activity, took its
toll on Euro-American relations. At such times different parties are

inclined to view their relations with economic partners in terms of a zero-sum game, which unavoidably leads to conflict. The unprecedented unevenness of the economic recovery, which succeeded it, did not lead to a substantial improvement of the general economic environment within which bilateral relations take place.

In fact, it can be argued that the very unevenness of the economic recovery had very much to do with the economic policies pursued on both sides of the Atlantic. The combination of a large fiscal deficit and a restrictive monetary policy in the United States and the excessive deflation imposed on European economies has surely contributed to macroeconomic developments and the strains that have been apparent in bilateral relations. Failure at the macroeconomic level is not put forward here as an explanatory factor to the exclusion of all others, such as, for instance, the notorious rigidities of European labour markets.

The general economic and political environment has not been conducive to co-operation between the two sides. American unilateralism, with its strong historical basis and aided by renewed confidence in the strength and vitality of the US economy, was reinforced by the general state of confusion and economic weakness in Europe, coupled with the poverty of political leadership and the now familiar lack of unity of the Europeans in relations with the United States. Furthermore, economic theories in current fashion did not attach much importance to international economic policy coordination. Mechanical rules and the automaticity of market forces were seen as sufficient to guarantee non-inflationary growth.

The approaches adopted on the two sides of the Atlantic to international trade and adjustment problems have also differed considerably. The differences were accentuated in recent years, or perhaps they were more noticeable simply because of the degree of adjustment required, itself a function of the macroeconomic environment and the continuous growth of economic interdependence. The gulf between economic reality and the order set up after the end of the Second World War has continued to widen. Existing international organizations and rules are manifestly inadequate to deal with problems arising in international trade. There are glaring gaps in other important areas such as international investment and taxation. On the other hand, the new monetary 'system', based on floating exchange rates and independent national macroeconomic policies, has not delivered the goods originally promised. This is most probably because its advocates had underestimated the degree of integration of the world economy. In general, as trade and financial interdependence has been constantly growing, governments and national political systems have been unwilling or unable to accept the implications and the constraints on national autonomy.

An additional factor, which has contributed to the recent tension in Euro-American relations, has been the divergence in the foreign policies pursued by the two sides and especially in their relations with the East. Foreign policy divergence has finally spilled over into the field of trade. Economic policies certainly do not take effect in a political vacuum. At times of serious East–West tension, increasing American assertiveness and European confusion, the links between trade and money, on the one hand, and foreign policy and defence, on the other, are perhaps bound to become more apparent. So are political and economic asymmetries between the two sides of the Atlantic. It has been argued that 'for the world economy to be stabilized, there has to be a stabilizer, one stabilizer'.[4] This is the well-known theory of hegemonic leadership as a prerequisite for a stable world economic order. Since a return to a balance of power situation like the one that prevailed in the aftermath of the Second World War is highly unlikely, not to mention undesirable, an effective management of global economic interdependence may need to rest on a more international and pluralist basis. One important step in this direction would be the creation of a more symmetrical relationship between the United States and Western Europe, not only in economic, but also in military terms. Whether such a step will be taken in the foreseeable future is an alto-gether different question.

NOTES

1   The title of an article by Nicholas Butler in *Foreign Affairs*, (Fall, 1983).
2   Stephen Woolcock, 'Atlantic trade relations', in Lawrence Freedman (ed.), *The Troubled Alliance: Atlantic Relations in the 1980s* (Heinemann, London, 1983), p. 100.
3   Harold Tittmann, 'The drawbacks of having the Pentagon in charge', *Financial Times*, 4 April 1985.
4   Charles P. Kindleberger, *The World in Depression, 1929–1939* (University of California Press, Berkeley, 1973), p. 305.

2

The EC–US Steel Trade Crisis

ROBERT W. CRANDALL

These are not the best of times for the world's steel makers. Since the 1973–4 oil crisis, they have suffered slow demand growth, low prices and constant warfare over market shares of world consumption. New entrants have disrupted their markets and competitive materials have shrunk them. Not exactly accustomed to operating in a fiercely competitive market, many have succeeded in convincing themselves that they now operate in an unfair world. They long only for the medieval 'fair' price and the quiet life. That they are unlikely to discover this nirvana is obvious. The consequences of their search for it, however, are serious and difficult to predict. This is particularly true for the ageing dinosaurs that produce steel in the United States and in Europe.

THE POST-1974 WORLD

Even before the 1973 Arab oil embargo, many of the developed world's steel makers were beginning to encounter difficulties. Steel is far from a high-technology industry that requires armies of highly trained workers. Nor are its principal raw materials confined to a few narrow areas of the globe. During the 1950s and 1960s, the real price of iron ore fell dramatically as new iron-ore deposits were developed.[1] Shipping costs for bulk materials, such as iron ore and metallurgical coal, also were falling. And the technology for building and operating steel works was increasingly available from numerous competitors in North America, Europe and (eventually) Japan. The result was that developing countries could now begin to build their own steel industries and rely less heavily upon imports from North America or Europe.

On the eve of the Arab oil embargo, the developing countries accounted for only 5.7 per cent of non-communist world steel production, but they were poised to expand this share substantially (see table 2.1). Countries such as Brazil, Mexico, Venezuela, Korea and Taiwan were preparing major expansion projects, and countries in the Middle East were to entertain similar notions in the next few years. At the same time, many European countries were expanding their capacity substantially – particularly the French, the British and the Italians. New coastal works at Fos and Taranto were built to serve a growing export market, and the events of 1973–4 seemed only to confirm the wisdom of these investments. Prices for steel products soared in 1974, following the first oil crisis, as buyers frantically bid for stocks of steel-mill products to satisfy booming demands for capital goods and consumer durables.[2]

TABLE 2.1   WORLD RAW STEEL PRODUCTION, 1973–83 (million tonnes)

Year	World	Western world	Industrialized countries	Developing countries
1973	691.7	490.5	462.2	28.2
1974	703.4	493.8	463.2	30.6
1975	643.4	423.6	391.1	32.6
1976	675.3	452.6	415.4	37.1
1977	675.4	443.2	399.6	43.5
1978	716.8	443.2	420.5	48.1
1979	746.6	468.6	442.4	54.5
1980	716.1	497.0	406.9	56.8
1981	707.6	463.7	401.8	58.2
1982	644.8	398.0	337.7	60.3
1983	662.0	405.2	341.6	63.6

Source: International Iron and Steel Institute.

In the United States, the effects of the 1973–4 euphoria were much more muted. The US industry had been suffering increases in import penetration throughout the 1960s, perhaps in response to an overvalued dollar, but also because of the failure of the US industry to keep pace with more dynamic producers such as those in Japan. The Japanese and European industries more than doubled their capacity in the 1960s, building numerous modern plants, but the US industry added only one new integrated plant during this period – and has added none since then.

Although some major US companies began to plan for new plants in response to the price explosion of 1973–4, the 1975 recession and its aftermath quickly cooled their ardour. Plans by US Steel and National Steel to begin new 'green-field' plants were delayed and then abandoned. New investments in huge iron-ore projects continued, and Inland Steel expanded its Indiana plant to nearly 9 million tonnes of capacity, but otherwise the denizens of Wall Street kept the US producers on a very short leash.

Since 1974, very slow economic growth in both OECD and developing countries has combined with a tendency of governments to shift away from 'infrastructure' investments and many consumers to substitute lighter materials for steel. The result has been negligible growth in world steel consumption from 1974 to 1979 and a disastrous decline from 1979 to 1983 (Table 2.1).

Most forecasters see little recovery of demand for the rest of this decade.[3] As a result, the world industry continues to operate with a substantial overhang of excess capacity in countries that have lost comparative advantage in steel production. These excess assets are being retired, 'rationalized', or simply operated as long as they produce steel that brings prices in excess of variable costs. Given the slow rate of technological change in the industry, this disequilibrium condition could continue for a considerable period of time.

The less developed countries (LDCs) have expanded their share of Western world steel output to nearly 16 per cent, generally reducing their dependence upon exports from the overbuilt developed-country industries. Although these LDCs remain net importers of steel, many have become important exporters of selected products. As the United States and European producers retrench, these developing countries will continue to expand their exporting capacity.

THE ROOTS OF THE CURRENT EC–US TRADE PROBLEM

Ever since the 1959 strike, the US steel industry has kept a wary eye upon imports. Because imports seemed to rise in a triennial pattern with the onset of wage negotiations, the industry assumed that it could buy protection from imports by suing for peace with its union, the United Steelworkers. In 1973–4, it entered into a costly 'experimental' agreement, guaranteeing the union at least a 3 per cent increase in real wages per year, if the union would forswear its right to strike. This agreement added enormously to the competitive disadvantage of the US industry vis-à-vis Japan, Canada and many developing countries. With no new plants, declining demand and soaring wage costs, the US industry was hardly prepared to fight an aggressive battle for market share even in its own country.

As a result of its rising labour costs (Table 2.2), non-competitive iron-ore costs and an ageing plant structure, the US integrated steel

TABLE 2.2 TOTAL COMPENSATION FOR PRODUCTION WORKERS
IN STEEL AND ALL MANUFACTURING IN THE UNITED STATES, 1960-80
($ per hour)

Year	All manufacturing	Steel
1960	2.87	3.82
1961	2.99	3.99
1962	3.06	4.16
1963	3.16	4.25
1964	3.29	4.36
1965	3.35	4.48
1966	3.50	4.63
1967	3.68	4.76
1968	3.94	5.03
1969	4.20	4.38
1970	4.17	5.68
1971	4.48	6.26
1972	4.83	7.08
1973	5.24	7.68
1974	5.72	9.08
1975	6.35	10.59
1976	6.93	11.74
1977	7.59	13.04
1978	8.30	14.30
1979	9.07	15.92
1980	9.89	18.45
1981	10.96	20.16
1982	11.79	23.78

Source: US Bureau of Labor Statistics; and American Iron and Steel Institute.

industry has high variable costs of production.[4] It has chosen to keep older plants open in the hope that demand would eventually revive, but by the 1980s this hope appeared vain indeed. Prices of US steel-mill products drifted upward from 1975 to 1977, while world export prices stagnated and even declined. The obvious result of this development was a surge of imports into the United States, first from Europe and Japan, and later from Canada and the developing countries (table 2.3).

The US industry could have chosen to wage a competitive battle with imports, slashing prices and beginning a major assault on costs. Instead, it began lobbying for trade protection in 1977, citing European unfair trade practices—initially charging that European and Japanese producers were dumping at less than 'fair value', and later that government subsidization unfairly reduced export prices and injured US producers.

With imports rising in 1977, as the 1976-7 recovery aborted, the US industry brought its trade complaints to Washington for the first time since the expiration of the 1969-74 Voluntary Restraint Agreements (VRAs), which had been instituted with the Japanese and Europeans.

TABLE 2.3 IMPORTS OF STEEL-MILL PRODUCTS INTO THE
UNITED STATES (million tonnes)

| Year | Total | As a percentage of apparent consumption from: | | | | Total |
		Japan	EC	Canada	Other	
1973	13.7	4.6	5.3	0.9	1.6	12.4
1974	14.5	5.1	5.4	1.1	1.8	13.4
1975	10.9	6.6	4.6	1.1	1.2	13.5
1976	13.0	7.9	3.2	1.3	1.7	14.1
1977	17.5	7.2	6.3	1.7	2.6	17.8
1978	19.2	5.6	6.4	2.0	4.1	18.1
1979	15.9	5.5	4.7	2.0	3.0	15.2
1980	14.1	6.3	4.1	2.5	3.4	16.3
1981	18.1	5.9	6.1	2.7	4.2	18.9
1982	15.1	6.8	7.3	2.4	5.3	21.8
1983	15.5	5.1	4.9	2.9	7.6	20.5

Source: American Iron and Steel Institute, Annual Statistical Reports.

President Carter, unfamiliar with the consequences of such a move, asked the industry to press trade suits under the 1974 Trade Act if it had legitimate grievances. The result was a welter of anti-dumping suits that created a major problem for the Administration, as it sought to complete the Tokyo Round of multilateral trade negotiations.

The Carter Administration's response to the industry's action was to erect a 'trigger-price' system, essentially placing a floor under import prices, in return for an agreement by the companies to drop their suits. The trigger prices were to be set at the Japanese cost of production plus freight from Tokyo, thus allowing Europeans and other higher-cost countries to sell at prices below their cost of production. The trigger-price system was extremely complex and easily evaded; therefore it could not have worked for very long. Indeed, Secretary Solomon, its architect, warned that it was to be no more than 'temporary', allowing the industry a respite from the drastic competition prevailing on world steel markets.

It was fortunate for policy-makers and steel producers that the trigger-price policy coincided with the beginning of a two-year decline in the value of the dollar. From the third quarter of 1977 until the end of 1979, the dollar declined by approximately 16 per cent on a multilateral trade-weighted basis. This allowed US steel import prices to rise naturally, but this rise was probably assisted somewhat by the trigger-price mechanism.[5] As a result, the pressure for trade protection abated somewhat in 1979–80. The narrowing of the differences between US and world export prices had reduced imports to the range of 15–16 per cent of domestic consumption. Nevertheless, in early 1980, the United States Steel Corporation filed anti-dumping suits against seven

European countries, apparently hoping for either higher minimum prices through anti-dumping duties or a revised trigger-price system.

In October 1980, US Steel received assurances of greater trade protection from a revised trigger-price system, and it suspended its suits. Had it been watching the foreign exchange markets, an unlikely possibility for a US steel company, it might have chosen to persevere.[6]

THE CURRENT SITUATION

The rise in the value of the dollar that began in the summer of 1980 has placed the integrated US steel industry in a desperate situation. Since 1979, the differences between US prices and world export prices have risen markedly. Once again, rather than reacting by cutting prices sharply, major US producers held prices relatively stable in 1982, and then cut prices by 5–10 per cent in 1983 as imports rose. However, the US companies did not match the sharp declines in (dollar-denominated) import prices in 1983, thus allowing imports to rise from 16 per cent of the US market to almost 25 per cent by early 1984. The degree of penetration is not the main cause of the US companies' concern. Rather, it is the depressing effect of imports upon prices and profit margins in their high-cost national market.

By 1982, the average price differential between US producers and the world export market had risen to over $100 per tonne, far more than the difference required to induce increased importation (see tables 2.4–2.6). As a result, US producers were unable to raise prices materially between 1981 and 1983.[7] Although they obtained modest relief in 1982 from their wage agreement with the United Steelworkers, their price-cost margins fell dramatically as demand plummeted in 1982 and then recovered mildly in 1983. In the first eight months of 1984, with prices far above world export prices, the US companies have been operating at about 75 per cent of capacity and barely covering their variable and (book value) capital costs. Even at full capacity, they would not be able to earn a remunerative return on their capital at these above-world-market prices.

Without trade relief, the pressure of import competition will depress US steel prices (unless Europe recovers strongly or the dollar declines) even further, as the dollar soars on the world's exchange markets. US prices could fall to 1980 nominal levels. The US producers are all too aware of this dismal situation, and they have responded by asking for more trade protection in three related actions. First, in 1982, they filed countervailing and anti-dumping duties against all European exporters and other large exporters in the world. These suits were largely settled by quantitative arrangements, the most important of which is the

TABLE 2.4   AVERAGE PRICES REALIZED BY US PRODUCERS OF
CARBON STEEL ($/tonne)

Year	Hot rolled sheet	Bars	Sections	Plates
1970	141.4	183.4	169.0	178.7
1971	150.8	197.6	183.2	193.0
1972	157.6	212.5	193.1	206.8
1973	169.4	225.9	203.3	220.3
1974	227.3	296.9	259.6	277.9
1975	244.3	324.2	302.4	322.8
1976	261.1	342.5	313.5	333.6
1977	283.7	370.0	319.3	356.7
1978	316.0	402.0	360.2	393.5
1979	348.1	443.1	411.7	435.8
1980	351.2	458.5	450.3	475.0
1981	389.9	489.9	473.0	525.9
1982	374.3	462.2	461.5	515.0

Source: US Department of Commerce, MA-33B, annual editions.

TABLE 2.5   PRICE DIFFERENCES: US-EC EXPORT PRICES ($/tonne)

Year	Hot rolled sheet	Bars	Sections	Plate
1970	17.7	54.7	24.8	24.3
1971	30.3	78.6	57.3	57.0
1972	37.8	95.3	71.0	69.1
1973	29.1	67.6	55.8	59.7
1974	−44.6	1.9	−10.4	7.9
1975	−23.0	60.2	49.0	−37.6
1976	5.2	107.5	57.0	31.3
1977	36.6	136.1	83.1	85.1
1978	40.8	142.1	85.0	57.1
1979	13.6	99.1	71.8	45.2
1980	−1.8	88.2	96.7	54.5
1981	69.5	176.2	141.4	147.4
1982	39.3	147.1	97.4	126.1

Source: US Department of Commerce, MA-33B, annual editions. Eurostat.

US–EC agreement, negotiated in October 1982, essentially limiting
Community exporters to about 5.4 per cent of US consumption of the
products covered by the agreement.[8] Pipe and tube shipments were
conspicuously absent from this total, an omission that has caused great
consternation among several major US producers.

TABLE 2.6   PRICE DIFFERENCES: US-JAPANESE EXPORT PRICES
($/tonne)

Year	Hot rolled sheet	Bars	Sections	Plate
1970	35.9	55.9	32.1	57.2
1971	48.8	84.2	61.3	78.5
1972	43.5	86.9	63.3	78.6
1973	20.2	40.4	23.8	58.8
1974	− 6.5	− 6.5	− 41.6	− 4.3
1975	53.8	114.5	69.6	66.4
1976	61.2	131.1	75.8	92.1
1977	78.2	127.8	54.0	82.7
1978	72.6	97.5	23.9	68.8
1979	43.2	107.7	58.8	103.3
1980	13.1	39.2	− 5.0	− 6.3
1981	52.6	180.3	76.2	90.9
1982	70.5	178.5	97.9	106.6

Source: US Department of Commerce, MA–33B, annual editions. Japanese Tariff Commission.

The US–EC agreement could not have helped the US producers very much by itself. Steel is an internationally traded commodity, and its price is determined in a market far larger than the US import market. It was predictable that European exporters would divert exports to other countries, while other exporters filled the void left by the agreement in the US. Imports into the US from sources other than the EC or Japan have soared since 1982, rising to 53 per cent of all steel imports in the first half of 1984 from only 35 per cent in 1978–82 (see table 2.3). With the dollar continuing to appreciate, imports have risen to almost 25 per cent of US steel consumption and continue to rise.

The US industry's second line of attack on imports has been to seek legislation, limiting imports to 15 per cent of consumption. This legislation languished for some time in Congress, perhaps awaiting the outcome of further trade suits and the 1984 Presidential election.

The third line of attack by the US industry has had two prongs. The United States Steel Corporation continues to pursue countervailing duty and anti-dumping cases against most exporters other than the Canadians, the Japanese and the Europeans. It has been successful in obtaining agreements or duties to reduce imports from such diverse countries as Korea, South Africa and Mexico. Bethlehem Steel and the USW, on the other hand, have used the 'escape-clause' provision allowed by the GATT to seek temporary relief from imports. In early 1984, they filed a section 201 escape-clause case with the Commerce Department, asking for a 15 per cent quota. This suit was timed to obtain a decision from President Reagan within a few weeks of the national election. On 19 September, the President announced that he would seek 'voluntary' export restrictions with steel-exporting countries in order to limit imports (excluding semi-finished steel) to 18.5 per cent of the US markets; however, he did not impose any restructuring requirements upon the industry as a *quid pro quo* for this protection.

RESTRUCTURING THE STEEL INDUSTRY

There is a widespread belief that the US and European steel industries can be returned to health through a policy of rationalization and restructuring. On both sides of the Atlantic, this restructuring process has begun. In Europe, capacity is being retired slowly, lately by Commission edict,[9] whereas in the United States, the large companies are withdrawing assets somewhat more rapidly. This gradual adjustment of capacity to demand should eventually help to alleviate some of the distress in both continents, but it is far from a solution to the difficulties in the steel sector.

The pace of plant closings has been rather slow in both Europe and the United States (see table 2.7). This is hardly unexpected in an industry with a relatively slow rate of technological progress. New facilities may be built to produce steel at costs that are below the full costs of some existing plants in Europe and the United States, but more than the variable costs of producing from these older facilities. As a result, it is not a sensible decision to close many of these older plants immediately. Instead, managements choose to operate them as long as prices cover their variable costs. Major capital expenditures in these old plants are deferred indefinitely, with the result that their capacities

TABLE 2.7   EFFECTIVE RAW-STEEL CAPACITY IN THE DEVELOPED WORLD, 1973–83 (million tonnes)

	US	EC	Japan
1973	134	152	117
1974	133	155	120
1975	131	172	122
1976	137	170	128
1977	132	167	137
1978	132	166	136
1979	130	166	136
1980	128	164	138
1981	130	160	138
1982	128	157	138
1983	114	153[a]	137[a]

[a] Estimated value.

Source: Peter Marcus and Karlis Kirsis, *World Steel Dynamics, The Steel Strategist*, no. 9.

erode slowly but steadily. This agonizing decline creates substantial political pressure for government assistance or trade protection *en route*, but it eventually generates a natural 'rationalization' of assets.

It is always difficult to measure the actual capacity of any industrial facility, and steel is no exception to this rule. Official data on crude steel capacity suggest that the US firms have been more successful than the Europeans in shuttering capacity during the recent steel crisis. Since 1976, US effective raw-steel capacity has fallen from 137 million tonnes to 114 million tonnes.[10] Given the increase in mini-mill capacity in recent years, this suggests that integrated companies have reduced their crude-steel capacity by more than 30 million tonnes, or nearly 25 per cent of their 1976 capacity.[11]

In Europe, on the other hand, the process of forming a cartel has created a variety of incentives to maintain, overstate and even increase capacity. Since 1976, the EC's crude-steel capacity has declined by perhaps 10 per cent. Beginning in 1980, the Commission sanctioned an outright cartel, replete with production quotas and (in 1982) with planned capacity reductions. In 1982, the Commission set a goal of reducing finished-steel capacity from 168.7 million tonnes to about 138.7 million tonnes.[12] Since the former number was probably an exaggerated estimate of production capacity in 1980, it is not clear how much of the decline will be phantom reductions on a Commission accountant's ledger and how much will represent real reductions. In any event, in 1983 the Commission 'increased' its pressure on the steel industry by asking for an additional 8.9 million tonnes of closures, over and above the 17.8 million tonnes already obtained.[13] This would bring the official finished-steel capacity down to 142 million tonnes, probably an exaggeration of effective capacity.

Unfortunately, it is not simply the overhang of excess capacity that plagues the older steel producers in Europe and the United States. Technological change may be slow in this industry, but there is some progress. New processes for casting or rolling steel have reduced energy costs and increased product yields substantially. Many of these processes cannot be accommodated at older steel plants with poor layouts. In addition, the new market for high-quality steels requires much greater investment in processes such as continuous annealing and electrogalvanizing. Investments in these processes are difficult to justify in plants with inefficient steel-making or hot-rolling facilities, but complete renovation of most of these older plants is simply not feasible. Thus, it becomes very important for firms to target their investments in improved product quality very carefully. In the United States, in particular, there is a serious risk that many companies will simply be unable to meet market demands for higher and higher quality steels in the next decade.

In short, restructuring of the steel industries of Europe and the United States is not simply a matter of reducing capacity, but rather of being able to supply at competitive prices the steel that the market will demand in the foreseeable future. Mini-mills in the US and Europe are likely to take an increasing share of the simpler products, leaving the integrated companies to concentrate on the higher grades of flat rolled products and the largest long products. But as long as there is a competitive group of highly-efficient new plants in Korea, Brazil or Canada to supply these products, the older integrated companies will find it difficult to seek refuge in higher prices.

With a strong US dollar, US producers are likely to continue to have a very narrow margin over variable costs. Clearly, without a weakening of the dollar, no amount of rationalization or restructuring will alleviate the US integrated firms' current plight.

SUBSIDIES, FAIR TRADE AND THE GATT

Under the General Agreement on Tariffs and Trade (GATT), export subsidies are treated more harshly than production subsidies. Thus, a programme of subsidizing export sales while maintaining domestic prices is more offensive than a general policy of production subsidies, such as those most frequent in the European steel industry. Under US law, however, all subsidies that affect US import prices are fair game for plaintiffs to attack under section 701 of the Tariff Act. It is only necessary to show that the subsidies are related to exports of a given product and that the low US import prices confer material injury upon US producers or their employers.

Given the state of the world steel industry, prices are not generally high enough to allow most integrated producers (regardless of location) to cover their full accounting costs of production, much less their full costs including the return on the reproduction cost of assets. In developing countries and in developed countries with declining steel industries, government ownership of the steel industry is pervasive. Were purely private firms operating in this environment, bankruptcies would be fairly common and operating costs would be substantially lower, as firms reduced inefficient manning practices and bargained aggressively over wages. It is entirely possible that in such an environment the true net worth of the European steel industry would be very low, perhaps as low per tonne of capacity as in the United States. But even if all existing government-owned steel industries were reorganized as private firms, it is far from clear that capacity and output would be much lower than at present. In the United States, Weirton Steel and McLouth have been reorganized and continue to operate and compete

with sharply lower variable costs. There is no reason why many inefficient government-owned companies in Europe or Latin America could
not enjoy the same result.

Few have grasped the importance of the above argument. It is far
from clear that government subsidies or government equity infusions to
the French, Belgian, British or Italian steel industries have had a major
effect upon capacity, output or export prices. These subsidies may
simply have allowed continued managerial inefficiencies, supracom-
petitive wages, and payment of debts to creditors who would otherwise
have been in line at the bankruptcy court. Obviously, it is possible that
some facilities enjoyed extended economic lives or that subsidies actually
reduced marginal costs, and therefore the offer price of steel on the
world market, but one may not blithely assume such a result.[14]

An obvious example of government subsidies that have been accompanied by prices above competitive levels is that provided by European
airlines. It would be foolhardy to suggest that government subsidies
have given Air France or British Airways the licence to drive fares
generally below competitive levels, thus threatening unsubsidized
firms in an open competitive market. In fact, were the Community to
open air transportation to competition, fares would plummet and subsidies would have to increase substantially to allow the continuation of
the incredibly inefficient operation of the flag carriers. Yet by the US
Department of Commerce's guidelines for trade cases, one can be certain that a large share of the government infusions of capital into these
firms would be deemed to constitute a subsidy under section 701 of the
Tariff Act of 1930.

There is only one approach open to the Community, if it wishes to
end the charges of unfair competition in the US market. It is simply to
reorganize each nationalized steel company into a firm capable of
standing alone. Establishing the true value of these firms' assets would
prove as embarrassing as the fact that all US integrated steel plants are
worth less than one efficient new plant of Japanese scale. In addition,
such a reorganization would require further downward pressure on
manning levels and wages. Given the political uproar that has accompanied employment declines in Belgium, the Lorraine and the Ruhr
valley, such a step is obviously not very likely.

It is quite clear, however, that world steel prices would not be much
affected by such a reorganization of the European steel industry. European output might not fall by very much. Even if it did, Brazil,
Taiwan, Korea, and even Canada and Japan have the ability to expand their output and their capacity substantially in response to any
upward movement in export prices. Thus, ending subsidies in Europe
is not going to relieve the pressure on the US industry that derives
from its high costs, the high value of the dollar, and excess capacity

throughout the world. It would not, therefore, reduce the cries for protection emanating from eastern and western Pennsylvania.

THE US GOVERNMENT AS CARTEL MANAGER

Unlike Europe, the US has chosen to avoid government-established
rationalization cartels. There are no minimum prices, no direct
government subsidies, no forced rationalizations and no incentives to
reduce employment. Rather, the US government has been a passive
recipient of difficult foreign trade suits from which it must continually
extricate itself. As the dollar has risen, the price of escape has also
risen.

The trigger-price programme was essentially an inexpensive concession to the US integrated carbon steel industry. It could not last. Since
that time, however, the industry has pressed for quantitative restrictions or the imposition of anti-dumping or countervailing duties. In
these proceedings, the industry (and other complainants) essentially
hold the US government hostage, requiring it to negotiate bilateral
agreements between US and foreign steel producers that would otherwise be illegal under US antitrust laws. But why does the government
not simply prosecute the cases to a conclusion, imposing the requisite
duties? The answer is quite simple to anyone with more than a passing
knowledge of cartel theory.

Under US trade laws, domestic interests may pursue anti-dumping
or countervailing duty suits against firms exporting goods to the United
States at less than fair value or at prices that are suppressed by subsidies
in the exporting country. These suits must demonstrate to the satisfac-
tion of the International Trade Commission that there has been
material injury to the US industry and/or its workers before the
Department of Commerce assesses the extent of illegal dumping or
subsidization. Once the injury determination is final, the Department
of Commerce completes its assessment of the duties required to offset
the dumping margin or the degree to which prices are subsidized by the
exporter's government. In either case, the corrective duties are applied
to all prospective imports of the product from the offending foreign producer until such time as he can demonstrate that he is no longer the
recipient of subsidies or that his prices are at or above fair value.

There are two important reasons why the anti-dumping and
countervailing-duty cases are rarely pursued to the point of imposing
the duties. First, the procedure is one that involves a host of arbitrary
determinations. What is 'fair value'? How can one determine the price
of like merchandise in the home market, if home-market products are
not identical in design or quality? If fair value is to be assessed by the

cost-of-production standard in the 1974 and 1979 Trade Acts, how can anyone determine the full cost of production over time of one product exported by a multi-product firm to the United States?

Similarly, the measurement of the effect of various government programmes upon export prices is devilishly difficult. How does the Department of Commerce estimate the cost of producing anything in a socialist enterprise? And how can this cost be translated into US dollars, if the exporting country maintains a multi-tiered exchange rate?[15] If a government nationalizes a troubled firm instead of allowing it to be reorganized through bankruptcy proceedings, is the government's investment a subsidy within the meaning of the GATT or the US trade laws?[16] In the last analysis, many of these determinations are necessarily arbitrary, a prospect that is more than a little discomforting to importers or exporters, who must wait months for this arbitrary judgement to be rendered.

Second, even if the parties in a trade case are patient enough to wait for an arbitrary decision on anti-dumping or countervailing duties, they would probably prefer a quantitative agreement to the imposition of a duty. If the quantitative agreement to limit imports is roughly equivalent to the effects of the expected duty assessment upon imports, the exporter avoids the duty by entering such an agreement, but retains the same market share. In addition, if a series of such agreements are pursued against all exporters of a given product to the United States, these agreements will have a more predictable effect than a set of *ad valorem* duties in reducing import competition. Quantity agreements are better than tariffs in cartelizing the industry and distributing the benefits among all sellers. Thus, US interests as well as exporters would both prefer quantitative agreements to duties, unless the duties were specifically earmarked to the aggrieved US industry for 'rationalization', 'modernization' or some other purpose.

In the case of the current steel market in the United States, the incentive for exporters to enter into restrictive trade agreements with the US government is even stronger than suggested above. As I have shown, prices of steel-mill products in the US are far above export levels in the face of the extraordinary performance of the US dollar since 1980, but exporters of steel will not be able to share fully in the fruits of the high prices, because they must compete against numerous other exporters for US market share. US steel buyers may be induced over time to shift away from high-priced domestic steel, but they need not pay more than the world price for this imported steel. If, however, a cartel agent were able to organize all steel exporters, each exporter might be able to obtain a very large share of the $100-plus per tonne price premium being enjoyed by US producers. The only available candidate for cartel manager who is not subject to US antitrust laws is the US government itself. Thus, the spate of suits filed by US Steel and others against most exporters of steel to the US may be seen as a god-send not only for beleaguered US steel producers, but especially for all of the firms competing aggressively in the world export market.

With both domestic firms and exporters interested in reaping supra-competitive prices from the US market, it is not surprising that the US government has found itself increasingly pushed towards negotiating 'voluntary' restraint agreements with exporters of steel. It is not an easy game, but its outcome is preferred by everyone (except US tax-payers) to countervailing or anti-dumping duties. As in the case of any cartel, however, the apportioning of market shares and enforcing them is no easy matter. It is for this reason that the US Department of Com-merce finds itself in much the same difficult position as ex-EC Com-missioner Davignon, assigning scarce market shares among numerous eager recipients.

The data in table 2.8 demonstrate that the nascent US import cartel managed by the Department of Commerce would be almost complete if only two major players would join – Canada and Japan. In addition, Korea would have to be restrained by more than the nominal duties levied on its steel exports in previous cases. Unfortunately for the US industry, these three countries are virtually unassailable under anti-dumping or anti-subsidy provisions of the US trade laws. They com-pete aggressively in the US market for a simple reason – they have relatively low costs of production. They can only be forced to join the fight for higher imported steel prices in the US by means of the section 201 escape-clause suit. But even if they join, the task of apportioning reduced market shares to those already under quota – such as the EC – will not be easy.

At present, most of the opposition to the imposition of quotas through section 201 or legislation comes from downstream fabricators, already in difficulty because of the appreciation of the dollar and the relatively high price of steel in the US, and from exporting sectors of the US economy. The latter have reason to be concerned, because the imposi-tion of a universal 15 per cent quota or President Reagan's prospective informal quota on carbon steel could generate claims for compensation under the GATT of nearly $2 billion per year at 1983 prices. For this reason alone, US trade authorities should view their role as prospective steel cartel manager as a mixed blessing at best.

THE CURRENT POLICY CHOICES

The above discussion of the US–EC steel policy problem is quite dif-ferent from that advanced by trade officials and industry spokesmen. They see the problem as deriving from the agonizing choices over

TABLE 2.8   IMPORTS OF BASIC STEEL-MILL PRODUCTS COVERED BY
TRADE MEASURES,[a] 1982-3 (thousands of net tons)

	Imports covered by trade measures, 1983	Imports of total basic steel mill products, 1983	Percentage of 1983 imports covered[a]
EC total	4039	4114	98.2
Japan	0[b]	4237	0.0[b]
Canada	0	2379	0.0
Mexico	578	651	88.8
Trinidad	64	66	97.0
Venezuela	0	158	0.0
Brazil	1011	1257	80.5
Argentina	189	273	69.3
Finland	85	196	43.5
Czechoslovakia	19	19	99.2
Poland	26	77	33.5
Spain	456	610	74.7
Romania	0	9	0.0[c]
Republic of Korea	1014	1728	58.7
China (Taiwan)	131	177	73.7
Australia	100	185	53.8
Republic of South Africa	487	557	87.5
Other	0	368	0.0
All countries	8199	17060	48.1

[a] Trade measures include the US–EC arrangements, the Mexican 'VRA', pending anti-dumping and countervailing duty cases, suspension agreements, and anti-dumping and countervailing duty orders.
[b] Carbon steel plate from Japan is covered by an anti-dumping order, but imports in 1983 were insignificant.
[c] Carbon steel plate from Romania is covered by an anti-dumping order, but imports in 1983 were insignificant.
The figures for total basic steel-mill product imports include tonnage for speciality steel products affected by a section 201 case. These amounts to about 1.3 per cent of total basic steel-mill product imports.
Source: Brief of the Japanese Steel Export Association, submitted to the US International Trade Commission in Investigation TA-201-51, 18 May 1984.

'restructuring' their respective industries. Firms and workers must be given aid (in Europe) or protection (in the US) to facilitate the adjustment of their industry to the new realities of the world steel market. In the interim, it would be nice if prices were 'stabilized' at levels far above world market prices. Davignon's attempts to elevate European steel prices have apparently not been very successful. In the US, however, the strong performance of the dollar and the intimidating force of scores of trade suits filed by the domestic steel industry have combined to keep steel prices far above world levels.

From my perspective, therefore, the US–EC steel trade dispute is simply part of a much bigger problem. US integrated steel firms have availed themselves of trade protection to elevate US steel prices repeatedly since 1968. Higher prices have been justified as necessary to ease the restructuring of the industry, but in fact they impeded the restructuring. As a result, the US industry is far from a stable equilibrium. At present, however, if US steel prices were to fall to world levels, US integrated producers would be decimated. Therefore, the current steel trade disputes with the US are simply a reflection of an industry with virtually insoluble problems trying to buy precious time.

Seen this way, the resolution of US–EC steel trade issues, regardless of the form they take, are irrelevant to the larger problem. It would not have mattered if the 1982 agreement had specified a target of 3 per cent or 7 per cent of the US market. It would not have mattered if the member countries of the EC had privatized their entire steel industries and ended subsidies overnight. No policy decisions within the EC can, by themselves, raise world steel prices. If the entire problem in the US is to relieve the unbearable downward pressure upon domestic steel prices, there is no bilateral agreement between the US and the Community that can succeed. It is for this reason that President Reagan's advisers have persuaded him to seek quantitative agreements with virtually all of the exporters of steel to the US.

If the dollar were to decline substantially, the details of subsidies, fair value and restructuring aids might become important once again. For instance, by the time the 1982 EC–US steel pact expires in 1986, there may be a more reasonable climate for trade discussions, if the dollar has fallen from its currently lofty level. It would be desirable at that juncture to find agreement on the types of subsidies that are counter-vailable, because they lower offer prices and increase exports. Dominick is quite right that the US approach on these issues is confused, but this confusion stems from the policy requirement of offering trade pro-tection on some *propter hoc, post hoc* basis, given the high value of the dollar.[17] It is naïve to suppose that such a discussion can even begin for a few years, however, given the press of current problems. US trade of-ficials are too busy trying to establish and manage an import cartel to be looking two or three years into the future.

CONCLUSION

Although it is easy to attribute the current problems in the US, EC and even Japanese steel industry to 'unfair' trade practices, these problems have much deeper roots. The world's steel industry is in the midst of a major shakeout, caused by slow growth in steel consumption and a shift

of production toward the newly industrialized countries. In the US and
in a number of European countries, this long transition has placed government authorities under strong pressure to fight against the inevitable.
In Europe, this pressure has led to a variety of measures to protect,
restructure and cartelize the industry. In the US, the only government
actions have been in response to trade suits brought by the aggrieved
steel companies and their employees in the face of a soaring dollar.
Among the 'targets' of these suits have been the European producers,
who are now awaiting the outcome of further attempts to raise US imported steel prices.

Unfortunately, there is no easy solution to the steel problem in the
US. A reduction in the value of the dollar would surely help, in the
short run, but it would not have a major impact on the long-run decline
of the integrated US companies. Steel production is shifting gradually
to the mini-mills in the US as world steel output moves equally slowly
towards the newly industrialized countries. One thing is sure: further
increases in the price of steel in the US while world steel prices remain
low will only serve to reduce the size of the US steel market in the long
run. Already, US motor companies are looking to Brazil, Mexico,
Japan and Korea for their US models or for components for these
models. Each country has a large steel industry that will benefit indirectly from trade restraints imposed upon steel in the US. If trade
restraints in the US are to help the US industry in the long run, they
must raise *world* steel prices. This would require very strong world
economic recovery or a world cartel. Neither seems likely in the near
future.

NOTES

1 For a discussion of these historical antecedents, see Robert W. Crandall, *The US
Steel Industry in Recurrent Crisis* (Brookings Institution, Washington, DC, 1981).
2 For the price trends in several basic carbon steel-mill products, see tables 2.4–2.6.
3 See International Iron and Steel Institute, Annual Report of the Secretary
General, Mr Lenhard J. Holscuoh, 11–13 October 1982.
4 See Crandall, *The US Steel Industry*; Donald F. Barnett and Louis Schorsch, *Steel:
Upheaval in a Basic Industry* (Balinger, Cambridge, Mass., 1983); and Peter Marcus
et al. *World Steel Dynamics* (Paine-Webber Mitchel Hutchins, New York, 1984).
5 For a discussion of trigger prices, see Crandall, *The US Steel Industry*.
6 A useful summary of these events may be found in Hans Mueller and Hans Van
der Ven, 'Perils in the Brussels–Washington Steel Pact of 1982', *The World
Economy* (December 1982).
7 For 1983 prices, see Marcus et al., *World Steel Dynamics*, or John Tumazos, *Steel Industry Review* (Oppenheimer, New York, 1984).
8 US Department of Commerce, International Trade Administration, Termination
of Countervailing and Antidumping Investigations, Appendix III 'The Arrangement', *Federal Register*, 29 October 1982.

9   See European Communities Commission, *Cutting Steel Capacity: European Commission's June 30 Decision*, Background Report, ISEC/B23/83, 19 July 1983.

10 See Marcus *et al.*, *World Steel Dynamics*. Official 'capability' estimates provided by the American Iron and Steel Institute, *Annual Statistical Report, 1983* (Washington, DC, 1984) show a decline from 145 million tonnes in 1977 to 123 million tonnes at present.

11 To some extent, this overstates their reduction in capacity to produce finished steel, given the modest increase in yields in the past eight years.

12 See European Communities Commission, *Cutting Steel Capacity*.

13 Ibid.

14 For an analysis of the effect of subsidies on prices, see John Mutti, 'Subsidized production, world steel trade, and countervailing duties', *Southern Economic Journal* (January 1984), pp. 871–80.

15 The US government once estimated the cost of production for Polish golf carts by analysing hypothetical costs for similar ones in Spain!

16 For a discussion of some of these issues, see Mary F. Dominick, 'Countervailing state aids to steel: a case for international consensus', *Common Market Law Review*, vol. 21 (1984), pp. 355–403.

17 Ibid.

Comment 1

PATRICK MESSERLIN

Robert Crandall proceeds to outline the major economic forces that during the past two decades have profoundly changed the world steel market and given rise to serious difficulties for the 'ageing dinosaurs' that the American and West European steel industries have become. In this comment, using my comparative advantage of being a European, I would like particularly to elaborate on the problems that are specific to the Community, to the extent that they also affect Euro-American relations. Two points appear to me to be essential both in order to understand the past and to be able to offer perspectives for future actions.

THE TREATY OF PARIS

The first essential is a proper understanding of the nature of the Treaty of Paris, which created the European Coal and Steel Community (ECSC): it cannot be overemphasized that this treaty, despite appearances to the contrary, is not based on free-trade principles.

In reality, the treaty establishes rules that are relatively close to those used (under the name 'basing-point system') in the 1930s by the American steel industry, when it tried to cartelize itself by setting factory-gate prices and also by laying down by convention the departure port for the products.[1] This meant 'transparent' transport costs, but also a large reduction in the possibilities of competition in this domain. It also required the publication of investment programmes, including future market shares. In practice, the treaty assured the permanence of 'spheres of influence' for each national steel industry, corresponding more or less to the frontiers of the member states.

Such an economic organization made good sense in the political context of Western Europe in the 1950s. It would have been suicidal – in a political context – to allow true free trade, since this would have introduced a certain specialization and thus differentiation between the member states. Indeed, the latter would without doubt have made the Federal Republic of Germany an even more important steel producer, taking account of the comparative advantage given to Germany by the technology existing in the 1950s.

During the 1950s, the Treaty of Paris played a fairly positive role, in that it allowed the creation of the Common Market and still only exerted weak pressures in the direction of national cartelization. The paradox of the Treaty of Paris is that it created a European dynamism in favour of free trade, while being itself fundamentally protectionist and anti-competitive. During the 1960s, however, the treaty gradually lost this dynamic role and, at the same time, continued to reinforce the tendencies to create 'national champions' at the centre of each national steel industry; this was so even in the Federal Republic of Germany, where this process of cartelization was taking place – already – under cover of 'nationalization'.

In particular, the Treaty of Paris gave rise to two types of behaviour, the combination of which was to have explosive results at the heart of each national steel industry. On the one hand, it slowed down the pace of the disappearance or elimination of firms by its tendency to stabilize market shares: the 'mavericks' never succeeded in destabilizing the established firms sufficiently to eliminate the most marginal of them and accelerate the writing-off of old plant. On the other hand, the treaty encouraged each state to act as a privileged or preferred investor and thus to increase production capacity by unreasonable amounts, since each state wanted to maintain future market shares at the existing levels.

These two factors together led to the overcapacity at the end of the 1970s and the beginning of the 1980s. Not only is this overcapacity characterized by global excess supply in comparison with the global demand for steel, but also, and most importantly, it is produced by great differences between the most efficient plant, scattered here and there by excessive investment, and the most marginal plant: in other words, in 1974 the West European steel industry appeared as an oligopoly that we have elsewhere qualified as 'imperfect',[2] where relatively small firms in relatively large numbers compete with each other with the state always coming between them.

THE INDUSTRIAL CHOICES OF THE COMMUNITY

Since the middle of the 1970s, under the combined pressures of the Treaty of Paris and political and social events, the 'adjustment' policy has been managed within the framework of a bicephal (dual leadership) structure headed by the Commission and the governments of the member states. The actions of the latter have constituted, above all, a classic policy of production and export subsidies, and have tended to delay or frustrate those measures undertaken by the Commission.

The Commission chose to be the organizer of the European steel cartel and also its secular arm. The rationing of exports to the United States, following the voluntary export restraints (VERs) imposed by the latter from 1969 onwards, had constrained the European powers to share out explicitly the markets that remained open: this export cartel, for markets that were equally important in terms of quantities and qualities of steel products, was the first step towards a cartel for the European market itself. This latter cartel proved to be difficult to establish for three reasons: the firms, even if they were already grouped in well-structured national oligopolies, still only formed an 'unstable' oligopoly at the European level; the states, through their investment policies, limited the area of possible agreement between different firms, and represented a major source of instability for the nascent oligopoly; finally, the crisis of 1974–6 revealed large differences between better than marginal and marginal firms.

What are the results of the cartelization policy 'imposed' by the Commission? Has this policy brought about a rationalization of plants, an incremental modernization and an adjustment of production capacity? It is difficult to give a definitive answer, but it is important to note that it is anything but certain, as indeed Crandall underlines. In this respect, according to J. Gandois, the difference between the cost price of the most efficient and the least efficient firms is, in 1985, 15 per cent for flat products and more than 30 per cent for long products:[3] little progress has thus been made in this respect during the last ten years, if this is really the position. Similarly, it is difficult to see how there can have been an acceleration of the modernization process, when certain steel firms, and not the least important, are announcing increases in research and development investment that are less than the increases of the same types of investment in those countries which are the most advanced steel producers. Does not such a situation imply an accentuation of the gap that already exists?[4] Finally, it is well known that it is especially difficult to estimate accurately the evolution of production capacities within the West European steel industry; this is so for two reasons. On the one hand, plant reductions are often designed to leave open the possibility of a later expansion in a situation of recovery; in other words, the newly rationalized plant, by being able to self-multiply, represents potential capacity that is all the greater. On the other hand, firms are encouraged to preserve as much capacity as possible by the means of cartelization used by the Commission.

In practice, the Commission plays the role of head office for the European steel cartel, using essentially quantitative instruments: quotas on imports (imitated from the American VERs), production quotas and strict limits on investments. However, these instruments all have the major fault of creating economic rents for the European producers, rents which will be bigger the more efficient are the producers. These rents can alternatively be absorbed by inefficient investment or management decisions, by failure to reduce wages, by high retirement premia and, above all, by the repayment of debts to creditors who would otherwise have had to bear their share of the burden of the inevitable bankruptcies, as Crandall also points out.

In view of these arguments, it is not at all clear that the Davignon plans, which combined concentration with cartelization, have accelerated whatever adjustment has actually taken place. This impression is reinforced by the fact that the firms that emerged from 'the red' in 1984 (Arbed, Hoogovens, Thyssen, Krupp, Boel, the Bresciani, etc.) were precisely the ones that appeared to be potentially viable in 1974. These firms have in fact lost money (especially between 1979 and 1984) solely because the other West European steel firms did not go bankrupt or into liquidation because of the 'discipline' of the cartel. Meanwhile, these latter firms still remain and seem to be just as far away from the leading group of the most efficient concerns.

If the results of the Davignon plans have been extremely limited, their cost has been extraordinarily high. As well as a European price 10-20 per cent higher than the world price, according to certain observers, large state subsidies have been poured into the sector: table 2.1.1 gives certain figures from the data established by the Commission in the framework of the 'Code of Aids' of 1981.

TABLE 2.1.1 AID TO EUROPEAN STEEL, 1980-5

	Total aid provided for (million ECU)	Aid granted (actual) by 15.10.84 (ECU per tonne)	Total aid per tonne produced, 1980-4 (ECU per tonne)
Federal Republic of Germany	4202	3503	17.8
Belgium	4188	2631	46.9
France	7613	3943	39.6
Italy	9089	8228	67.9
Luxemburg	527	383	11.9
The Netherlands	469	375	14.8
United Kingdom	5763	2674	37.9
Others	319	161	20.3
Community	32970	21898	

Source: P. Lamm, Les Echos, 22 November 1984.

Apart from the financial costs, there are also non-monetary costs of considerable significance. The member states are seen to be at least as important as the market as originators of risk and uncertainty: thus in France, the nationalized group Sacilor set aside 600 million francs for the building of a heavy product line, even though the government had refused permission for its construction several months earlier. As for the Commission, one must fear that it has become a prisoner of the very cartel it created, providing a new example of the well-known role of the 'regulator regulated'.

CONCLUSION

The future of Euro-American relations in steel would be considerably different if the Community adopted two new approaches of very different significance. The first, the most essential and the most difficult, would consist of placing steel and coal within the normal framework of the Treaty of Rome. The abandonment of the Treaty of Paris can be seen as a deregulation of the two industries concerned. The Treaty of Rome provides at least as many instruments for pursuing a policy of adjustment as does the Treaty of Paris. Furthermore, these instruments have many fewer perverse effects than the quantitative measures implied by 'the state of crisis' (in the ECSC sense).

The second approach is to continue in the direction of the 'Code on Aids': after all, budgetary constraints on the part of member states became even more marked during periods of slow growth; this may lead one to suppose that those states with tight budgets would be only too happy to see reminders of the limits on subsidies.

If the Community does not undertake these two measures, there is a danger that American protectionism in steel will be used as an alibi by the Community to justify its agricultural protection or its strategy of 'reprisals', while persuading itself that it is still the champion of free trade. This attitude can only damage the overall interests of the Community, precisely because it is the largest trading power in the world.

NOTES

1   For an analysis of the 'basing-point system' of cartelization, see F. M. Scherer, *Industrial Market Structure and Economic Performance* (Rand McNally, Chicago, 1970); for an opposite analysis, see D. D. Haddock, 'Basing-point pricing: competitive and collusive theories', *American Economic Review* (June 1982), pp. 289–306.

2 P. A. Messerlin, 'The European steel industry and the world crisis', in Y. Mény and V. Wright (ed.), *Local and National Management of Industrial Problems: The Case of Steel in the 1970s* (European University Institute, Florence, forthcoming).

3 J. Gandois, 'L'Europe et son acier', *La Tribune de l'Economie,* 2–3 March 1985.

4 See, for example, *Le Rapport d'Activité d'Usinor* (1984).

Comment 2

WILLIAM T. HOGAN

There are two points of view concerning the future of the steel industry in the United States and, to some extent, they apply to the industry in the EC. The first is definitely pessimistic and refers to the integrated companies in the steel industry as ageing or dying dinosaurs. In the United States, it points to import penetration, the ageing plant structure, the decline in demand, and the general lack of adequate capital to bring the industry's technology to a competitive level with that in Japan and the Third World. It also singles out what is called an excessively high level of wages in comparison with other countries. The average hourly employment cost in integrated plants in the United States is approximately $21.00, as compared with $12.00–13.00 in Japan and $3.00 in South Korea. With all of these disadvantages, this view sees little hope for a long-term revival of the integrated segment of the industry and looks to the Japanese and the Third World, as well as the mini-mills, to provide much of the steel in the United States in the decade ahead.

Without question, the aforementioned difficulties present major problems for the integrated companies in the United States, and the survival of a few has been called into question. The recent negotiations conducted by the US Trade Representative's office with the steel industries in those countries that export large tonnages to the United States will result in the reduction of these exports to approximately 18.5 per cent of the US market, from 26 per cent in 1984. This will unquestionably bring some relief, since it will increase output by the American steel industry over the 1984 level by some 7 million tons. Nevertheless, according to the pessimistic view of the industry, this will only bring temporary relief.

There is another view of the integrated segment of the steel industry in the United States which is less pessimistic; in fact, it could be termed mildly optimistic for the long run. While recognizing the aforementioned problems, as well as the decline in certain segments of the steel industry, proponents of this view maintain that the worst days of the integrated steel companies in the United States are behind them and that, given any increase in demand, a number of the companies, not necessarily all, can return to profitability in the next year or two.

Many of the integrated companies have taken steps to solve their problems. These include the closure of plants or parts of plants; reductions in the workforce, both hourly and salaried; programmes to reduce costs in almost every phase of their operations; diversification into non-steel activities to protect themselves on the downside of the steel cycle; mergers; a considerable number of joint ventures; and investments in facilities such as continuous casting, which will permit more efficient operations and improve steel quality. Under the pressure of the market, they restructured themselves to a point where they differed markedly from their 1980 appearance.

In terms of plant closures, some 21 million tons have been abandoned by the integrated steel producers between 1981 and 1984. This has reduced overall steel capacity in the country from 154 million net tons to less than 135 million net tons. The process is by no means complete, and a reduction of at least 5–7 million tons more can be expected by the end of 1986. Virtually all of these abandoned facilities were relatively obsolete and high cost. Consequently, those that remain are more modern and can produce steel more efficiently and at a more competitive cost. Further, with the reduction in capacity, the companies, with less tonnage, will operate at a higher rate of capacity, which will enable them to reduce costs.

An added improvement is the investment in continuous-casting facilities, which is overdue. However, it will bring the proportion of output continuously cast from a relatively low 31 per cent in 1983 to more than 55 per cent in 1986, when all of the units are in place and operating. Every major integrated company in the United States has either recently installed, has under construction, or has firmly committed itself to substantial continuous-casting units.

A major development in the US steel industry in the past year has been the formation of joint ventures among steel companies. These involve some five electrolytic galvanizing lines that are under contract or construction at the present time. The facilities are directed to satisfy the recent requirements of the motor industry for galvanized sheets in the exposed parts of the car bodies to resist corrosion. The companies involved in these joint ventures include Bethlehem and Inland, United States Steel and Rouge Steel, LTV and Sumitomo, National Steel and

Nippon Kokan, and Wheeling-Pittsburgh and Nisshin. Only Armco is installing its own facility. This move is a particularly astute one, since it allows the major companies to participate in the motor industry market for galvanized sheets without the need for each company to construct its own facility; a circumstance which would have led to a large overcapacity. Further, joint ventures will be pursued in the near future in other aspects of the industry, particularly in the production of iron, where blast furnaces as joint ventures are practical.

It is questionable whether there will be any mergers among major integrated companies in the next year. The merger between Republic and J&L, as well as the purchase by Nippon Kokan of 50 per cent of National Steel, leaves only two possibilities among the major integrated companies, namely Inland and Armco.

MINI-MILLS

In the last twenty years, the mini-mill has achieved a significant position in the steel industry in the United States. At present, it accounts for 20–23 per cent of steel production and, as these mills increase in size, their output could well grow to more than 25 per cent of the US total. They are currently confined for the most part to a relatively narrow range of products, including concrete reinforcing bar and small structurals. Within the last few years, some of the mini-mills have ventured into other product lines. One has installed facilities for medium structural shapes, whereas another produces rounds for seamless tubes and forgings. A third produces special-quality bars. There has been considerable discussion about the production by mini-mills of sheet products. This, however, will require an improvement in technology so that thin slabs of 1 inch or 1½ inches can be cast and, at best, the finished product will be a commercial brand of sheets. Very few mini-mills will be involved in the production of sheet within the next five years, so that, although the mini-mills have achieved a very definite position in the US steel industry, their expansion into the areas dominated by the integrated mills is highly unlikely. The one exception to this is wire rods, where mini-mills have virtually taken over the field, as a number of the majors have ceased production.

The steel industry in the United States, in spite of capital expenditures of over $40 billion in the past two decades, still faces problems in a number of areas. Considerable progress has been made toward their solutions, although much remains to be done.

Comment 3

FRANK S. BENYON*

In order to complement Mr Crandall's paper and to give an element of balance thereto, it would seem necessary to:
1) highlight the disadvantages of an industrial 'policy' composed solely of import controls;
2) complete and correct the description of the adjustment policies of the European Community;
3) situate the 1982 US–EC arrangement in its context and evaluate how much it solved, or will solve, steel trade problems, at least those across the Atlantic.

THE US APPROACH

It is beyond dispute that the US government's approach to its industry's mounting costs and diminishing markets is based entirely on external protection, either maintaining prices by the trigger-price mechanism, countervailing duties, etc. or keeping foreigners' market shares down by 'voluntary export restraint' agreements. The major disadvantages of this are, first, that a sovereign government is thus held hostage by its steel industry complainants and, second, that the imposition of duties, or the allocation to importers of fixed market shares, is in no way made dependent upon the fulfilment by the complainant industry of restructuring measures. More important, however, the tortuous evaluation methods used by the US authorities

---

* The views expressed herein are entirely personal to the author.

in these procedures and the often arbitrary decisions which result, not only do nothing to solve the underlying industrial problems, but, on a much broader scale, throw into question the international trade rules negotiated with such difficulty within the GATT, and in particular the Subsidies Code of the Tokyo Round, for all products.

As for real results of the 'spontaneous' restructuring by the US mills, one must recall that the apparently favourable position shown in table 2.7 concerns raw steel capacity and not rolled products. (The latter are those with which purchasers – and thus supply, demand and the level of prices available to the producers – are most concerned.) Indeed, it is in this sector that the Community reductions are more important, from 168.6 million tons in 1980 to 140.3 million tons in 1985, or about 17 per cent, including cuts made both within and beyond the framework of the Community Aids Code referred to below.

THE COMMUNITY APPROACH

The EC, in contrast, has adopted a complete, coordinated and multi-faceted approach to its steel industry's problems. Indeed, it was the existence of such comprehensive and calculated restructuring policies that prompted the Community to object so fiercely, both before the US authorities and the GATT, to the approach adopted by the US in its countervailing procedures. Let us first recall that the European Coal and Steel Community (ECSC) established, by the Treaty of Paris of 1951, the first common market in these two important heavy industries. The Commission administers this community in close co-operation with those concerned, respecting the principle of limited interventions contained in article 5 of the treaty, and exercising a preference for in-direct actions (article 57). On occasions, however, and especially in crisis situations, direct interventions in production and markets are foreseen, and the Commission has used these powers to the full in the 1970s and, increasingly, in the 1980s. It has taken actions in the five following areas.

First, it cannot be denied that the Commission is fully aware of the problems that imports can create. Accordingly, it has established close monitoring procedures and a revised anti-dumping mechanism, and concludes annual voluntary arrangements with major suppliers. How-ever, the strict import barriers foreseen in article 74 of the treaty have not been resorted to, no doubt since the Community realizes that its position as a net exporter would thus be too greatly harmed.

Second, the Commission has provided a comprehensive mechanism for restructuring. Its 'subsidies code', adopted in 1980[1] and strength-ened in 1981,[2] provides for subsidies only to be granted if the recipient

undertaking is cutting capacities, is engaged in restructuring and specialization programmes, and is able to restore viability without any
public aids being paid after 1985. The very step which Mr Crandall
sees as 'obviously not very likely' namely that each company should
stand alone without subsidies, is precisely what the code – respected
fully throughout its application – foresees after December 1985!

The third measure taken to assist the industry's restructuring has
been to subject production to quantitative quotas, thus maintaining
prices. Unlike what is implied in Crandall's paper, this system is an act
of sovereign authority, specifically foreseen in article 58 of the treaty,
upheld entirely by the European Court of Justice, and is in no way the
'sanctioning . . . of an outright cartel'. As in the USA, in the Community also there is a clear distinction between public and private production controls.

To ensure further that certain revenue levels for the steel-makers are
maintained, the Community's price publication rules have been policed
strongly, steel dealers were included within the controls for the first
time in 1981, and at different times[3] minimum price systems have been
introduced.

Lastly, the whole policy has been accompanied by extensive social
measures for the reconversion of, or granting of assistance to, the large
number of workers laid off by the inevitable plant closures.

As a general comment, it must be conceded that in so far as it is the
Community and the Commission which are given all powers by the
treaty, and in so far as the Commission does not (unlike a US president) depend so directly upon the approval of a national electorate, it
may have been somewhat easier for the Commission – as opposed to
a national government – to carry through these often unpopular
measures.

THE US – EC ARRANGEMENT OF 1982

It was in this context of two diametrically oposed approaches to the
same fundamental industrial problems that the 1982 arrangement was
negotiated and concluded. This arrangement was to be welcomed for
different reasons: it showed what favourable results could be achieved
when the Community as a whole acted as negotiator; it avoided im-
perilling the Community's entire restructuring policy by ensuring
a fair share of the US market for more than three years; and it created a
new precedent in relation to the classic voluntary export restraint
agreement, where only the exporter undertakes to limit supplies,
because the US government also undertook obligations, namely to control the imports by virtue of a new section 626 added to its Trade Act in

1982 and to enter into consultations before any other actions, discretionary or more 'automatic', were taken.

Unfortunately, however, the arrangement has its negative aspects too. Not only did it not solve all import problems – since special steels, tubes and some other products were left out, which led to annoying discussions both in Congress[4] and in new countervailing, etc. procedures[5] – but, more important, it did not solve the underlying problem of the US industry. Although the arrangement referred to giving 'time to permit restructuring', it nowhere specified how and when, on the US side, this should take place! In addition, it was yet another step away from free trade towards the 'organization of world trade', which was no doubt not without significance in the subsequent US decisions to introduce controls on imports from other countries or for imports of other products (for example, the pipes and tubes arrangement concluded with the Community at the beginning of 1985).[6] Lastly, it did nothing to solve the fundamental differences of approach to the interpretation of the GATT and its subsidies code, and thus to the general problem of the compatibility of government actions in ailing industrial sectors with the general code of conduct for world trade.

Overall, however, it is submitted that the Community has the correct and coherent approach to the basic problems of steel production in developed countries. Although it is true that 'no policy decision within the EC can . . . raise world steel prices', it is submitted that the policy decisions already taken and put into practice, namely draconian capacity reductions and increasing product specialization, accompanied for a short period by temporary measures to guarantee acceptable revenues and fair market shares, will produce an industry with greater productivity and thus lower costs, and with the technology and ability to produce a more sophisticated product which will not always even need to compete with the often simpler product from countries with cheaper labour.

What one can say with certainty is that an approach consisting of raising import barriers even higher is not the right one, since, as Mr Crandall concedes, its success would require a world cartel or a very strong – and fast? – world economic recovery: not very sure bases on which to build one's hopes!

NOTES

1   Decision 257/80/ECSC OJ 1980 L29.
2   Decision 2320/81/ECSC OJ 1981 L 228.
3   As at present, Decision [3715/83/ECSC] OJ 1983, L 373.

4 For example the Gaydos Bill limiting imports introduced in November 1983.
5 Gilmore steel in September 1983, Bethlehem steel under S.201.
6 Giving a 7.6 per cent share to Community exporters with certain flexibilities for the
   coming two years.

Agricultural Policies and World Trade: The US and the European Community at Bay

TIM JOSLING

INTRODUCTION

The European Community and the United States are the two superpowers in world agricultural trade. In keeping with this status, agricultural trade relationships between them are characterized by suspicion, hostility and rivalry, tempered by the awareness of mutual dependence and shared interests. The resulting atmosphere of confrontation and mistrust spills over into other areas and threatens the harmony of the Atlantic alliance. If the continual sparring were about issues of small moment, one could attempt to relegate agriculture to the back room of commercial diplomacy and get on with more important things. Such an option is foreclosed by the growing significance of trade in agricultural products, both to the developed countries themselves and to the world economy as a whole.

Trade relationships in agriculture are bedevilled by the high political priorities given by almost all developed-country governments to maintaining the income level of domestic farmers. Yet the working of the trading system for temperate-zone commodities is of fundamental interest both for the developed countries, among whom a large part of the trade takes place, and for developing countries, who use such trade as an essential supplement to their own domestic production. The US and the EC can and do, by their domestic policy actions, influence the conditions of trade in agricultural products and hence the environment in which other countries frame their own policies. Superpower status carries with it obligations as well as opportunities. It is not too far-fetched to suggest that US – EC conflicts over agricultural trade are among the most important issues facing world agriculture today.

This paper begins with a discussion of the 'agricultural trade problem' in broad outline, and the macroeconomic environment in which this problem must be seen. The current state of US and EC agricultural policy forms the backdrop for the discussion of trade relationships, and is briefly described. The main trade issues are then summarized and the role of the GATT in dealing with such issues is reviewed. The paper ends with some comments about the future course of trade relationships between the US and the EC in agricultural markets.

ANATOMY OF THE AGRICULTURAL TRADE PROBLEM

Governments are ambivalent about trade. Some of their most vocal constituents are against it – or at least that part of trade that appears to threaten their incomes and employment prospects. In general, however, governments agree with the proposition that obtaining goods from the cheapest source and selling into the most profitable markets makes - sound sense for all countries. Agricultural trade is a particularly obvious and profitable form of international division of labour, essential to the reduction of the real cost of providing food and the stabilization of food supply. However, the temptation to use trade policy to create rents for domestic interests is perhaps greater in agriculture than in other sectors. Such policy responds to mercantilist as much as to liberal pressures. Protectionists in importing countries argue that they should provide for the domestic market and spread fears of undersirable dependence on foreign sources of supply. Export interests, in turn, persuade governments to help them find markets abroad for produce in excess of domestic requirements. The result is an agricultural trading system riddled with government-imposed distortions, but functioning under reluctant acquiescence with the underlying logic of the division of labour.

Although this problem of government-distorted trade is not unique to agriculture (the steel industry provides another example of a similar conflict), it has perhaps reached its peak in this sector. Ironically, the agricultural industry in most industrial countries is one of the most competitive. Despite some growth in corporate enterprises, the sector is characterized by small independent units making individual decisions based on local conditions. The government stands back from the production process, but takes charge of market conditions, at least for the major crops and livestock products, thereby hoping to create a favourable environment in which the farmer can make a respectable living.

The size of this market can be manipulated with a variety of instruments, including state-purchasing, the discouragement of overseas

supplies, the subsidization of exports and the granting of aids for
domestic use. The role of the government in such activities immediately
conflicts with the interests of other governments similarly engaged.
State-buying, unless it is simply for smoothing intra-seasonal supply,
leads to subsidized disposal on other markets. Import restrictions are
seen by foreign governments as hindering their own market objectives.
Even consumer subsidies, which should be beneficial to all farmers, are
often linked with trade measures to concentrate the benefits at home.
In short, unless by chance the favoured commodities differ by country,
domestic policies geared to enhancing income opportunities for domestic
farmers immediately run foul of those of other countries. In view of this
seeming incompatibility between trade and domestic policy, it is surprising that so much trade in farm products exists among industrial
countries, and that farm policy conflicts are not more widespread.

Before fleshing-out this anatomy, it is interesting to observe the
macroeconomic conditions under which the conflict will be most intense and the situations which are likely to ease tensions. One could
easily sketch out a 'worst-case' scenario for agricultural trade problems, where the exporting countries faced problems in their overseas
markets caused by slow income growth, high exchange rates *vis-à-vis*
the importers' currencies, and high support prices in those importing
countries. Add to that a weak domestic off-farm employment situation
(and perhaps pressure from forthcoming elections) and one has a
recipe for heightened agricultural trade problems as seen by the exporter. This will translate into diplomatic pressures on the importing
countries for trade liberalization. If those countres in turn have, as a
result of budget pressures or low farm incomes, been trying to expand
the markets for their own producers, this additional external pressure
will be resisted and trade relationships strained.

The situation in the early 1980s seems to correspond to this dismal
scenario. The highly valued dollar, due largely to the US decision to
finance budget deficits by offering attractive debt instruments, rather
than by increasing taxes – thus shifting foreign demand away from
wheat and corn towards treasury bills – has hit US farm exports at a
time when economic growth in other countries is still sluggish.[1] Price
levels in importing countries have followed their own path, dictated by
domestic events, rather than reflecting the generally lower real prices
on world markets. Persistently high interest rates hamper a now capital-
intensive US agriculture, and exacerbate the burden of the budget
deficit. Firms are reluctant to take on new workers, thus limiting the
off-farm opportunities for rural workers. Protectionist sentiments
abound in many sectors of the economy, making it more difficult to
espouse a credible foreign commercial policy of liberalization. As a
result, agricultural trade disputes seem further from resolution than for

many years. If these events are merely a temporary phenomenon, born of the 1981–2 'Great Recession', then one might be tempted to look past them to a normalization of trade relations, if and when the dollar falls back to more normal levels. The revival of economic growth, at home and abroad, may remove some of the problem for the exporter, although the importer may find it more difficult to reverse the rhetoric and deprotect the domestic agricultural industry.

Before turning to the specific problems created for agricultural trade, and the possibilities of resolving some of those problems, it is worth while to review briefly the domestic policies which dictate trade relationships. In keeping with the focus on US and EC trade issues, this review is limited to policies in those two areas. A fuller treatment of the relationship between agricultural trade and domestic policy would require a similar examination of the policies of other countries.

US FARM POLICIES

Modern US farm policy is usually considered to have had its origin in the depression, specifically with the Agricultural Adjustment Act (AAA) of 1933. The AAA introduced a new level of government involvement, setting up the Commodity Credit Corporation (CCC), which could both purchase and sell commodities directly and also grant loans to farmers using their products as collateral.[2] In addition, acreage allotments were authorized, which would specify the area that each farm could devote to particular crops. Later in the decade the mechanisms for implementing this form of acreage control were refined, and the groundwork was laid for the establishment of marketing orders. With the vote of two-thirds of producers for a particular crop, acreage allotments could be set up along with associated marketing quotas tied to average yields.

The early post-war period saw an intense debate on mechanisms to be used for farm income support and market management, centred around the 1949 Brannan Plan for direct (i.e. deficiency) payments. In the end, the old won over the new, and the 1949 Agriculture Act settled for acreage allotments and marketing quotas as the main instruments for market adjustment. CCC direct-purchasing activities continued for many commodities and the non-recourse loans provided a floor to the market. The post-war and Korean War periods of high demand alleviated income and surplus problems, and took much of the pressure off policy instruments. The agricultural sector responded with increased output and by 1954 surpluses were back – not because of depression conditions, but as a result of a surge in production.

The year 1954 saw two major developments in farm policy: the introduction of flexible price supports – i.e. price reductions – for surplus commodities, and the establishment of a surplus disposal programme, the Agricultural Trade and Development Act, usually known as PL 480. Unable to stem the tide, these measures were reinforced in 1956 by the Soil Bank, designed to take land out of production. This differed from the earlier acreage-allotment programme in several respects. It was not crop-specific: whole farms could be removed from the productive base. Farmers were paid to make such adjustments, rather than penalized if they did not. Farms could be retired for several years at a time, essentially being leased to the government in return for a rental payment. The conservation reserve, in particular, proved successful in this regard and removed 30 million acres from production by 1962.

By the beginning of the 1960s, further measures were needed to control output. The 1962 Food and Agriculture Act attempted to introduce mandatory production controls, where these were agreed by a vote of growers of a particular commodity. In 1963, the wheat growers soundly defeated such a programme in a referendum, and mandatory controls have never been tried since. In their place appeared direct income supports for farmers *choosing* to participate in certain programmes. Loan rates were lowered to attempt to clear markets, but farmers could avoid the impact of this by 'signing up'. This led, by 1970, to the notion of making it a condition of receiving such payments that farmers 'set aside' a proportion of their acreage otherwise destined for surplus commodities. In place of government payments specifically to retire land into the Soil Bank, the 1970 Agricultural Act thus offered income-support payments to those farmers that voluntarily reduced acreage, and withheld payment from those that chose otherwise. In addition, payment limitations were imposed, which attempted to contain the amount paid to individual farmers.

The next major initiative in farm policy came in 1973, when the Agriculture and Consumer Protection Act of that year introduced deficiency payments linked to a target price. The loan rate could now be reduced to clear the market, and the use of export subsidies could be ended. This orientation of market prices towards those obtaining on world markets was made easier by the rapid escalation of world prices at that time. Nevertheless it marked a significant shift in US policy, which was to have implications for the growth in exports later in the decade.

In 1978, a new policy of subsidizing on-farm storage was introduced. This 'farmer-owned reserve' scheme was incorporated into the 1981 Farm Bill. To get the (quite generous) storage subsidy, farmers have to hold grain placed in the reserve for a period of up to three years, or until prices have risen to a predetermined release-price level. In return, farmers receive a higher loan rate (the entry price): the government on its part can 'call' this loan, if prices rise to some point above the release price. Then, in 1982, the government introduced a novel 'payment-in-kind' (PIK) programme, which compensated farmers who held land out of production by releasing to them government grain stocks rather than paying them cash. This strange procedure is best regarded as a temporary measure designed both to reduce government storage costs and to avoid direct budget allocations at a time of financial stringency.

This narrative holds in large part for the field crops, although each commodity has had its own peculiarities over the years. With the exception of some early attempts to incorporate pig-meat production, the meat sector has not been supported by internal market measures. In the mid-1950s, the Meat Import Law encouraged 'voluntary' restrictions by exporters to the US market of beef and sheep-meat, but in general the livestock sector is left unprotected from the effect of feed costs, cyclical production swings and demand variations. Milk is of course the exception, as in all developed countries, with extensive programme to support farm incomes. The US employs both of the standard mechanisms for supporting the dairy sector: price discrimination to exploit the less price-responsive liquid market, and support-buying to clear milk products from the market. Imports of milk products are also controlled. Price discrimination is operated through local milk-market orders, which establish prices for different classes of milk: producers receive a blend price for their output. Federal programmes require the CCC to buy up surplus butter, cheese and skimmed milk powder, and place limits on the prices at which these products can be released onto the market. Milk policies have become expensive in recent years, leading successive administrations to attempt to find ways to control programme costs. Direct-supply control has now been instituted as a temporary measure, and a producer tax, similar to the EC co-responsibility levy, is also 'on the books'.

A number of factors have heightened the importance of trade issues in US domestic farm policy. One such factor is the much greater dependence upon export markets of the US farm sector. Domestic agriculture has the capacity to export $45–50 billion worth of farm products. It seems unlikely that government programmes can for long afford to hold that capacity in check. And yet if the markets are not there, the producer will have to make the painful adjustment. The remarkable growth in exports during the 1970s has left US agriculture more exposed and more dependent upon trade than in previous periods. The stakes in the agricultural trade game are much higher this time around.

Along with the greater dependence of the US farmer on foreign markets has come increased competition from other suppliers. Market shares, as well as total market size, are under pressure. Much of the growth in exports came from a policy of competitive pricing at home

and a relatively cheap dollar abroad. US foodstuffs were a bargain in
overseas markets. Now other countries, anxious to move their own
products onto these markets, find it relatively easy to undercut US
prices. The US had refrained, quite properly, from an all-out subsidy
war, but the result has been the loss of outlets to those that are less
restrained. The US has instead borne much of the adjustment through
storage programmes and set-asides. This, combined with a generous
deficiency-payment programme that shielded farmers from the
weakness in foreign markets, has led to formidable budget costs.
Again, this willingness to finance agriculture over a period of slack
demand has raised the political temperature of the farm trade debate.
The need to control government spending has arguably a higher weight
in the political balance than the need to indemnify agriculture for past
investments. If other exporters have different priorities, then even a
recovery in export markets may not be enough to prevent further
weakness in farm incomes.

EC FARM POLICIES

The European Community's agricultural policies are sufficiently well
known to need little introduction. The Common Agricultural Policy
(CAP) stems from decisions in the early 1960s as to the implementation
of the objectives of the Treaty of Rome (1957), which set up the European Community. The treaty singled out agriculture as worthy of exceptional treatment: although free internal trade was still to be
respected, a common policy of market management was to be implemented largely by means of import levies against third countries and
support-buying on the domestic markets. This structure was put in
place by 1962, for most commodities, and prices were aligned in the
period up to 1967. The policy has resisted major modification since
that time, despite growing pressures for reform.[3]

The European Community's Common Agricultural Policy leads a
double life. On the one hand, it is an income-support system for EC
agriculture, subject to the same pressures and limitations as other
similar policies; on the other hand, it is part of the complex pact among
member states forged over twenty-five years of negotiation on common
policies. As a support programme, its main distinguishing feature is
that it relies on border instruments to a larger extent than that of many
developed countries. The cornerstone of the policy over much of its life
has been the variable levy, a device that effectively isolates EC
agricultural markets from world price changes. For some minor commodities, direct producer aids are given, and for sugar a system of production quotas has been in existence for some years. In the main,

however, the levy on imports has been the principal device for protecting farm incomes. The policy has been nothing if not successful. Sheltered from the winds of competition, agriculture has responded impressively to the generous price incentives afforded it by the CAP. The present problems reflect this success. For commodity after commodity the Community has become a net exporter. The weight of market support has shifted from the regulation of imports to the subsidization of exports. This has become at the same time increasingly expensive and increasingly irritating to overseas countries. Viewed as an agricultural policy *per se*, it should be reformed to take account of the new realities.

It is the role of the CAP as an intergovernmental pact within the EC that makes the conduct of agricultural trade policy much more difficult. As a result of the fact that levy revenues are paid to the Community, high prices, to importing countries, imply high import costs whether or not imports come from partner countries or from the rest of the world. Those same prices, to exporting countries, mean greater incomes from foreign sales, irrespective of their destination, as the EC picks up the cost of subsidies. Importing countries no longer face the option of buying at the world price: the usual economic calculus of comparing such prices with the cost of domestic production is irrelevant. Exporting countries also have no interest in the world price levels: the higher the common price, the more they get for their sales. As a result of the quite logical financial structure of the Community, world prices become largely meaningless to the individual countries of the EEC. By extension, any discussion about world trade problems in agricultural products loses its immediacy: the level of the common price becomes the main focus for each individual country. The CAP as a support mechanism isolates EC farmers from world market trends: the intergovernmental arrangements for common policies and common finances isolate EC governments from world market concerns. As a recipe for frustrating trade relations it is hard to think of a more potent mixture.

Does this mean that the CAP is condemned for ever to be hostage to the internal struggle between the importing and the exporting interests within the Community? There are signs that the impermeability to outside events may be coming to an end. For the first time, the budget cost of the CAP has become a real factor in determining the change in annual farm prices. The CAP is financed, along with other Community programmes, from the revenue from customs duties and import levies and from the proceeds of a uniform tax of up to 1 per cent on the value-added base in member states. This last component has acted as a balancing item, being paid by member countries only as required to meet expenditure. This year, such expenditure is expected finally to exhaust the available finance. The issue of control of spending under the CAP (usually known, not too accurately, as CAP reform) is now, together

with the topics of increasing available finance for EC programmes, correcting the imbalance in the burden of such financing (the UK budget
contribution issue), and preparing for the enlargement of the EC to include Spain and Portugal, at the top of the agenda for the Community.

Just as agricultural trade has become more crucial to the US farm
economy, so the EC is finding that world markets are no longer merely
a useful safety valve for the occasional surplus. Much of the Community's livestock population feed on US corn, soya beans and corn
gluten meal, and cassava from Thailand. The managers of the European
compound feed industries, more concerned with low cost and high
quality for their raw materials than with their country of origin, have
shown an impressive facility for searching out foreign sources of supply,
taking advantage of new trade opportunities until they become an embarrassment to domestic farm policy. Livestock farmers, burdened by
the need to buy high-cost domestic feeds, have shown a willingness to
take advantage of the natural cost advantages of large-scale arable farming in North America in reducing their feed costs. Employers in the
domestic pig and poultry industries, encouraged by their compound
suppliers, have located their enterprises near population centres and
have practised their skills in transforming plant material into high-
quality consumer foods. This internal specialization within agriculture
is at once a force for trade expansion and an embarrassment to the
market managers in agricultural ministries.

On the export side, the EC has emerged as the third largest supplier
of wheat to the world market, not far behind Canada, and is now a
major exporter of meat, sugar, dairy products and wine. The world
price for these commodities governs programme costs and makes the
CAP more vulnerable to fluctuations in overseas demand and to
exchange-rate variations. The strong dollar in recent years has assisted
the Community in finding overseas markets, and an arrangement with
New Zealand on keeping up world dairy-product prices has controlled
somewhat the cost of dairy-surplus disposal. But these events themselves are likely to change rapidly. A decline in the value of the dollar,
seen by many as inevitable once the US federal deficit is brought under
control, would leave EC price levels looking much higher relative to
world prices. The dairy price could fall dramatically, if the US and
New Zealand were to decide to release accumulated stocks onto the
world market. Wine sales, particularly to the US, have also benefited
from a strong dollar and from the lack, so far, of a policy to protect US
wine producers against imports. The countries of the Soviet Union
have had a succession of poor grain harvests: better weather, or better
management, in that part of the world, coupled with greater production in developing countries, could expose EC cereal markets to heavy
support costs in the future.

Some market expansion can be obtained by limiting imports or consumption of oil-seeds, cereal replacers, corn and tropical fruits, though not without economic and political cost. It is in any case doubtful whether these actions would delay the needed price and output adjustments in the EC for more than a few years. Additional finance and higher consumer prices are also temporary palliatives, and ones that threaten the whole political basis for agricultural policy. Storage policies, though desirable as an aid to stability (and having significant external benefits in terms of international stability), clearly cannot influence long-run market balance in the Community. The pressures on the Community to reorient its policy towards that of an exporting area, with the range of options that such a move implies – primarily supply control and price reductions – are unlikely to be denied. Coupled with the US problems noted earlier, the time seems to be at hand for a resolution of some of the major issues in agricultural trade. It is those issues that are summarized in the next section.

ISSUES IN AGRICULTURAL TRADE NEGOTIATIONS

Several different trade issues can be identified that are likely to form the backdrop to any international discussions on agricultural trade over the next few years, and to the continuing dialogue between the US and the EC. These include the issue of competitive export subsidies, the protection of domestic markets, the emergence of new trading arrangements, the granting of preferences to certain groups of countries, and the question of price stability.

Developed exporters face serious conflicts regarding export subsidies and export credits in the markets for such items as wheat and dairy products. These issues also involve developing-country exporters as well for such products as beef and sugar. The use of aggressive exports aids (including liberal export credits) to expand markets and dispose of surpluses is a major distinguishing feature of agricultural trade. In no other major sector is so much production put into world markets at less than domestic production cost. If one country engages in such practices, other exporters have to follow the lead or lose markets. The risk of allowing these practices to continue unabated is that they tend to sour trade relations in other fields. In addition, the uncertainty generated in agricultural markets by such subsidies gives confused signals to other producers, including developing countries attempting to put their own agricultural sectors on a sound footing. The US and the EC share a common interest in the avoidance of costly subsidy wars. The problem is that neither can afford to give up their policies unilaterally.

The more traditional trade problem of access to import markets raises particular problems at a time of high domestic unemployment and relatively low-farm incomes. Negotiations on this issue involve developing-country exporters as well as developed-country suppliers. The products involved include cereals, oil-seeds, dairy products, meats, sugar, and fruits and vegetables. Protectionism is now generally recognized as significantly greater in agricultural than in manufactured trade, although the degree of protection afforded to developed-country agriculture tends to rise and fall with world market prices. The reduction in trade barriers in manufacturing has left agriculture out on a limb. The heart of the matter has always been the unwillingness to force painful adjustments onto the domestic farm sector. Some liberalization in agricultural trade could occur, if consumer opinion were to object to the hidden taxes which they pay to protect weak sectors, and if the rest of the economy were to grow fast enough to offer genuine alternatives to rural people who might be displaced.

Both the US and the EC protect those sectors of their agriculture that they consider to be vulnerable to foreign competition. In the EC, this process has been carried further as a result of the attempt to stimulate productivity through protected markets, rather than improve efficiency by means of exposure to competition. The reluctance of the EC to use various forms of direct payments to farmers has exacerbated the market-access problem.

Specific US–EC issues of market access have undergone some modification as trade flows themselves have changed. With the emergence of the EC as a cereal exporter, access to European grain markets has become less of an issue. But the non-grain feeds, imported in part to replace high-cost grains in Europe, have also provided an adequate replacement in the diplomatic diet. The EC would like to control such access, presently guaranteed under the GATT, to ease the burden of cereal surpluses. Similarly, the EC is seeking to support the market for domestic olive oil by taxing substitute vegetable oils. The US is naturally resisting this as an affront to the massive soya-bean trade with Europe. Access questions also arise with respect to EC goods entering the US, in particular wine, dairy products and processed meats.

Some of the more recent problems of agricultural trade are related to the emergence of trading arrangements not adequately covered in the GATT. These include the problems arising from state-trading, the proliferation in certain markets of bilateral agreements, and the negotiation of 'orderly marketing' arrangements and other voluntary export restraints. State-trading is not a serious issue of contention between the US and the EC, since both are committed to the notion of allowing the private sector to handle international trade. Bilateral trade agreements are common in commercial relations with central-plan economies, for which trade is an adjunct of policy rather than a result of private decisions within a policy-determined framework. Trade works best with a free flow of information: predatory behaviour by those with a monopoly on certain types of information is disruptive. Such bilateral agreements seem to offer information on future import intentions on the part of the central-plan countries, and at the same time fit in with the predilection for quantitative advance planning by those countries themselves. Attempts by the EC to broaden agreements to include developing countries pose more problems for the US, but the consequences of such trade agreements for US–EC trade relationships have yet to be put to the test. More problematic are voluntary export restraints and orderly marketing arrangements, which serve as alternative protectionist devices to import quotas and pose analogous problems for agricultural trade relationships.

A further set of trade issues are related to the granting of preferences for developing countries, the emergence of trade groupings and customs unions, and other departures from the GATT concept of unconditional, most-favoured-nation tariff schedules. The EC has a highly-developed preference structure among developing countries and those that it considers part of a regional market. Much of the preference is in markets not competitive with EC domestic supplies. The main exceptions are for sugar from the Lomé countries and the preferences granted to the Mediterranean Basin on a variety of fruit and vegetable products. The US has generally avoided preference schemes for agriculture, although the Caribbean Basin Initiative has elements of a regional approach to trade. Any preference scheme puts a strain on the multilateral system, but so long as clear development objectives are involved the issues seem to be non-contentious. Enlargement of the EC will involve changes in the Mediterranean preferences, and it remains to be seen whether this will cause further EC–US tensions.

The issue of market stability is closely linked with other trade issues, but may be conveniently separated. Commodity markets where instability problems are serious include cereals, oil-seeds, sugar and tropical products. The problem of price instability is of broad concern to all trading countries. However, its manifestations are different in different situations. Many developed-country importers, as well as the centrally-planned economies, have devised effective ways to shelter their economies from the direct effects of international market instability in temperate-zone commodities, through border mechanisms which neutralize world price movements or through state-trading policies which have the same effect. Exporting countries are often forced to employ stock policies or production adjustments to neutralize variability in world markets. To the extent that they are successful, they have a legitimate complaint that they are unfairly burdened by absorbing such fluctuations. If they fail, world market prices are more volatile than would otherwise be the case.

Variable world prices might be considered by some to be an essentially harmless by-product of 'successful' domestic stabilization policies. This has at least three disadvantages. A volatile world price is a much less reliable indicator of efficient resource allocation; the allocation of burdens and benefits from world price fluctuations is arbitrary, leading to further tensions in the trade system; and such instability will tend to destabilize other related markets where domestic isolation is not so complete – in particular, the livestock sector. Some degree of stability in world markets is of interest to all trading countries, even those that are importers. Individual countries are naturally reluctant to give up their stabilization objectives and policies: collective action is necessary to allow a widespread sharing of the burden of market stabilization to the general benefit. The EC in particular, as it becomes a larger grain exporter, will be under increased pressure to participate fully in the regulation of world markets through domestic policy adjustments.

GATT AND AGRICULTURAL TRADE

The institution most concerned with the conditions under which goods are traded internationally is the General Agreement on Tariffs and Trade (GATT). Set up after the Second World War, the GATT provides a set of rules which the 'contracting parties' agree to observe, and acts as a forum for the negotiation of changes in trade barriers. The basic propositions embodied in the GATT are plainly liberal in intention, emphasizing the mutual benefits of freer trade, outlawing export subsidies and quota restrictions, and encouraging mutual reductions in consolidated tariffs. It preaches non-discrimination among member states, through the extension to all other contracting parties of the market access granted to the 'most-favoured' nation – subject to defined exceptions for customs unions and developing countries. It allows for conflict resolution, for compensation and for trade sanctions against violators of the agreement. Though originally oriented largely toward industrial countries of the OECD bloc, its membership has now expanded to include many developing countries and some central-plan economies. Seven rounds of negotiations have been successfully completed since the inception of the GATT, which have led effectively to a low-tariff system for manufactured products in developed-country markets.

Agriculture from the start proved a problem area for the GATT system of more liberal trade. Agricultural policies were largely excluded from the agreement's strictures against non-tariff restrictions on trade (article 11), as a response to the feeling, particularly in the United States, that domestic policy measures should not be subject to international limitations. Although other parts of the agreement do require that governments manage their domestic agricultural policies so as not to harm the legitimate interests of others, and oblige governments to consult on agricultural trade problems, these provisions have been rarely applied. Waivers were frequently sought to exempt particular policy actions from the GATT code. Most notable among these derogations was the waiver granted to the United States in 1955, which effectively removed the major elements of US agricultural policy from international scrutiny. More recently, the tacit acceptance by most countries of the Common Agricultural Policy of the European Community has reinforced the notion of the primacy of domestic policy in international trade discussions.

The relative ineffectiveness of the GATT to deal with illiberal elements in national policy has not prevented the incorporation of agricultural discussions in the various GATT rounds of trade negotiations. Although many of the important agricultural trade issues were not on the agenda, a modest degree of liberalization has been achieved through the reduction of tariffs and the establishment of tariff-free quotas for certain products. A number of tariffs on (at the time) minor traded goods were 'bound' in the Dillon Round of trade talks in the early 1960s, when the newly-formed European Community negotiated the necessary changes in member-state duties on imports from third countries. Many of these commodities, such as soya beans, protein meals and cassava, later became big-ticket items in international trade – to the discomfort of EC policy-makers.

In the Kennedy Round, later in the 1960s, a major divergence of views emerged about the nature of agricultural trade policy, with the United States arguing for a return to the GATT notion of a market-oriented trading system, and the Community generally favouring managed markets through commodity agreements. The EC proposed a temporary binding of support levels (relative to negotiated reference prices), but this was rejected by the United States as perpetuating protectionist policies in importing countries. Finally, an 'agricultural component' of the Kennedy Round was agreed, which included, in particular, an International Grains Arrangement (IGA) (1967), a modified version of earlier International Wheat Agreements. The stabilization provisions of the IGA had a short life, as surplus grain production pushed prices below the established minimum, and countries proved unwilling to hold domestic output in check.

In the most recent round of talks, the Multilateral Trade Negotiations (MTN) – also known as the Tokyo Round – which were concluded in 1979, agriculture was again on the agenda. The underlying issue was again the extent to which agricultural trade was to be subject to the same rules as trade in manufactured goods. Should markets be free or managed? Should domestic policies be the subject for negotiations? Should export subsidies be banned or otherwise controlled? Should quantitative trade barriers be phased out? And, should importers be able to shield their markets from disruption? Disagreements on these fundamental issues persisted through the MTN, and prevented any substantial progress towards liberalization. Some quantitative restrictions were relaxed, two commodity agreements were concluded (for dairy products and for meat), though neither was endowed with the instruments to stabilize markets, and an attempt was made to incorporate a code of conduct for export subsidies.[4]

This last development, the attempt to bring agriculture within a set of rules governing export subsidies and countervailing duties, held out the most promise for liberalization. The code obliges countries to avoid export subsidies that lead to an 'inequitable' share in world markets or that undercut prices. However, the implementation of the code, through the repeated challenge within the GATT of certain practices (such as the EC's export refunds), has not been as successful as might have been wished. Interpretation of such concepts as an 'equitable' market share lead inevitably to conflicts and can render meaningless the spirit of the original agreement.

Whether the GATT can improve its effectiveness in dealing with agricultural issues is likely to be put to the test shortly. Countries are discussing a new GATT round of negotiations, which will surely include agriculture, and a special committee has been set up to look into the agricultural issues. How far this initiative is likely to proceed is dependent upon whether the countries concerned, particularly the EC and the US, have confidence in the GATT mechanism for resolving trade issues in agriculture. The various options, of which the GATT is but one, are discussed in the next section.

THE FUTURE OF AGRICULTURAL TRADE RELATIONSHIPS

If the analysis of the earlier part of this paper is correct, the inherent conflict of interest among countries in agricultural markets will continue as long as governments are directly involved in managing the markets for domestic producers. At one level, these issues can be dealt with in traditional trade policy terms. Liberalization of import regimes, for instance, would doubtless help the consistency of agricultural policy, as well as consumers' wallets. But it is difficult to argue effectively that the EC, say, should not protect its grain market against a surge of non-grain feeds, if injury to domestic interests can be cited by the US as reasons for excluding foreign goods in their own markets. And the case against deliberate, open and predatory export subsidies in third-country markets is likewise more difficult to make, if others grant export credit terms generous enough to avoid the need for explicit subsidies.[5] Ultimately, the issue is the reconciliation of domestic policies with the requirements of an international trading system that has brought widespread benefits to world agriculture.

In this quest for global responsibility in domestic policy-making, the US and the EC have a key role to play. Although other countries such as Japan, Canada and Australia will be deeply involved in the process, it is difficult to see any outcome that does not effectively reconcile the interests of Europe and the United States. They can essentially agree on the agenda, the location and the pace of any negotiations on agricultural trade and domestic policy. The range of options that are open to countries include a continuation of present attitudes towards the sanctity of domestic policies, a move towards agreements among groups of countries, and the search for improved global practices. These three approaches might be called 'unilateral', 'bilateral' or 'multilateral', depending upon the degree of inter-country coordination involved. They are discussed briefly below in the context of US–EC trade relations.

Unilateral policy

Despite the interrelatedness of national concerns in agricultural trade, it is still possible to think of trade policy as being essentially unilateral and reactive. A country can take as given the state of world markets, including the impact of other countries, and fashion its own policies accordingly. Both the US and the EC are dominant enough in agricultural trade that they can force others to react to their own policy decisions – with or without any international discussion of such adjustment. Two variants of the 'unilateral' approach seem to be on the cards at present, one emphasizing confrontation and the other emulation.[6]

Confrontation implies the use of policies that deliberately lead to a state where other countries must modify their behaviour. One example of confrontational policies would be to use targeted export subsidies to replace other countries, in particular overseas markets. Such subsidies could be effected by the use of the various export-credit programmes already in existence. In this way the US could drive the EC out of, say, the wheat flour market in Egypt and Algeria, the wheat market in China and the Middle East barley market. Targeted subsidies tend to cost less than those of general applicability, and such an approach

would allow the US to regain some lost market shares. Another variant
of confrontation would be to use the mechanisms set up under the
GATT to counter the excessive use of export subsidies not just for obvious and blatant cases, but as a form of policy harassment. The EC
may already be vulnerable in certain markets to charges of violation of
the GATT; the decision to press complaints at every turn would indicate a heightened level of confrontation and tension.

Confrontation could also occur in the area of US/EC trade flows
themselves – rather than in the struggle for third-country markets. The
EC might take action on soya beans and corn gluten, for instance, as a
direct way of resolving its own policy problems. The US could relieve
some of the problems of surplus Californian wine by limiting imports
from Europe. Such policies have strong domestic appeal, and in the
absence of other action may win the day by default. Similarly appeal-
ing is the notion of retaliating on imports of other commodities for the
harmful effect of agricultural policies. The 'chicken-war' of the 1960s,
was a notable case of such retaliation, and could be repeated in the
1980s.

The main feature of such confrontation strategies is that they tend to
spread ill will to other areas of commerce and international relationships. Predatory subsidies, the harassment through the GATT, the use
of market power and the act of retaliation would each sour relationships to an extent that is difficult to foresee. Taxpayers foot the bill for
subsidy wars; retaliation hits domestic consumers; GATT challenges
weaken support for that body, and undermine the structure of liberal
trade. In short, the baby may disappear with the bath water.

Emulation has a somewhat less threatening ring. If the EC dumps
dairy-product surpluses, then why should the US not do the same? If
EC wheat is sold on world markets at a fraction of the domestic price,
then why should the US not counter with general export subsidies of its
own? And if other countries make use of variable levies to counter import competition, many not such an approach be feasible for the US in,
say, meat, or for the EC in the case of oil-seeds? The selling of grain by
state agencies is common to Australia and Canada: why should the US
and the EC not set up their own selling agencies? And perhaps the EC
needs export-credit systems like the US, or a system of voluntary export
restraints for sensitive imports.

Unfortunately, emulation of the trade policies of other countries is
not an easy or costless option. It is, in effect, a toned-down form of confrontation, hiding behind a shield of acceptability. It is unlikely that
major changes in policies would be brought about by such a strategy.
Instead, as with a confrontation strategy, the costs to the protagonists
would increase, including substantial budget costs in the US, to the
advantage not of domestic farmers, but of countries such as the USSR,

which pick up surpluses in the world markets without having to worry about the objections of their own domestic farmers. In particular, a switch to EC-type policies by the US would remove much of what remains of rationality and cost advantage in world markets. The unilateral approach has domestic support, and seems to fit with a 'tough' foreign policy line presently in vogue. To those with a professional interest in diplomacy and with a concern about the deterioration of trade relationships, such autarchic policies slide quickly into anarchic ones.

Bilateral policy

Another approach, which is enjoying some popularity at present, is the search for bilateral solutions. If the US has a problem with the EC, or vice versa, why not settle the matter bilaterally, through regular ministerial meetings and negotiations? The success of US bilateral talks with Japan is a sign that such an approach can work; the lack of success in US–EC talks makes one wonder about its general applicability.

The bilateral approach rests for its effectiveness on one of two premises: that the subjects under discussion are of major interest only to the two countries; or that a broader agreement, even if desirable, is less likely. The first condition is presumably met fairly often in specific cases where issues such as quality standards are under discussion: it seems less likely when discussing price policies in widely traded commodities. As a fall-back when multilateral talks fail, bilateral approaches have some merit, but can also cause further problems by their success. Australia, for instance, has reportedly taken exception to the notion that the US is the logical source of increased beef imports into Japan.

What might such a bilateral approach cover? Two different types of agreement need to be distinguished. The US or the EC could enter into more or less formal pacts with other *exporters*, such as with Canada for wheat, Australia for beef, or New Zealand for dairy goods, in order to avoid 'costly' competition. This idea has been current in various guises for some years among producer interests. What stops such notions from gaining too much ground are the implications for domestic policy, that a high degree of control over domestic production and trade is necessary, and the doubtfulness of the longevity of such pacts, when all evidence suggests that the result is to stimulate production in other countries. On the other hand, the US or the EC could negotiate bilateral agreements with *importers*, in the sense of bargaining policy modification, for either guarantees of supplies (which might appeal to Japan) or of export restraint (as requested in corn gluten by the EEC). It is difficult to argue against bilateral or regional approaches when other action fails, but they remain in the world of 'second best' when the problems themselves call for wider action.

Multilateral policy

If the bilateral approach is largely an admission of failure at the multilateral level, the issue facing US and EC trade policy is whether any multilateral approach can succeed in the present era of commercial confrontation and diplomatic mud-slinging among allies. Although it is not necessarily the case that all trade questions are amenable to multilateral discussion, the broad direction of the trading system can hardly be discussed at any other level. Hence the issue of agricultural trade, rapidly becoming isolated as a major problem for the GATT, cannot be forever swept beneath the rug. Some start has been made on establishing the basis for trade negotiations in agriculture, though with considerable reluctance in the case of the EC.[7] The OECD, with a more limited membership, has also organized a set of studies designed to lead to negotiations. It is possible that the bilateral talks can themselves speed up the multilateral negotiations by allowing issues to be clearly identified. Though it is not yet clear what the scope of any future negotiations will be, the ducks are slowly being brought into line.

The main question for such a negotiation will be the same as has haunted previous attempts at multilateral discussion of agricultural trade. To what extent can national agricultural policies be discussed directly, as opposed to being held sacrosanct? The US is in a position to make a bold move to change the rules on such procedure. It could, for instance, release the well-known waiver granted to it by other countries which recognized that domestic policy needs could dictate trade policies, even when those policies were out of line with GATT procedures. This in turn would require a modification to section 22 of the Agricultural Adjustment Act, which mandates the supremacy of domestic policy. This would imply a willingness to bring national policies into accord with the needs of trade relations. Such a move would have been unthinkable with only a small interest in trade: with exports providing the balance wheel for domestic producers, however, the gamble might be worth taking.

Countries under such a scenario would essentially be agreeing to, and asking other countries to agree to lay the certain aspects of domestic policies on the negotiating table. No sovereignty would be given up: no domestic policy decisions would be made collectively. But the reality of the influence of domestic policy over trade flows would be recognized. Countries would no longer have to negotiate with a mandate already so circumscribed that no progress is possible. Rather than saying to the negotiators 'gain some markets for us, but do not compromise our cherished national programmes', the mandate would be 'search for agreements which will lead to a constructive improvement in the international environment in which our agriculture must compete, even if it means limiting our freedom of action on domestic policy'. The glimmer of hope for such an approach, and it would be misleading to be any more positive about the chances for success, is that both the EC and the US are searching for ways in which their domestic policies can adapt to the increasingly trade-oriented nature of markets. Progress would be slow, but a corner would have been turned in the search for a better climate in agricultural trade relations between the US and the EC. The benefits to the Atlantic alliance could be substantial.

NOTES

1 For a discussion of the macroeconomic factors behind the US agricultural trade situation, see G. Edward Schuh, 'Future directions for food and agricultural trade policy', *American Journal of Agricultural Economics*, vol. 66(2) (1982).

2 Two amendments to the 1933 AAA have achieved a prominence presumably not foreseen by their authors. Section 22 authorizes the use of trade controls to underpin domestic price-support schemes. Obligations under this clause, as amended in 1951, led to the famous (or infamous) agreement in the GATT in 1954 which effectively removed from international scrutiny the import policy of the US with respect to agricultural products. Section 32 set aside 30 per cent of all import-duty revenue to be available for schemes which stimulate demand for farm products, including both domestic and export subsidies. Much of the financial burden of these subsidy programmes was thus absorbed by a fund set up specificallly for that purpose.

3 For a recent and authoritative discussion of CAP reform prospects, see Graham Avery, 'Europe's agricultural policy: progress and reform', *International Affairs*, vol. 60(4) (1984).

4 For a discussion of the progress on agriculture in the MTN, see T. K. Warley, 'Agricultural trade policy issues in the 1980s' (mimeo, November 1980); and T. E. Josling, *Agriculture in the Tokyo Round Negotiations* (Thames Essay No. 10, Trade Policy Research Centre, London, 1977); and for earlier history of agriculture in the GATT, T. K. Warley, 'Western trade in agricultural products', in A. Shonfield (ed.), *International Economic Relations of the Western World 1959–71* (Oxford University Press, London, 1976).

5 The EC view of the conflict over subsidies is given succinctly in Derwent Renshaw, 'Issues in the European Economic Community's agricultural trade policy', in J. Paxton Marshall and Howard McDowell (ed.), *Issues in Agricultural Trade Policy: The US, Japan and the EC* (Virginia Co-operative Extension Service, September 1984). The broader perspective on US–EC agricultural relations is given by Nicholas Butler, 'The ploughshares war between Europe and America', *Foreign Affairs*, vol. 62(1) (1983).

6 Some detail of possible confrontation strategies is found in Jeremy A. Sharpe and Philip L. Paarlberg, *Japanese and EC Agricultural Trade Policies: Some US Strategies* (USDA/ERS, IED Staff Report, Washington, DC, December 1982).

7 For a recent discussion of the agricultural agenda for the next GATT round, see
   Charles E. Hanrahan, Penelope Cate and Donna V. Vogt, *Agriculture in the GATT:*
   Toward the Next Round of Multilateral Trade Negotiations (Congressional Reasearch
   Service, Library of Congress, Washington, DC, September 1984).

Comment 1

MICHEL PETIT

Tim Josling's paper is particularly useful as it provides us with a clear and synthetic analysis of the complex set of problems linked to the confrontation between the United States and the European Community about the international trade of agricultural products. The author properly emphasizes the importance of these problems for both parties and for the world economy as a whole.

It is because of the economic nature of his approach that Josling can deal with so many problems. But, at the same time, as a result of a too narrow economic stand, his analysis suffers from two serious limitations which must be pointed out. Before discussing these limitations, however, let me indicate first the results, which appear well established and which, in my opinion, are particularly important.

MAIN RESULTS

1) The economic difficulties of exporting countries (slow growth in importing countries; overvalued exchange rate, particularly for the dollar; weakness of the domestic labour market) are serious; they can be expected to be the source of political pressures and international tensions.

2) The burden of stocks has indeed been carried mainly by the United States. Stocks have had dramatic consequences for the federal budget, and this is another major source of political pressure.

3) The fact that the Community has become more and more a net exporter of several major agricultural products exerts growing pressure on the Common Agricultural Policy.

4) The economic classification of issues between the United States and the European Community proposed by Josling is very useful:
   a) export subsidies;
   b) market access;
   c) growing importance of 'special arrangements' not covered by GATT, such as the long-term bilateral agreements;
   d) stability of world markets.

5) Multilateral negotiations involving agriculture are likely to start relatively soon. Let us note in passing that this opinion does not result from a strictly economic analysis, but more from observation of current political trends.

6) Ultimately, the main issue is that of the compatibility of domestic policies with the requirements of an international trade system, which has brought widespread benefits to world agriculture.

7) Finally, Josling's classification of unilateral, bilateral and multilateral approaches to solving trade problems is enlightening and probably very useful.

Beyond this agreement on very important points, I think that the author gives too much weight to the effect of prices in the explanation of the growth of agricultural production. This criticism applies to both the European and the American cases. In Europe, agriculture has undergone a tremendous process of modernization since the end of the Second World War. Admittedly, such a process was not independent of agricultural prices, but it has been a multi-faceted phenomenon and the impact of product prices has not been straightforward. The main forces behind this evolution of agriculture have been the demand for labour outside agriculture and the availability of new techniques. In this context, do we know for sure whether the modernization of agriculture would have proceeded at a faster or at a slower rate, had farm prices been lower than they have been? In economic terms, the modernization process can be essentially interpreted as the substitution of capital for labour. With lower product prices, one could expect that more labour would have moved out of agriculture, thus accelerating the substitution; but less capital would be expected to have moved in, thus slowing down the substitution! Of course, in a world of perfect input markets, the optimum input combination would be immediately achieved at all times. But in a period of very rapid change and with most agricultural inputs provided directly by the farm family without going through a market, it is impossible to know for sure whether the agricultural modernization process would have been faster or slower.

In the United States, it is not justified, in my view, to write that in the 1970s 'much of the growth in exports came from a policy of competitive pricing at home and a relatively cheap dollar abroad'. Actually there was a tremendous growth in world demand, perhaps related to the price of agricultural commodities, but also, and more importantly to events in the USSR, the oil crisis, the take-off of the newly industrialized countries, etc.

TWO MAIN LIMITATIONS

In addition, Josling's paper suffers from two major limitations: an insufficient attention to the policy decision-making process, and a constant reference to a free-trade norm. These are directly related to his orthodox neo-classical economic framework.

Regarding the policy-making process, I am convinced that the analysis must be conducted in political economy terms. Policies can be interpreted as resulting from the complex and dynamic play of conflicts and alliances among economic interests, organized in pressure groups with the purpose of influencing the policy decision-making process.

This is not the place to develop fully the plea made earlier for an analysis of agricultural policy issues in terms of political economy.[1] It will be sufficient to illustrate here how a political economy approach can help us understand phenomena that are only described by Josling without any explanation. For instance, the process of reform of the CAP leading to the March 1984 compromise, so aptly presented by Avery,[2] can indeed be interpreted as resulting from the interplay of economic and political factors.

British governments had been putting pressure on their partners for several years to reform the CAP and to revise the financial arrangements, arguing that the UK was bearing a disproportionate share of the Community budget. It was only when it became obvious that the Community was going to run out of financial resources, because of the growth of export restitutions to be paid, that a real negotiation leading to a reform could begin. The pressure was so much greater because the application of Spain and Portugal for membership in the EC had been pending for several years. Because of broad geopolitical reasons, European leaders wanted Spain and Portugal admitted, in spite of the fact that their admission would compound the financial and CAP reform problems. Admission of two countries, poorer on average than the current members, could only be a financial drain on the Community budget. In addition, the admission of Spain and Portugal will disrupt the markets for such Mediterranean products as fruit, vegetables, wine and olive oil. These products, being generally less easy to store than those of northern Europe, such as cereals, butter or milk powder, benefit from a lesser degree of protection. This will add pressure for reforming the CAP towards a more even geographic distribution of its benefits. Thus the three issues of CAP reform, Community budget and Community enlargement were closely interrelated and could only be solved as part of a global package.

This explains why the recent CAP reform process was so closely interwoven with successive summit meetings in Stuttgart (June 1983), Athens (December 1983), Brussels (March 1984) and finally Fontaine-bleau (June 1984), after a very complex sequence of negotiations which, for the CAP reform, culminated at a meeting of the Council of Ministers (Agriculture) at the end of March 1984. With this back-ground, one can also understand why the reform process can never be complete and, as a result, is a continuing one of recurring negotiations among the Community member states. Thus one can probably answer in the affirmative to Josling's question: is the CAP condemned for ever to be hostage to the internal struggle between the importing and the ex-porting interests within the Community? More precisely, probably like all economic policies, it is the product of continuously evolving conflicts of interests. An analysis of the same type can be conducted to under-stand the evolution of US policies described by Josling.[3]

Finally, and most importantly, an analysis in terms of political econ-omy can help us to understand the rigidity of the policy-making process on both sides of the Atlantic. This rigidity leaves very little room for international negotiations. As a result, the relationships between the United States and the European Community about the trade of agri-cultural products have been and will continue to be contentious and confrontational. Whereas both parties would clearly benefit greatly if they were able to find a mutually acceptable arrangement, such an out-come is unlikely.

The second major limitation stems from the norm used by the author to judge international trade. One must stress that he is very careful and did not present a purely doctrinal paper. Space is not sufficient to note here all the places where the free-market ideal is proposed. It will be sufficient to quote the contrast drawn between industry and agriculture for which GATT has been 'ineffective'.

The problem is that this free-market stance is not neutral in the debate between the United States and Europe. It espouses the American point of view in a confrontation where ideological differences regarding the pros and cons of market adjustments are prominent. These differences play a prominent role in the tensions between the United States and Europe.

Some observers point out that these ideological differences, however great, must not matter very much, since policies on both sides of the Atlantic have many common features: they vary greatly from one product to another. On each side, one may find some that are very protectionist and others that are much closer to free trade. But such an argument misses the role of doctrines in the policy process. An economic doctrine can be defined as a set of beliefs and a set of values. The beliefs relate to the existing interrelationships among economic variables, which are viewed as relevant for a policy. The values relate to the choice of policy objectives and the order of priority among them. Both sets are closely interrelated. The beliefs are usually consistent with a broad acceptance of a general economic theory, but without worrying about the limitations of that theory and about the questions it leaves open.

Most stands taken on policy issues by participants in policy debate use either explicitly or, more often, implicitly a doctrine as a reference. It happens that in the debates about the international trade of agricultural products most US participants refer to free trade as an ideal, whereas most continental Europeans dealing with agriculture would prefer a coordination at the international level of national government interventions, hence their recurring proposal to set up grandiose schemes of international commodity agreements. This leads to a dialogue of the deaf: Europeans point out that Americans preach free trade in agriculture, but do not practise it. Americans point out that international commodity agreements do not work . . . There is little doubt that this ideological divergence plays an important role in the continuing confrontation between the United States and the European Community.

In conclusion, I should emphasize that for Josling to promote a free-trade ideal seems to me to be perfectly proper. But I believe also that it may be appropriate for an economist from the continent, particularly from France, to point out in a friendly manner to his Anglo-Saxon colleague, that his analysis is influenced by his ideology, as is true for all of us.

NOTES

1 See M. Petit, 'For an analytical political economy. Relevance to the study of domestic and international trade agricultural policies', Paper presented at the Theodor Heidhues Memorial Seminar, Göttingen (Proceedings to be published). See also D. Hathaway, *Government and Agriculture – Public Policy in a Democratic Society* (Macmillan, New York, 1963).
2 Graham Avery, 'Europe's agricultural policy: progress and reform', *International Affairs*, vol. 60(4) (1984), pp. 643–56.

3   For a comparison of French and US policies of intervention on agricultural markets since the 1930s, see M. Petit, *Determinants of Agricultural Policies: Analytical Framework and Selected Case Studies from the United States and the European Community*, (IFPRI Research Report, Washington, DC, 1985).

Comment 2

D. GALE JOHNSON

I have little basis for disagreeing with Josling's paper. Both the European Community and the United States, along with Japan, bear major
responsibility for the current controversies and conflicts in agricultural
trade. They are each separately and collectively responsible for the
failure to improve the trading system for agricultural products in the
past two decades. In spite of the nil movement toward liberalization of
trade in farm products, trade has continued to grow – and at a very
high rate in the 1970s.

I find it surprising that the United States has failed to do more, given
the increasing dependence of US agriculture on world trade during the
1970s. By the beginning of the 1980s, the output of two acres out of five
was exported and exports accounted for about a quarter of the total
final demand for US farm products.

The US did move, as noted by Josling, to a more market-oriented
domestic policy from the mid-1950s to the 1970s. However, the 1981
Farm Bill, combined with the high exchange value of the dollar, has
resulted in a significant loss of exports. There is a tendency to blame
the loss in the volume of exports upon the increase in the foreign-
exchange value of the dollar, but the greatest degree of responsibility
lies with the price-support levels set in the 1981 legislation. That legislation provided for almost no downward flexibility in establishing price
support or market intervention levels. Even when it became obvious
that the minimum price-support levels were encouraging production
and reducing exports, Congress was unwilling to do more than make
minimal changes in the price supports and target prices.

In addition, the US has done almost nothing to induce or assist
resource adjustments in those sectors that have been and are protected

against import competition – dairy, sugar, wool and peanuts. Beef is protected, even though there is now no evidence that the support provided by import limitations has any significant effects upon domestic prices or production of beef. The legislation that permitted controls over the import of beef and veal was passed in 1964, in reaction to the EC reductions in meat imports during the early 1960s. This case illustrates that protectionist actions by one actor often calls forth similar actions by another.

In 1955, the United States obtained a waiver from the provisions of article 11 of GATT concerning the conditions under which quantitative restrictions could be imposed on the imports of agricultural products. In the three decades since that time, the US has not taken the necessary domestic policy measures that would permit it to return the waiver. The US pays a high price for having the waiver. By keeping the waiver, it greatly reduces its bargaining power in agricultural trade negotiations. It is difficult to see how other countries can take seriously US efforts to reduce trade barriers, while the US retains its waiver of article 11.

In dairy production, the United States has started some small efforts to reduce production incentives. But all that the present programme is designed to achieve is self-sufficiency in dairy production. There is nothing in the programme that is designed to make the US dairy industry low cost and more competitive in world markets.

The US sugar programme is clearly out of hand. Domestic sugar prices are four to five times the world price. However, the major beneficiaries may not be sugar producers and refiners, but a small number of producers of high-fructose or iso-glucose sugar from corn.

I wish to add some comments to those made by Josling concerning the controversy over the EC proposals to limit the imports of non-grain feeding materials, including soya beans, manioc, corn gluten feed, alfalfa meal and a variety of other products. In the early 1960s, the EC bound the duties on the above-mentioned feeding materials at zero or nil levels. The consequences of this decision have been a heavy cross to be borne by the CAP. Imports of cereal or grain substitutes, excluding soya beans and soya bean products, increased from nil in 1960 to 4 million tonnes in 1970 and to 16 million tonnes in 1982.

The imports of soya beans, soy meal and soy oil have reduced the demand for cereals in the EC and competed with domestically produced fats and oils, such as butter, olive oil, rape-seed and sunflower seed. The imports of the non-grain feeding materials and soya beans have significantly increased the cost of the CAP. Almost no duties are collected on these products. The level of production of grains has now reached the level at which the EC has become a net exporter of all grains, in part because of the entry of the non-grain feeding materials. The EC has indicated that it intends to restrict the importation of certain non-grain feeding materials, such as corn gluten feed. It has already negotiated a limit on the amount of manioc that it will import from Thailand.

The United States, not too surprisingly, has strongly objected to any quantitative limitation on imports of corn gluten feed. But the US does not resist the EC proposals to control the access of non-grain feeds with entirely clean hands. Corn gluten feed is available, in large part, because of the high domestic price of sugar and the subsidized production of alcohol. Thus corn gluten feed is a result of distortions in the pricing of products in the United States. And almost all of the corn gluten feed is exported, due to its duty-free import into the EC. It is very probable that the duty-free import of corn gluten feed is largely at the expense of corn imports by the EC. Thus the gain to US corn producers from the duty-free import of corn gluten feed is very modest indeed. The primary beneficiaries are the corn processors. Up to the present, most of the effects of the imports of non-grain feeds have been at the expense of grain exporters, not at the expense of the EC farmers. However, as noted above, these imports have resulted in a loss of revenue or an increase in expenditures due to the subsidized export of grain. The cost of the non-grain feed imports to the Community budget has now become a major factor in EC policy deliberations.

It is appropriate to note that the EC has not publicly announced any proposal to compensate exporters for loss of future markets. It is not enough to provide favoured treatment of existing import levels, since, if present policies continued, imports would probably continue to increase. If this were not the case, the EC would not be interested in limiting such imports.

An important point that I wish to make is a supplement to Josling's paper; it is a point that I believe he agrees with. In the long run, and one might say in not such a long run, how much income the farming population receive for their labour and capital depends upon alternative earnings in their economy. High farm prices (or subsidies) are not enough to increase the returns to farm labour or capital, except in the very short run. High prices can have some effect upon the number of people engaged in agriculture or the amount of capital employed in farming and, of course, upon the price of farm land, but not upon the rate of return on the investment in that land.

The effect upon farm employment of farm prices that are significantly above world market prices appears to have been modest. The reduction of farm employment in the EC and Japan has been as fast or faster than in the US and Canada since the mid-1950s. One of the reasons for the CAP was to maintain the rural way of life, but the CAP has been no more successful in maintaining a large farming population than the policies of any other industrial country. Nor does price policy contribute to reducing income inequality in agriculture, something that the Commission of the European Communities has recognized by noting that regional inequalities in incomes from agriculture has actually increased since the beginning of the CAP. What does reduce income inequality in rural areas is ready access to non-farm jobs, either through migrating to non-farm areas or by creating part-time farm households that supplement their agricultural incomes by non-farm incomes.

I wish to address an argument that is often made by policy-makers to justify significant protection of agriculture. This argument is that international market prices are so distorted that it is necessary to protect one's farmers from having to compete with the low international prices created by subsidies to agriculture in other countries. Those who make this argument universally fail to substantiate it by careful analytical studies. Studies have been made that indicate that, except for dairy products and sugar, the distortion in international market prices is modest, probably no more than 10 per cent. It is true that international market prices are highly variable, but much of this variability and instability results from the policies of domestic price stabilization followed by the European Community, the centrally-planned economies and many developing countries.

The heavy budget costs of high price supports, when output is not limited, as has been true in the European Community, or production limitation is voluntary, as in the United States, have led some policy-makers to favour output quotas. This is the route the EC has instituted for dairy products very recently. Before this path is accepted, however, there should be an evaluation of the Canadian experience with output quotas as the method of increasing farm incomes, while greatly reducing governmental costs. Milk quotas provide an illuminating example. In the province of Ontario, the current market value of the quota for a family-sized dairy farm of 40 cows is $180000; in British Columbia, the market value is $400000. These figures do not include the value of the cows! Nor any of the capital costs of operating a dairy farm. The figures are the cost of the right to produce milk from 40 cows. Consequently all or most of the benefits of the quotas go to the farmers who were in business at the time the quotas were instituted. But given the enormous capital investments that many farmers have made in the quotas, there is enormous resistance to abolishing the quotas.

I shall conclude with the major point that I made earlier, namely that government policies of protection, price supports and subsidies do little to determine the incomes of farm people. People's incomes depend upon the resources they own and the conditions of the factor markets, especially the labour market.

Comment 3

PAUL LUYTEN

The presentation by Professor Josling of the problems of agricultural policies and world trade is well balanced. It stresses the fundamental point that order in world trade in agriculture is inextricably linked with disciplines on domestic policies. It is a refreshing and penetrating analysis of the problems that beset the world agricultural scene.

Trade in agriculture has, from the very beginning of the GATT, been treated differently because of its specific characteristics. Field crops fluctuate with weather conditions. This is not the case with industrial or mineral production. The offer is highly atomized and price elasticity of demand is low. Non-economic factors such as security and environmental concerns play an important role. Sanitary and phytosanitary preoccupations offer plenty of scope for undercover protectionism. To these material and economic features must be added a sociological characteristic: the electoral constituencies of agricultural areas – consisting not only of farmers, but of the whole of the rural population and the industries and services supplying agriculture – are well defined and highly organized. They therefore play a more than proportionate role in democratic processes.

The specificity of the agricultural sector explains why widespread and intensive state intervention in agricultural production has been a universal characteristic for quite a long time. Massive government assistance has been bestowed everywhere for several decades, especially in industrialized countries and also in many developing countries, not only through price support and product and income subsidization, but also in the form of irrigation and land-reclamation assistance, research and development, education and training, state-financed export

market promotion, etc. This has stimulated a staggering progress of
productivity and has turned agriculture in many countries into what is
more and more a kind of high-technology activity, with several sectors
such as the livestock, poultry and pig sectors progressively losing their
agricultural characteristics. These developments, in turn, have modified the comparative advantage: from 'natural' it has become more and
more an 'acquired' advantage, thereby allowing countries to claim
competitivity on the basis of past subsidization. These trends are
bound to persist and even to accelerate. The more agriculture becomes
'industrial', the more difficult it becomes to continue to support it in
traditional ways without risks of considerable overproduction and unsustainable budgetary costs.

During past rounds of negotiations, the developed countries have
liberalized trade and reduced tariffs to a substantial extent for processed
agricultural foodstuffs and products other than the major ones such as
grains, sugar, dairy products and meat. But even in these product
areas, the traditional GATT negotiating techniques for agriculture
have gone as far as they could, and for the major products they have
not led to substantial progress. So far the GATT rounds of negotiations
in the field of agriculture have too often aimed at finding traditional
neat solutions and have ended up with no solutions at all, or only the
fourth or fifth-best solution. What is required now is to introduce in the
ambit of negotiations elements taking account of the link between
domestic policies and trade measures. This will require a major effort
on the part of all participating governments.

The time has come to face reality and to create a new basis for
negotiations: for example, by looking at some kind of agreement about
the policy instruments governments are allowed to use to achieve their
domestic agricultural objectives. What is also required is a change in
the outlook of some of the participants. The tendency in the past has
too often been for 'agricultural exporting countries' to argue for
disciplines from the 'importing countries', while claiming that their
own production, support and protective policies were not relevant.

At the beginning of such a new negotiating process, one should not
aim for more than obtaining marginal changes in the management of
national agricultural policies. Excessive disciplines, if ever agreed,
would be circumvented or even breached. Rules could gradually be
tightened up over time to bring about a pattern of production and trade
which moves progressively closer to a more rational and fairer division
of labour.

4

The Bickering Bigemony: GATT as an Instrument in Atlantic Trade Policy

JACQUES PELKMANS

The US and the EC continue to maintain their ambivalent and at times puzzling attitudes towards GATT. Although the US had a dominant influence on the agreement's articles, in both 1947 and 1955, the legal status of GATT in the US was fundamentally in doubt. GATT is a 'contract', not a treaty, and the profound constitutional and related consequences have continued to bewilder non-US negotiators, especially in cases of long-run commitments. The EC came into being in 1958 and – as such – was never formally recognized in GATT. A debate, on the GATT article 24 waiver for the EC customs union, was adjourned without ever being recommenced and without any conclusion being reached. Subsequently, the EC built up a galaxy of preferences[1] with little, if any, serious regard for GATT's fundamental principle of non-discrimination: free-trade areas with EFTA countries and a few Mediterranean countries; preferential trade agreements with other Mediterranean countries; complex, preferential arrangements with the ACP (Lomé Convention) countries. At the same time, the EC and the US together dominate the functioning of GATT and have a decisive influence on issues of GATT reform. They at least seem to care, whereas many others are content with little more than token representation, with 'special and differential' treatment or no membership at all.

Both trading powers have proved to be rather skilled in combining a highly publicized claim of respect for GATT rules with ingenious techniques for getting round them. Yet, since 1960, both have also led two GATT rounds, while dominating a third one, bringing tariffs down to uninterestingly low levels. In addition, they have forged ahead to broaden the scope of the shaky and incomplete agreement by improving codes and formulating new ones. But they have also been on the verge of jettisoning the results during a stormy truce that was prevented only with difficulty from exploding into a trade war.

US and EC trade policy cannot be properly understood without reference to GATT. Similarly, neither the functioning of GATT nor the reform debate can be discussed without taking full account of the constants in both power's trade policies as well as their short-term priority interests. This chapter attempts to analyse this interaction and draws a few tentative conclusions about GATT reform. After examining the EC and US weight in GATT, and the role of GATT in Atlantic trade conflicts, a few constants in both trade powers' policies are identified and linked to GATT reform. The chapter ends with a short perspective on GATT reform itself.

It is not the aim – given the subject and the structure of this book – either to provide a full treatment of GATT reform, or of US–EC trade relations nor will it be possible to analyse the underlying economics of the issues. Restricting the subject matter to the role and significance of GATT in Atlantic trade policy provides quite a rich topic in itself.

US AND EC WEIGHT IN GATT

GATT membership covers nearly all countries of some importance in international trade, with the exception of a few OPEC countries, the USSR and a few socialist countries.[2] It is therefore appropriate to look first of all at the weight of the EC and US in world trade. The preponderance of what is now the EC–10 and the US in world trade at the time of the Dillon and Kennedy Rounds is clear from the fact that in 1963 they had a joint share of 50 per cent of world trade. By 1982, this had declined, but only to 45 per cent, despite the rapidly increasing economic openness of many newly industrializing countries. In manufactured goods trade, the 1982 share was 53.5 per cent, however; excluding intra-EC trade, it was still 42 per cent; excluding, in addition, East European exports of manufactures – as they are not really subject to material GATT rules – the share was approximately 47 per cent. In other sectors also, the two played a major role: in the food sector (including unprocessed agricultural goods), the combined EC and US share in 1982 was 48.5 per cent; without intra-EC trade it was 33 per cent. By comparison, the next biggest trading partner was Japan, with a 1982 share of 7.5 per cent of world trade, and 12.7 per cent of world manufacturing trade.

GATT negotiations on product-related tariff reductions and, later on, across-the-board (industrial) tariff reductions have been based on the rather obvious diplomatic understanding that the 'principal suppliers' would have to call the tune. There would be little point in trying to negotiate bilaterally between any two small suppliers, and then extend the result to others by MFN treatment,[3] in the absence of previous negotiations with the trading partner(s) that took a large share of the country's external trade. This was also true for the EC and the US itself. In the 1962 US Trade Expansion Act, this understanding was taken so far that the President's negotiation mandate for tariff cuts went further in situations where the two principal suppliers had a world market share of 80 per cent or more (not counting Eastern Europe). This was a clear reward arising from the expected accession of the UK to the EC, because, in that event, the joint US–EC share would have been beyond 80 per cent in a number of important manufacturing sectors; in manufacturing as a whole, it would have been a little above 70 per cent. Of most GATT contracting parties, the US and the EC are almost always the most important trading partners. Table 4.1 gives the EC and US shares in the foreign trade of a few selected countries. For the US, the EC is the biggest trading partner with 24 per cent of US exports; for the EC, the US is the biggest trading partner with nearly 15 per cent of extra-EC exports. These figures show, however, that it is primarily predominance in world trade that leads to EC and US predominance in GATT and not transatlantic trade itself. While undoubtedly still of major importance, the days are long gone when transatlantic trade itself was the core of the (manufacturing) trade in the world.

TABLE 4.1   EC AND US SHARE IN TRADE OF SELECTED COUNTRIES
(per centage for 1982)

	Share of exports to:			Share of imports from:
	EC	US	(EC + US)	(EC + US)
Argentina	22	13	35	45
Australia	13	10	23	43
Brazil	27	21	48	28
Canada	9	65	74	76
Egypt	44	5	49	59
Hong Kong	17	29	46	23
India	27	16	43	38
Indonesia	5	18	23	32
Israel	31	20	51	50
Japan	12	26	38	24
Mexico	11	56	67	78
South Africa	24	9	33	51
Spain	46	7	53	45
Sweden	47	7	54	59
Switzerland	48	8	56	73

Source: IMF, Direction of Trade Statistics, 1983.

Ever since the start of the EC there has been something of a 'big-emony'[4] over activities in GATT, with the US frequently in the role of initiator and the EC as the responding party. This was certainly the case during the 1960s, when the Dillon and Kennedy Rounds were taking place. The EC showed its willingness in the Dillon Round by carrying through a massive harmonization programme, converting nearly 20000 tariff lines in the four respective tariff schedules[5] into some 3000 Community tariff lines, in order to be able to negotiate reduction of the common commercial tariff, even before it had formally come into being. Co-operation during the Kennedy Round was perhaps less easy, but ultimately rather successful in cutting tariffs significantly further and agreeing upon an anti-dumping code. In those days, and even more during the 1950s, the co-operative bias was strengthened by the hegemonial position of the US in the Western system: its role in all international economic organizations, its predominance in defence and security affairs (and its readiness to 'buy off' free riding in trade or monetary affairs by 'sweeteners' in the realm of security), the near-monopoly of the dollar as an international currency and its strong position in hi-tech trade, expressed in what was called the 'technology gap'.

The continuing erosion of the economic basis for such a hegemonic role became even more visible during the 1960s. As a result, the EC was less constrained in aligning its common trade policy position more closely with what it considered to be its priority interests, while the US sought more and more to combine the role of custodian of the world trade order with outright deviations from the underlying principles. The US obtained a waiver on agricultural trade in 1955, on the basis of a curious 'consensus' that would certainly not have been possible even ten years later. The US pioneered 'voluntary export restraints' (vis-à-vis Japan) in 1957, and took the initiative in negotiating the Short (1961) and Long Term Arrangement on Cotton Textiles (1962–73), which went against the notion of non-discrimination, while undermining article 19 of GATT on safeguards. Typically, the EC – traditionally rather protectionist in textiles and clothing – had no difficulty in negotiating a Dillon Round with the US as principal supplier in many products, while at the same time joining with the US in blackmailing the newly industrialized countries of the day into undermining the GATT in cotton textiles. The more assertive attitude of the EC could also be seen in a small, but significant conflict: the Atlantic trade war over chickens and brandy in the same period. The chicken war was a signal that the emerging bigemony would not necessarily be stable: without hegemonic 'sweeteners' and the deterrent of effective sanctions, it might well evolve into a competitive duopoly. Given the fact that both were each other's principal suppliers, trade warfare would be extremely costly for both and ruinous for the GATT order. Hence the declining input of hegemonic 'stabilizers' came to be replaced more and more by informal attempts at Atlantic trade conflict management. Although the GATT principles were not altogether ignored, they took secondary priority. The prime objective was to stabilize, or at least not to endanger, in general, the degree of market access already achieved, while containing, and if possible accommodating, the domestic political pressures with specific deviations. Thus, the EC left a few conspicuous holes in its otherwise extremely protectionist variable-levy system for agricultural imports, which happened to be of particular importance for US farmers. It has created the remarkable situation whereby the EC is by far the largest market for US agricultural exports, and yet the US considers the CAP to be about the greatest evil in world trade relations. Similarly, the US felt compelled to negotiate an EC export restraint in steel in the late 1960s that infuriated the Community.

Being neither a harmonious bigemony, nor a competitive duopoly, the two powers spent most of the 1970s bickering as well as co-operating in and outside GATT. When they were determined and joined forces, it turned out to be decisive: they called the tune for the first Multi-Fibre Agreement (MFA) in 1973, which carved out an even larger part of manufacturing trade from GATT. Although the launching of the Tokyo Round was stimulated by Japan as well, the conduct of the actual negotiations depended critically on US–EC agreement – in particular, the painful negotiations on safeguards were finally broken off as a result of the stubbornness of the EC's preference for selectivity, without any serious attempts being made by the US, Japan and the major NICs to formulate a code that the EC would be asked not to block (since GATT works with a 'consensus' procedure). When they strongly disagree, nothing happens, as in agriculture and in the GATT's dispute settlement procedures, no matter how much others try.

The fundamental facts have to be kept in mind in any discussion on GATT reform. Considering their preponderance, the EC and the US jointly hardly need GATT. Between the two of them, mutual respect for GATT constraints can be very useful, but it is, from their policy-making point of view, not always the most convenient and expedient alternative medium. In many cases, however, the trade policy issue will not neatly fit these two extremes: positions may partly overlap, or the problem may have important external effects on other GATT partners with possible feedbacks. GATT can then be appropriate as a setting in which the EC and the US can make deals. There are also good functional, as opposed to political-strategic reasons to prefer GATT as the existing framework and as the proper forum for enlarging the scope of international trade rules. In this chapter, no attempt is made to probe deeply into the ideals of lawyers and economists,

who seek to establish a Utopian world trade order. Their main arguments are assumed to be known to the reader. They are not unimportant, because they linger in the minds of a large number of (though
not all) trade policy-makers as a framework of reference for the basics.
Nevertheless, to give priority to functionalism would prevent us from
understanding and assessing the functioning of GATT and the reform
debate.

GATT AND ATLANTIC TRADE CONFLICTS

No history of Atlantic trade conflicts will be provided. The idea is to
relate a few recent trade policy issues to the rules or actual functioning
of GATT as the world trade organization. Reference will be made to
some important instances where work in the GATT had a pacifying
influence on the Atlantic trade policy front, but also to some recent
ones where GATT remained peripheral in the process of conflict
resolution.

First, the Tokyo Round (1973–9) was moderately successful. Besides
a further series of modest tariff cuts, with the US agreeing to reduce
(some of) the disparities in its tariff schedule, the Subsidy Code and the
Customs Valuation Code removed two serious obstacles between the
EC and the US. Both codes ended the use of 'grandfather' clauses by
the US, which had led to endless bickering across the Atlantic for many
years. The US Tariff Act of 1930 contained a mandatory provision for
automatic imposition of countervailing duties in the case of subsidized
foreign exports to the US, with no proof of (what) injury necessary or
even relevant. The other outdated provision, the so-called American
selling-price system of customs valuation going back to 1922, had
already been abolished in the Kennedy Round package, but this had
never been agreed by the US Congress. Acceptance of the new code by
the US removed that anomaly. An interesting EC concession was the
agreement to abolish all tariff duties on trade in airplanes, helicopters
and certain components. Given the US position in the world aerospace
industry, and the then still highly uncertain position of Airbus Indus-
trie, this can certainly be described as a pacifying gesture.

Second, measures have been taken in response to complaints about
practices not in conformity with GATT principles. For instance, the
US had been complaining about the so-called 'reversed preferences' in
the two Yaoundé Conventions between the EC and (mostly French-
speaking) African countries. The case for allowing the (very) poor
countries protection can perhaps be made on economic grounds, but the
GATT basis is somewhat muddled. After all, article 24 of GATT permits a free-trade area (which the Yaoundé Conventions essentially
were), but only after a formal waiver by the GATT Council. However,

the US made it clear it would not agree to viewing it as a free-trade area, but rather as a preferential agreement between poor and developed countries; in the case, neither other poor countries nor the US could be discriminated against, when trying to enter the Yaoundé countries' markets. This led to the Soames–Casey agreement, to apply GATT rules without GATT. What happened in 1975, with the first Lomé agreement, meant that the discrimination against the US in ACP (Africa, Carribean and Pacific) markets was ended (both EC and US now face the same protection), but that the preferential access of the Lomé countries to the EC is better than the GSP (Generalized Scheme of Preferences) treatment other less developed countries get.

Third, dumping has been dealt with increasingly in a 'judicial' fashion, based on the GATT Anti-Dumping Code. This has certainly depoliticized the operation of a part of trade policy that, if dealt with in a political fashion, can be easily manipulated. In the first EC report since 1980 on dumping cases,[6] US (especially chemical) companies appear to be the worst offenders, followed by Comecon exporters. Yet, given the public nature of every case, the procedural safeguards for both parties and the detailed prescriptions for calculation of the 'normal value', dumping has ceased to be a trade-policy problem, except in highly exceptional cases.

In other instances, however, GATT has either little to offer or is ignored. The major case in point is obviously agriculture. Virtually every country in the world is protectionist in agriculture, just like the US and the EC. A workable truce for two decades between the US and the EC has meant that the EC does not fundamentally question the GATT waiver of 1955, while the US is (grudgingly) content with the big loop-holes in the variable-levy system, such as for corn, corn gluten, soya beans, tapioca and manioc. Underlying the truce were the following facts: the US can substitute corn and soya-bean cultivation for wheat-growing (wheat has a high variable levy) without much difficulty; EC import needs in these feedstock products are very great; the EC is a net importer of many agricultural products that the US exports; there is no serious competition in the world market to supply the EC with non-variable-levy feedstock.

None of the four implicit assumptions still holds true completely today. The US wheat surplus is growing structurally and no substantial further substitution can take place; put differently, the substitution of wheatland for corn/soya-bean land is no longer capable of putting a brake on the continuing rise in wheat output, since the EC market is more or less saturated. It is ironic, to say the least, that it is the inefficiency of Russian wheat-growing that enables Washington to choke off the pressures from the Mid-West farmers to act tough on CAP protectionism.

The EC import need has been growing to a lesser extent, because of the possibilities offered by the distorted CAP price structure of growing feedstock products in comparatively disadvantaged regions. More problematic is that there is continuous pressure in the Community to 'close' the loop-holes in the CAP's external protection. One source is obvious: since domestic EC grains can also be used as feedstock, the huge imports of corn gluten and tapioca tend to suppress the demand for domestic grains. Dairy-producing EC countries, especially the Netherlands, would resist 'closing' the loop-holes not only for cost reasons, but also on productivity grounds, since today's feedstock mixtures lead to a much higher milk output. Formally GATT is involved, since corn gluten carries a GATT-bound zero tariff that the EC asked to be temporarily suspended, and to be replaced with a tariff quota equal to current imports (from the US). The US refuses this. It is interesting to note that the sharp increase in US corn gluten exports to the EC (an addition of 300 per cent in volume since 1974) pushes EC grains *exports* to higher levels as well!

Also, the third assumption is becoming decreasingly correct. The EC has become a net exporter in more and more agricultural products, even in certain lower qualities of wheat. In many instances, it is doubtful whether this has anything to do with comparative advantage; mostly, both the surplus and the sale on the world market are artificially subsidized by the CAP. This must tend to depress the world price level to the detriment of all other agricultural exporters, and it might squeeze out US exporters or decrease their market shares.

Finally, the fourth assumption has been undermined by rapidly increasing EC tapioca/manioc imports, from Thailand in particular. Abiding by the unwritten rules of the truce, US pressures led the EC to impose a voluntary export restraint on Thailand's exports of the feedstock products.

GATT has proved itself incapable of taking serious action on any of these points. Many countries regard their agricultural protection as un-negotiable. In the EC, where after all members states have fully exposed their agricultural markets to each other (albeit under common price guarantees), there is no prospect of a CAP reform which would lead to external protection being significantly decreased or surpluses being turned back into deficits. The fundamental political significance of the CAP is decreasing slowly, but it may take perhaps another half a generation before it can be replaced without risking a breakup in the EC fabric itself. Rather, it may be the budgetary pressures on the CAP that will enforce incremental change. In any event, the only possibility for GATT to facilitate conflict resolution is the multilateral surveillance on export subsidies (in the CAP, called 'restitutions'). In agriculture, such subsidies are not forbidden as long as they do not lead to more than 'equitable' shares of the market. Since the world market – as a residual of many near-insulated and distorted national markets – is volatile both in volume and price, and since bad harvests shift around the globe irregularly, it is exceptionally hard to prove the 'inequity' of the market share or the causality with the restitutions (that may vastly differ over time and space). Yet, it is obvious how damaging such exports subsidies must be to traditional exporters. Two GATT dispute-settlement panels, on wheat flour and on pasta (following US complaints on CAP export subsidies), had difficulty, in deciding whether the world market could not be divided into regional markets, some of which were 'traditionally' supplied with subsidized EC products. This amazing stalemate, ignoring the fairly simple economics of export subsidies,[7] has infuriated US trade policy-makers. Left without any remedy in GATT, they opted for a limited subsidy war in wheat flour, thus hoping to force the EC to the negotiating table.

Without CAP reform, no doubt conflicts will intensify. The EC faces the GATT waiver exempting the US even from scrutiny in GATT panels, however ineffective they may be. The Community's wine and dairy exports to the US are sources of controversy, which must therefore be treated outside GATT.

A second case where GATT has hardly played any role is steel. In late 1977, the Solomon and Davignon plans to curb steel imports and introduce trigger prices as anti-dumping remedies were coordinated between Washington and Brussels. Later the situation changed. The US forced the EC to accept voluntary export restraints in order to prevent litigation to obtain countervailing duties on US steel imports from the EC. Of course, many EC steel firms were (and are) heavily subsidized. Whether this had caused export prices to be so low and volume increases to be so big that (serious or material?) injury had been inflicted upon American steel makers is another matter. In July 1983, specialty steels from the EC were also hit. This time, however, a link to GATT was possible. The US International Trade Commission gave a formal recommendation about dumping and EC subsidies which the President followed by imposing tariffs and quotas. This led to compensation claims in GATT: since the US could not hope to satisfy the EC with their offer of 4 million dollars, the EC retaliated by raising tariffs on certain chemicals.

There are other cases of some importance where the GATT has little to offer. Security-related exports are subject to a restrictive surveillance or to prohibitions under the so-called COCOM-regime (Coordinating Committee on Multilateral Export Controls). European politicians were incensed at the extraterritorial application of US law, prohibiting US affiliates in the EC from exporting hi-tech components for the Soviet–Siberian gas pipeline. Major cases of voluntary export

restraints to third countries are also in this category, because of the
fear of trade deflection. By definition, voluntary export retraints are
bilateral and outside GATT; so must their repercussions be. Thus,
when President Reagan imposed such a restraint on Japanese car exports to the US, there was some anxiety in the EC, which may ultimately have contributed to the more protectionist stance *vis-à-vis* Japan
in the February 1983 'accords'. Finally, the future of the Multi-Fibre
Agreement also depends to a critical extent on the US and the EC, and
not on GATT (as it is outside its legal realm – although, oddly enough,
the GATT Secretariat is more or less compelled to assist the Textile
Committee and the Surveillance Board to manage the MFA).

CONSTANTS IN US TRADE POLICY AND GATT REFORM

The usual picture that is drawn of commercial policy is one of ad-hoc
responses to immediate pressures. This notion is surely correct in a certain sense. Indeed, many trade policy officials in the EC and the US
compare themselves with men from the fire brigade. Nevertheless,
there are a few constants in trade policy-making on both sides of the
Atlantic, which exert a powerful influence on the *modus vivendi* of the
bigemony and shape their respective view of GATT reform.

In the US, there have been four constants underlying trade policy-
making for at least several decades. In the first place, US trade policy is
subject to a high degree of legalization. The reasons behind this strong
preference include the reduced discretion of the executive branch of the
federal government – fitting the US constitutional system with its
'checks and balances' – the desire for openness so as to avoid 'back-
room deals' and to provide a basis for well-informed public debate and
a search for ways to assist officials to 'fend off' special interests.[8] Certainly, conflict management between the EC and the US (and between
Japan and the US) is regularly subjected to severe strains due to the
inability of US trade policy officials to act at all during one or the
other investigation, or due to cumbersome domestic deals between
the Executive and special interests to keep them from using the various
complaints procedures. Big industry, on the other hand, can pur-
posefully manipulate the system by complaints about dumping, foreign
subsidies, etc., creating anxiety abroad that is bound to find its way
to the US trade policy-makers; in so doing, firms or sectors may increase the leverage they have on the US government. Another
drawback of the system is the tendency to litigate in foreign trade
policy, which is not well understood in many other countries.[9]

The constant of legalization appeals to deep-rooted American con-
victions about how society ought to be organized. The drawbacks will

not be considered a sufficient argument for dismantling the many statutory formulae or the various institutions involved. Rather, legalization is verbally 'exported' as an important principle for GATT reform. Although the author is not aware of any official detailed proposal, through the years repeated references to stricter procedures, more authority and a wider scope for GATT dispute settlement have been made. Vague suggestions of a world trade court have also been heard. One may wonder whether GATT is ready for even a modest version of these ideas. But another serious problem raised by these ideas is also rarely mentioned: if extensive legal procedures at the GATT level were to be introduced, would the US legal trade policy system subject itself to them in all relevant cases? Or would it merely lead to a GATT system of voluntary arbitration?

In the second place, the political economy of US trade policy is, *ceteris paribus*, more inclined to border protectionism than in many other countries. Border tariffs, quotas and countervailing duties have a number of imperfect substitutes with economic effects in a similar direction, such as subsidies, government guarantees, public participation in firms and public procurement. Only some of these are utilized in the US; in particular, public subsidies for social purposes during adjustments and during severe crises or for large-scale, risky projects are seldom found in the US. The US practises a paler shade of the 'mixed economy' and (industrial) subsidies at the federal level are minimal. At the state level, the inclination to intervene tends to be somewhat stronger, but the distorting nature of state subsidies would cause immediate problems with the severe regime of intra-US market integration, as maintained by the Supreme Court. The result is an unrelenting call for border protection, with the federal government having little else at its disposal than all or nothing. A further disadvantage is that subsidies appear on the public budget and hence create greater pressures for conditional policy action than tariffs or ('voluntary') quotas. Indeed, now that tariff protection has become less of a problem to US importers, and tariff peaks have been planed off in two GATT rounds, incidental tariff or quota protection is more easily resorted to, and is rarely tied to stringent conditions. Though protection is usually temporary, it tends to become semi-permanent, or may come back so soon as cyclical pressures cause a new profit squeeze; no systematic surveillance of adjustment efforts is employed. Also, border protection necessarily applies to all firms, whereas subsidies can be fine-tuned. The latter create further pressures from domestic competitors for the removal of the subsidy as soon as possible. The US propensity to resort to border protection may have increased further, after the dismantling of the trade-adjustment assistance programme at a moment when US unemployment reached a post-war high.

In the third place, US protectionism tends to increase markedly in times of dollar overvaluation.[10] Probably this characteristic is not particularly American, since exports in an overvalued currency would face an across-the-board competitive disadvantage, irrespective of their origin. When defining the equilibrium exchange rate as that real rate that is expected to generate a surplus (deficit) on current account equalling the outflow (inflow) of financial capital over one business cycle, one should first ask what the accompanying macroeconomic policy is, since different mixtures of monetary and fiscal policy will have different impacts on current and capital account, certainly in the short run. If domestic macroeconomic policy is imagined to be geared toward low unemployment and low inflation through an unconstrained mix of monetary and fiscal policy, one can make a subjective (but not necessarily worthless) judgement about the order of magnitude of misalignment. Such a judgement can be squared with purchasing-power-parity calculations, at least if the statistical base of the commodity basket is not too old.

If we ignore currencies that are overvalued merely because their price is kept artificially high by means of exchange and trade restriction, it must be said that currencies that are substantially overvalued for several years are rarely found. This is to be expected, since self-correcting forces are at work that cannot be resisted indefinitely. None the less, at the time of writing the dollar is breaking all post-Bretton-Woods records *vis-à-vis* currencies such as the D-mark, which orginates from a non-inflationary country with a surplus on current account; at the same time, the US has a yawning trade deficit. Apparently the combination of high (real) interest rates and an underlying confidence in the US economy (relative to other economies) is capable of keeping the dollar at a rate which is closer to 30 per cent than 20 per cent overvaluation, without any sign in the past three years that the downturn – which is bound to come – has started.

One might wonder whether this phenomenon is a 'constant'. By definition, it does not seem to be. But persistent dollar overvaluations have occurred in the past and they were always accompanied by an upsurge in protectionism.[11] The present overvaluation is a bad omen. It might lead to protection that survives the overvaluation by many years. It might lead to trade policy conduct in which GATT is ignored or marginalized, because of the search for quick and visible results. It might cause politicians to overemphasize 'fair' trade – a value laden and plainly political term – as against 'malpractices' of Japanese and Europeans, while neglecting the main cause of the export squeeze: the macroeconomic policy at home.

The fourth constant worth mentioning is the firm belief in the bicycle theory of trade liberalization. This is the conviction of the need to give domestic trade policy-makers a believable excuse for inaction on the protectionist front, as this would inflict damage on the fragile, but large international negotiations. Without such believable excuses, protectionist pressures cannot be fended off for long, putting a brake on further progress in dismantling barriers, leading eventually to the bicycle of trade liberalization falling over. The view is only consistent with the US desire for a more legalized GATT, if the latter would merely lead to voluntary arbitration; a stronger GATT with enforcement capacity would, of course, render the search for excuses for inaction superfluous, and hence the bicycle theory. Ever since the Dillon Round, the US has sought to get beyond ordinary 'further' tariff reduction for which GATT is best suited. In the Kennedy Round, the first talks on nontariff barriers were initiated and new, more radical negotiation techniques for tariffs (now across-the-board) were practised. During the Tokyo Round, the emphasis was largely on a number of non-tariff distortions, as tariff reductions were no longer considered sufficiently interesting in the light of substantial exchange-rate volatility and the rate of subsidization in some countries. Increasing the scope and strengthening the dispute-settlement capacity of GATT seem to be the forces that pedal the bicycle so as to prevent it from falling over. The coverage should be increased mainly by: progress in subjecting world agricultural trade to GATT rules; negotiating a framework of GATT rules and a standstill in domestic regulation with respect to international trade-in-services; and finding an international solution for 'targeting' in hi-tech products, as well as the specific consequences for trade in hi-tech goods. What all three topics have in common is that they are even more difficult than any of the codes of the Tokyo Round, with the possible exception of subsidies. This chapter cannot hope to deal with them in any detail.

The idea of subjecting national (or EC) agricultural trade policy measures to GATT rules obviously reflects a US strategy to overcome the piecemeal arbitration approach that the first Reagan Administration followed, mainly (but not only) *vis-à-vis* the EC. Without a profound knowledge of the actual interpretation of articles 11 and 16 in particular of GATT, and full knowledge of all the waivers, derogations and exceptions that currently apply, it is impossible to gain an insight into what today's GATT rules really mean to agricultural trade. Moreover, as noted before, enforcement is weak and the review of the temporariness of measures is frequently lacking. The declaration after the ministerial GATT session of November 1982 stated that 'the following matters be examined, in the light of the objectives, principles and relevant provision of the General Agreement and also taking into account the effects of national agricultural policies . . . all measures affecting trade, market access and competition and supply in agricultural products, including subsidies and other forms of assistance'.[12] In 1983, a Committee on Trade in Agriculture was established which reported in the early summer of 1984. If serious negotiations ever come about, they will not only be protracted, but they will not, in any case, lead to immediate changes in actual agricultural trade policies. It is also important to realize that both the EC and the US have an interest in output restraints, and some of their far-sighted politicians and civil servants may actually look to GATT as a constraining force, in addition to a budgetary one, that might help to keep the farm lobby in check. This is unlikely to be achieved by the paper agreement itself, but rather by the permanent insertion of considerations of conflicting international interdependence in national policy formulation to which a GATT consensus, and GATT's review system, would supposedly lead.

International trade-in-services negotiations are also a long shot, to put it mildly. The OECD Code on Invisibles Trade has never worked, because the national-treatment idea had been diluted from the start by so many exceptions that the idea itself got lost. A few brief comments on how to proceed in this difficult area are made on the final section of this paper. In any event, no matter how firmly one believes in the bicycle theory, liberalization of international trade-in-services must be a long shot, if only for the reason that virtually no across-the-board (as against 'sectoral') expertise is available in many countries, and very few countries have taken a strong, overall interest in the domain. To some extent, this reflects the very different levels of development of GATT's contracting parties; it is well known that the level of economic development is a dominant explanatory variable for the importance the service sector has in the economy. But even the EC and Japan are not well prepared – in a functional sense – to enter serious negotiations. For instance, do responsible US policy-makers not know that the EC Commission has neither a Directorate-General for Services, nor a Directorate, nor even a Division? After the GATT ministerial of November 1982, which merely decided to call for national studies on services trade, 'to review the results of these examinations . . . and . . . consider whether any multilateral action in these matters is appropriate and desirable',[13] the Commission set up an internal task force on international trade-in-services, which had representatives from no fewer than nine Directorates-General, plus the legal service and the statistical office. Seemingly simple matters such as the proper EC statistics or a comprehensive economic view on EC services, its internationalization and its strengths and weaknesses had to be pioneered. At present the Community is developing a perspective on the topic, which might eventually result in a clear negotiating position, for which a Council mandate can be requested. However, one might question the wisdom of US negotiators in asking for a standstill pronouncement by the ministerial session in 1982. It is doubtful whether the US itself could have lived up to such a promise, given the vast complications and the substantial notification machinery which would have been needed.

The US ideas on 'hi-tech' trade and industrial targeting may simply be an attempt to diminish pressures from Congress to 'do something' there. There are a few Bills in Congress on this topic, but, of course, they would lead to a unilateral US response with unknown consequences. The ideas are not well worked out, as far as the author is aware. They remind one of the EC frustrations on Japan – indeed, the main culprit here, as far as the US is concerned, is also Japan – that led to complaints under article 23 of GATT about the broad government/ industry relationships in Japan, or even the private/public balance, formal and informal, in that country, supposedly causing a comparatively low aggregate import ratio. Such actions tend to be unproductive, if not counter-productive, both inside and outside GATT. Not only do countries rightly refuse to submit their socio-economic construct and traditions as such to intergovernmental scrutiny, but they also have lots of opportunities to point to similarities in so many other countries, including the US, so that no judgement can ever be a useful guideline for a world trade organization. If industrial targeting is a serious problem in international trade, remedies should be sought in the curtailment of crucial instruments used, and in the assurance (and enforcement) of equal market access.

CONSTANTS IN EC TRADE POLICY AND GATT REFORM

The EC has had a common trade policy for just over twenty years, has grown in membership and gone through quite a remarkable socio-economic transformation during its existence. None the less, the properties of the EC impose behaviour upon it in trade policy with at least three constants. Typically, the Community does not excel in putting forward important initiatives on the trade front; it has a complex regime for dealing with import pressures, allowing for a range of internal substitutes of external border protection; for deep-seated reasons the EC also has an ambivalent attitude, and excessive sensitivity, to international judicial review.

The European Community is a 'pre-federal' conglomerate of nations that have great difficulty in accepting all the consequences of joint trade policy-making. There are legal competence problems between the Commission and the Council; there are great difficulties about whether the Commission should be given mandates, and what the appropriate balance of interests ought to be (given the veto practices in the

Council); there are legal safeguards (article 115, EEC), which cause
the common commercial policy not to be truly common; what is worse,
the policy is not implemented by a Community customs system, but by
national customs systems, providing ample scope for differences in
administrative handling and for implementing national deterrent
measures so as to impose 'voluntary export restraints' upon specific
target countries anywhere in the world; finally, an overall trade policy
is hard to formulate in the EC, because there is no hierarchical structure
or effective coordinating device to align the positions of the Councils of
Ministers of Trade and Industry (or Economic Affairs), Foreign Affairs
and Agriculture. This is quite apart from anomalies such as the lack of
provision for a common trade policy in the European Coal and Steel
Community Treaty, which had to be compensated for by judicial
review, at least in so far as intra-EC (steel) measures require commercial policy measures at the same time. It is quite obvious that such a
Community is not suited to lead the world into new, grandiose initiatives of GATT reform, or, in general, to initiate a substantial liberalization of trade. The sometimes naive or brusque way in which US trade
policy is conducted is often criticized in EC circles, oblivious of the fact
that the Community itself has done little if anything, to establish more
appropriate GATT rules or to enhance their effectiveness. The EC
trade policy system is sluggish: once having adopted a liberal policy
towards a certain product market, it tends to prove very hard to undo
the underlying compromise; similarly, once having gone protectionist,
the vested interests need to lobby for only one, or a few, no-votes and
liberalization will require a much higher price or might not even be
negotiable. Fortunately, in industrial trade the EC is still fairly liberal
and the 'ratchet effect' makes this very difficult to change. In desperation, France introduced the infamous strategem of relocating video-
recorder imports to Poitiers in order to upset the frozen coalition in the
Council that prevented joint protection against Japan. But one cannot
re-create 'Poitiers' all the time without disrupting the co-operation that
all member states desire in their own interests. Another interesting
example is the insistence of the Commission on the need to be able to
act more quickly against 'unfair' trade practices by means of a 'new
Community instrument'. For months this proposal was blocked by
what are traditionally called the 'liberal' countries, mainly out of a fear
that the Commission would become more protectionist than they
would like; such vetoing action can be effective because it can prevent
any protectionism in the Council. It is a typical example of what 'pre-
federal' means in EC practice: although the liberal trade policy countries
(such as the Federal Republic of Germany and the Netherlands) claim
to be in favour of more integration, also by transferring more power to
the EC institutions, they tend to do precisely the opposite as soon as it

does not suit them. Conversely, the so-called protectionist EC countries (admittedly an exaggerated label and perhaps too simple a classification) consider that they cannot always wait until the unwieldy EC
machinery outlines a trade policy response that suits them, and tend to
break the unity of the 'common' trade policy, if they feel it is really
necessary, even at the cost of creating *intra*-EC barriers to prevent trade
deflection. Such a Community is expected to sponsor GATT reform. It
might do this, but it will never be the true initiator.

A second constant of EC trade policy is the access to substitutive instruments of relief or support on the part of import-competing producers
and their employees. One version, which is not possible in the US, is
the occasional permission of one-country protection against highly-
targeted imports. A well-known example is the temporary US export
surge to the UK in synthetic carpets in 1980, caused by a temporarily
low dollar, a high pound (having previously moved upwards *vis-à-vis*
EMS currencies) and the then subsidy to US gas supply. The UK
demand for temporary emergency protection was accommodated
under Commission surveillance, without other EC countries engaging
in protection. Other possibilities include *de facto* national protection via
'amorphous' protection such as voluntary export restraints to national
submarkets of the Community, national subsidies in various forms,
manpower and other market policies facilitating adjustment, and various forms of state involvement, ranging from the underwriting of loans
to public purchases of shares of firms. Also, in certain cases regional
policy may offer alternative forms of employment in the very areas
where import competition might appear to hurt. As noted in the section
above, the US either does not deploy some of these instruments or
does not utilize them to anywhere near the same extent. On the other
hand, the contrast is certainly not one of black and white. As has been
argued elsewhere at greater lengths,[14] the surveillance function of
the EC Commission generates (*ceteris paribus*) pressures for more external protection, comparable in kind, though not in intensity, to the
pressures within the US for external protection. A stricter Commission
surveillance of national subsidies, as has taken place since the early
1980s, and a closer inspection of the financial relation between public
enterprises and 'their' governments, would cause protectionist pressures to seek for other, or additional, forms of relief, or adjustment
'pauses', or perhaps merely quasi-rents; hence, they will tend to turn
to the EC, directly or via their country's ministers. An explicit mani-
festation of this tendency is the recently proposed 'deal' to trade off
more external EC protection for a full consolidation of the EC's internal market. This idea is mostly directed against imports from Japan
and the newly industrialized countries, and carries subjective over-
tones that come rather close to the 'targeting', 'domestic contents' and

'reciprocity' Bills of Senators Danforth, Helm and others in the US Congress. One wonders what would remain of GATT, if the 'bige-mony' were to embrace these proposals on both sides of the Atlantic.

Third, the EC seems to be wary of any proposals aiming at stricter judicial review in GATT. The attitude is usually explained by a Euro-pean tradition of seeking socio-political accommodation of trade prob-lems. This explanation, however, overlooks the fact that the Community itself has developed an elaborate and – for a pre-federal system – sur-prisingly effective judicial review for major domains such as customs matters, indirect taxes, technical standards, subsidies of all kinds, cross-frontier and national business collusion, dominant firm behaviour, crisis cartels, trade policy instruments as well as derogations, and lately public procurement, public enterprises and even certain services and exchange controls. The judicial review by the European Court of Justice is a cornerstone of EC market integration, and is undoubtedly recognized as such by all EC member states. To claim that the EC would merely perceive transnational judicial review as a 'typical' US export of its own constitutional system cannot, therefore, be correct. The Community's internal judicial review system has created a pro-found awareness of the ambition, but also of the complications, such a review would bring. Different 'layers' of law may well be inconsistent and confusing, if there is no hierarchical relationship. Within the EC, the concepts of the 'supremacy' of Community law and the fact that EC competences and measures lead to 'pre-emption' secure such hier-archy; enmeshing the EC judicial review with national adjudication procedures completes the system. The Community will be very anx-ious not to damage its own ambitious, but nevertheless fragile, system of judicial review.

It is probable, however, that there is more to it. Policy-makers and observers in the Community tend to be sceptical about the infusion of international economic organizations with a high degree of judicial am-bition. The higher the ambition is set, the more damaging the defiance will be. There is a lingering doubt as to whether large trading partners – EC, US, Japan possibly – will ever accept too tight a judicial review, given the political and retaliatory alternatives they have at their dis-posal. The point does not only relate to the present debate on GATT reform, it can also be exemplified by the much weaker GATT of the last ten to fifteen years. The EC has insisted for a long time on inter-preting article 19 of GATT – a safeguard clause in case imports 'disrupt' the domestic market – in a way that allows for selective (i.e. discriminatory) protection. Leaving aside for the moment what would be the ideal and economically optimal safeguard provision, this is merely to register that what the EC wishes to 'legalize', and what is opposed by many other developed GATT partners, including the US, is exactly what all of them have been practising for decades now. Also, the Multi-Fibre Agreements (MFAs) do not augur well for more sweeping attempts to legalize the GATT. The MFAs violate the non-discrimination and article 19 provisions, leave a lot of room for what are, in fact, bilateral dictates with 'sweeteners' of a rent-seeking kind for the exporters, and have tended to become more restrictive, due to ad-hoc insertions such as the 'reasonable departures' clause (1977) and the cut-backs for major suppliers and the 'surge' mechanism (in 1981), leaving little possibility of pursuing the commendable objectives of an 'orderly' and 'equitable' development of trade and a 6 per cent import growth rate in volume. Also, the issue of graduation – a term not to be heard in Geneva – may not be susceptible to judicial review.

A PERSPECTIVE ON GATT REFORM

A comprehensive GATT reform would raise so many legal, economic and diplomatic issues, with so many domestic constitutional, legal and political ramifications, that it would not be realistic to expect it in the foreseeable future. At the same time, however, the present situation is so lamentable that the reasonably satisfactory functioning of the world trade system should be attributed primarily to the dominant position of the EC and the US, and possibly Japan, with GATT as a mutually accepted and mild constraint.

The slow, but steady erosion of the trade dominance of the 'bigemony', and the continuing increase in trade openness of the EC and the US constitute fundamental arguments in favour of a strong and effective GATT in the long run. The theory of trade warfare seems to me to be a far too simple analytical construct to deduce policy-relevant guidelines for *unilateral* actions to discipline presumed sinners. Recently, two political scientists[15] advocated a 'tit for tat' retaliatory strategy with trading partners that violate 'explicit' (?) GATT rules. They claim that 'tit for tat' is 'not aimed at starting a trade war. It is a programme that should elicit cooperation and freer trade . . . The US should meet protectionism in kind. We *cannot* defend liberalism unilaterally; without pressure, our trading partners *will not* act in accordance with GATT norms'. If they imply that trade theoreticians have failed to develop tariff war analysis, together with the co-operative alternatives, they are right;[16] the theory is not about how to deter and then liberalize, it is (still) about how to acquire a terms of trade gain. However, if they imply that it is for the US, or for that matter the EC or any other country or group, to determine whether and when to retaliate, the world trade system will soon collapse. Rather, retaliation should be used as a deterrent (sanction) in a multilateral framework. The wheat-flour subsidy 'war' between the EC and the US was a carefully controlled warning, which does not lend itself to generalization.

There are three major components of GATT reform, which complement each other. The first volet of the triptych consists of institutional and procedural reforms. It includes such fundamental issues as the conversion of GATT into a true international treaty, the question of whether and how to amend GATT in its present form (this now requires two-thirds of the equally weighted votes; with application only for those countries having voted in favour), the relation of the many codes that have emerged from the Tokyo Round and have legal status as separate treaties (only for the signatories) to the General Agreement as it stands, and the improvement of the weak and malfunctioning dispute settlements procedures. It is not possible to deal with all these questions within the context of this paper; some of these questions are in any event better left to more competent specialists.[17] It has already been noted that the EC is not very outspoken on these matters. The US has thrown in at least three 'concepts', which provide a rough indication of the desired direction. One is GATT-Plus, a group of (probably industrial) countries, moving on to more ambitious forms of trade liberalization and institutionalization, outside the strictly GATT framework. As Jackson shows, this has in fact already happened with the recent codes.[18] The relationship with the GATT itself, and especially the reduced significance of the most-favoured nation clause, are major questions that ought to be posed again, since they have not been answered. Another idea is the Super-GATT: this is an attempt to broaden the 'bigemony' towards hierarchical co-operation, led by the group of eighteen. Today the group of eighteen changes composition every year, although the big traders are always included. The group operates at the highest level of civil servants. The US notion of it would make it a political directorate, but whether it would be comparable to the IMF group of twenty or a derivative of the Western Economic Summits, or tied to the OECD, or be comparable to the construction used for the North/South dialogue in 1976/7 is not clear. Finally, a GATT-of-the-like-minded would introduce a sort of sectoral à la carte progress, with groups of changing composition; this bears some similarity to the concept of *géometrie variable*, as applied to EC integration. It is hard to escape the impression that the US was launching these ideas out of frustration with the non-result of the GATT ministerial of 1982.

The second volet is an incremental improvement in the effective implementation of present GATT rules. Of course, this component is not unrelated to the first one, but can be developed separately, if genuinely desired. It could include better implementation and judicial review of the Subsidy Code – a serious bone of contention, particularly between the US and the EC (and Japan) – and a more satisfactory approach to a cluster of issues relating to the treatment of present and new NICs by developed countries. Both major issues may either be tackled gradually by the GATT Council (i.e. at ambassador level, and lower working parties and committees, occasionally helped by panels), or by a separately announced negotiation round. The subsidy question deserves a (lengthy) separate paper in order to do justice to the technical-economic and socio-political aspects.[19] The present author's recommendation is that EC Commission surveillance and the EC Court's judicial review of national public aids be used more extensively, because they teach a number of lessons which are highly relevant for effective GATT surveillance.[20] Although undoubtedly not in full conformity with prevailing US views (although there is not really 'one' US view on the question of adjustment aid to sectors and on subsidies to advanced 'frontier' industries), it would go a long way towards minimizing disputes internationally. In agriculture, however, export subsidies must be subjected to much more stringent controls; ad-hoc panels, manned by diplomats who happen to be stationed in Geneva for a few years and relying on 'proofs' of inequitable market shares, cannot possibly give proper results.

The cluster of problems surrounding NICs' access to developed countries' markets suggests a *package* that could perhaps be worked out in a major negotiation. It would tie selectivity with respect to article 19 firmly to criteria such as temporariness and degressive stringency of protection, and restructuring plans, subject to GATT surveillance and possible sanctions; at the same time the MFA ought to be phased out, based on the same criteria and with explicit encouragement to NICs to organize themselves *in GATT* so as to deter the EC and the US effectively, when necessary; criteria for graduation of NICs should be established and a timetable for implementation set. This package may sound ambitious to some, but it would seem to represent a reasonable balance of interests. In any event, there would appear to be no advantage in continuing with the informal bilateralism or in keeping near-developed NICs outside the material obligations of GATT. It should also be remembered that export surpluses of the EC and the US with NICs as a group have decreased steadily, and that some of the NICs need secure market access in order to pay their debts.

The third volet comprises an extended GATT coverage of agriculture and services trade. The recent report by the new GATT Committee on Trade in Agriculture is restricted, so nothing can be assessed. What is fairly certain is that, probably for the first time, the full 'horrors' of departing from formal agricultural trade rules will become intelligible. In services there are a large number of very difficult issues, such as domestic competences for trade diplomats (versus technical ministries), the place of developing countries, the link with a possible new GATT round, the question of conditional most favoured nations (like the Tokyo Round Codes) and the so-called new 'mini-GATT', and the realization of the most important principles of a future liberalization negotiation. With respect to the most important principles – in GATT jargon, the '*châpeau*' – three questions must be answered in my view. One is the adequacy or utility of 'national treatment' and 'non-discrimination' as the guiding principle. GATT has the national-treatment principle in article 3, once goods have received customs clearance. Article 3, subsection 4 applies this explicitly to domestic regulation. But GATT applies to products, not services, and it invariably assumes border protection.

The central difficulty with *services*, rather than products, is that the prior condition of border protection is frequently not fulfilled and, more importantly, could not effectively or usefully be imposed in certain service sectors. Regulation, sometimes combined with a discretionary system of authorizations, is *the* instrument of protection. Therefore, the inherent logic of the General Agreement breaks down.

To propose national treatment for services as the underlying principle (as the US seems to be doing) renders the services trade unnegotiable (as it assumes that the removal of protection implicit in domestic regulation is a feasible political option in a sufficiently large number of countries), unless accompanied by concrete proposals for (negotiable) forms of border protection in services trade, that can substitute (somehow) for today's domestic regulations. Both possibilities should be seriously examined. The present author is not aware of any breakthroughs with respect to the second possibility. If this is correct, and if the implicit political feasibility assumption on national treatment does not hold, we ought to search for alternative organizing principles of negotiation.

The liberalization approach of the EC Internal Market offers some suggestions for such principles – without, of course, implying the same degree of ambition for worldwide negotiations. The EEC Treaty provisions for the Internal *product* Market, in so far as they are concerned with domestic regulation (articles 30–6), are based on three ideas:

general prohibition of 'measures having equivalent effects' as quantitative restrictions;
a positive list of *legitimate exceptions* (article 36);
a proportionality rule, that is, the legitimate regulatory objective should be achieved with *the least protectionist (i.e. discriminatory) instrument* or provision (in other words, proportional to the task).

For the *châpeau*, this would imply:

the appropriate formulation of a general prohibition on discriminatory services regulation (national treatment);
the appropriate formulation of what is agreed as a 'reasonable (minimum) regulatory protection', that is, legitimate exceptions to
national treatment.

Further negotiations would then have to concentrate on:

appropriate multilateral surveillance of the proportionality rule;
step-by-step approaches to reduce domestic regulation to the 'reasonable' level.

Another element of the *châpeau* should deal with the 'quantifiability' of
concessions, given serious statistical problems and little clarity about
the effects of internationally negotiated deregulation. Finally, the efficacy of codes as a vehicle for implementing the services trade liberalization should be addressed. Given the experience of intra-EC services
liberalization, in a legal and political environment which is far superior
to anything the GATT will achieve in the 1980s, it is difficult to be optimistic about the prospects of agreement even on a *workable châpeau*.

In conclusion, it would seem that the better functioning and broader
coverage of GATT will have to be traded off with ever-changing groups
of signatories to a variety of agreements, with a small core of (mostly)
OECD countries moving farthest. How attractive that is to the GATT
parties at large, and what the material difference would then be with
the OECD, are the key questions left unanswered.

NOTES

1 This expression can be found in A. Cairncross, H. Giersch, A. Lamfalussy,
   G. Petrilli and P. Uri, *Economic Policy of the European Community* (Macmillan, London, 1974).
2 In 1983 GATT had 90 'Contracting parties', and another 30 applying *de facto*
   GATT rules or having provisionally adopted GATT as a reference for trade
   policy.
3 MFN = 'most favoured nation'. See, for instance, K. Dam, *The GATT, Law and
   International Economic Organisation* (Chicago University Press, Chicago, 1970).
4 The word 'bigemony' was introduced by Fred Bergsten in 1974, when advocating
   the bilateral hegemony in international economic – in particular, monetary
   – affairs that the Federal Republic of Germany and the US could exercise together
   in order to stabilize the world economy. However, I utilize it for the EC and the
   US together in trade matters.
5 Four, because Benelux had already achieved one common tariff schedule.
6 EC, *First Annual Report of the Commission of the EC on the Community's Anti-Dumping
   and anti-Subsidy Activities*, COM (83) 519 final; 12 September 1983.

7   See G. Sampson and R. Snape, 'Effects of the EEC's variable import levies', *Journal of Political Economy*, vol. 88(5) (1980).

8   See J. Jackson, 'Perspectives on the jurisprudence of international trade', *American Economic Review*, vol. 74(2) (1984). According to Jackson, this legalization has important domestic and international drawbacks, the most problematic one is the following dilemma: 'the more one maximizes the goals of a legalistic system (predictability, transparency, corruption minimization, minimization of political back-room deals), the more one will sacrifice other desirable goals such as flexibility and, in international relations, the ability of government officials to make determinations in the broad national interest' (p. 280).

9   See J. Steenbergen, 'Subsidies in international trade regulation', paper presented to a Conference on International Trade Law organized by the Georgetown University Law Center, in Estoril, Portugal, 22–24 June 1981 (unpublished). As Steenbergen puts it: 'It reflects a different legal culture and basic differences in the concepts of state and society. Most European entrepreneurs consider a problem to be settled by litigation as a case lost, regardless of the outcome of the procedure. A system depending on litigation is therefore from their point of view an effective deterrent to trade. They will react this way even if they do not dispute the fairness of the rules and the independence of the court. But their reaction is of course even stronger when they have to litigate abroad . . .'

10 See F. Bergsten and J. Williamson, 'Exchange rates and trade policy', in W. Cline (ed.), *Trade Policy in the 1980's* (MIT Press for the Institute of International Economics, Cambridge, Mass., 1983).

11 Ibid.

12 As published in *Focus, GATT Newsletter*, December 1982, p. 5.

13 Ibid., p. 7.

14 See J. Pelkmans, 'Trade policy as industrial policy in the EC', paper presented at the Euro-American Trade Policy Colloquium, European University Institute, Florence, 2–4 April 1981. See also J. Pelkmans and H. Van der Ven, 'Communitarian industrial policy and the nature of industrial change' (in Dutch), *Maandschrift Economie*, vol. 45(5), (1981).

15 See J. Goldstein and S. Krasner, 'Unfair trade practices: the case for a differential response', *American Economic Review*, vol. 74(2), (1984), pp. 284–5; italics in original.

16 But see C. Kindleberger, *International Economics* (Irwin, Homewood, Ill. 1973), pp. 196–8; and W. Mayer, 'Theoretical considerations on negotiated tariff adjustments', *Oxford Economic Papers*, vol. 33(1), (1981).

17 See J. Jackson, 'GATT machinery and the Tokyo Round agreements', in W. Cline (ed.), *Trade Policy in the 1980's* (MIT Press for the International Institute of Economics, Cambridge, Mass., 1983).

18 Ibid.

19 For a good guide through what he denotes as a 'morass of detail', see G. Hufbauer, 'Subsidy issues after the Tokyo Round', in W. Cline (ed.), *Trade Policy in the 1980's* (MIT Press for the International Institute of Economics, Cambridge, Mass., 1983).

20 See J. Pelkmans, *Market Integration in the European Community* (Nijhoff, The Hague/Boston/Lancaster, 1984).

Comment 1

MIRIAM CAMPS

The first four sections of Professor Pelkmans's essay seem to me to present an excellent quick survey of some of the main features of US–EC trade and of the more or less enduring characteristics of the rather different trade policies that these two major trading entities pursue, characteristics which, given the preponderance of these countries in world trade, severely constrain the process of GATT reform. Although here and there questions might be raised about particular points in his analysis, it seems to me not only broadly correct, but also illuminating; I shall therefore limit my comments to the last section of his paper, in which he deals more specifically with questions of GATT reform.

Let me begin by saying that I very much agree with Professor Pelkmans's contention that a unilaterally-determined retaliatory policy, even though it might be adopted in the belief that it could be used to induce others to adhere to a liberal trading system, would – almost certainly – lead instead to the collapse of today's system which, though far from perfect, is nevertheless far better than nothing.

Much has been written about GATT reform, and there are so many different aspects of the problem which might be explored that anyone's short summary of needed action is bound to seem inadequate to others who have thought about the problem. Inevitably Professor Pelkmans's treatment of these questions seemed to me too perfunctory; my comments on his comments are open to the same criticism.[1]

Professor Pelkmans groups his comments on GATT reform into three clusters, his three 'volets' of a triptych of reform: procedural and institutional questions; improvements in the implementation of existing GATT rules; extension of GATT rules to agriculture and services.

I should summarize and group the needed reforms a little differently, and the kinds of changes I should like to see made would, probably, extend the role of the GATT somewhat beyond what he has in mind, although, for reasons I touch on below, I think the logic of his suggestions would take him further down the road of institutional reform than he may realize.

Under his first 'volet' he lists, but says very little about, constitutional questions, such as turning GATT into a true international treaty, the relation of the codes to the General Agreement, and voting arrangements. He refers to the need to improve dispute-settlement procedures, and also, somewhat disparagingly, to various ideas that have been floated unofficially in the US from time to time about a GATT-Plus, a Super-GATT, or a GATT for the like-minded. From his brief discussion, I am far from clear just what changes under this heading he would advocate, other than improvements in the dispute-settlements arrangements, although from the discussion in the body of the paper I infer that he would like to see the GATT given a firm constitutional base. In my own view, it is an illusion to think that one can do much to improve the GATT as the centrepiece of the international trading system, unless governments are prepared to make rather more changes in the organizational side of the GATT than even some of the stoutest supporters of the GATT like to contemplate. Like Professor Pelkmans, I think it desirable that the GATT be put on a firmer constitutional base. But it is, in my view, even more important for the key governments to decide that they want the GATT to become a trade *policy* body, not simply an organization that essentially provides the framework for tariff reductions and the negotiation and enforcement of a set of commercial policy rules. To enable the GATT to perform this broader role, they should also agree to make changes in the way their own policies are formulated and conducted, and in the structure of the organization. I am not suggesting that the GATT should cease to improve and enforce the rule-system embodied in the General Agreement and the Codes; nor am I saying that it should abandon efforts to agree on new rules or modified rules for new areas. But I am suggesting that, in addition, it should become the main forum for the discussion of the many problems affecting trade that do not lend themselves to settlement by the quasi-legal means typical of today's GATT approach. In particular, I think that the international staff of the GATT needs to be strengthened and given more independence and more rights of initiative; that there should be a higher-powered, more broadly gauged policy committee than the Committee of Eighteen has yet shown itself to be; and that member governments should send to discussions in Geneva more frequently than they now do high-level representatives who are not only directly concerned with commercial policy formation within their own governments, but are also competent to discuss questions which, although they give rise to conflicts in commercial policy, can only be solved if they are looked at in relation to other policies – monetary policies, debt settlements, etc. – or as aspects of domestic 'industrial' or structural adjustment policies.

Turning to Professor Pelkmans's second 'volet', it seems to me to be clear that substantial improvement in the two areas he identifies under this heading – subsidies and the problem of the newly industrialized countries (NICs) – is likely to be made only if the GATT becomes a more policy-oriented organization and the international staff is given more of a role than is now the case. Although I found Professor Pelkmans's discussion of subsidies rather imprecise, I think he is recommending that something like the system followed in the European Community (surveillance by the Commission of the public aids given by member countries and judicial review by the Court) be adopted by the GATT. There probably are lessons to be learnt from the Community's experience and, like Professor Pelkmans, I think that surveillance by an international body is an important element of an improved approach to the subsidies problem. But there are, as he recognizes, important differences between the action that can be taken within a Community which has accepted the goal of forming an economic union (even in the imprecise way that goal is today accepted by the ten countries involved) and the action that can be taken by a wider universe of states with widely divergent political and economic systems and which has no such ultimate goal in sight. The kind of 'effective surveillance' Professor Pelkmans seems to have in mind implies far more in the way of agreement among key governments about the conditions that legitimate resort to public aid, and far more understanding of and agreement on questions related to the process of structural change within states and between states than today exists. It seems to me that the better surveillance we both want will only come about if there is an almost continuous interaction between a strong staff identifying problems and a high-powered policy body capable of profound and wide-ranging discussion of the underlying problems.

When he turns to the problem of the NICs, Professor Pelkmans sketches out a package designed to bring these countries into the GATT as full participants. I, too, think the time is ripe for a package deal, and many of the elements in my package are very similar to those in his: agreement on the part of the advanced industrialized countries to phase out the Multi-Fibre Agreement (MFA); acceptance by both groups of countries of a safeguard arrangement (an improved article 19), which permits selectivity in application, but at the same time ties resort to safeguards (i.e. protection) to steps to improve competitiveness and to a timetable providing for the progressive dismantling of the special protection, and, of course, adequate international surveillance of the process; agreement on criteria for 'graduation' and on timetables for the progressive acceptance by the NICs of the obligations of the GATT and the Codes. But again, as in his short discussion of subsidies, I think the result desired by Professor Pelkmans will only be achieved if there are rather more changes in the way the GATT functions and in the way the key member governments regard its role than perhaps he realizes. For example, although in a 'new GATT round' it might be possible to negotiate some kind of 'framework' package providing for a new approach to safeguards, the winding down of the MFA, criteria for 'graduation', and the basic timetables that would apply on both sides, I suspect this would have to be followed up by a series of specific 'packages' based on country-by-country reviews, taking into account such things as the debt problems of the country concerned and any special constraint (e.g. voluntary export restraints) to which its trade was subject. If I were a member of an NIC government, I should wish to see a strong 'international' element 'hold the ring' in this negotiating process. Furthermore, I suspect that most of these negotiations will result not in agreements that can be implemented more or less automatically, but in various kinds of 'best endeavour' formulae, with provisions for consultation and negotiation in the event of difficulties. In short, I see the 'graduation' process as involving protracted negotiations on a range of interconnected issues which, like progress on the subsidies front, will call for a rather different view of the role of the GATT Secretariat and a rather different kind of GATT representative than we have known in the past.

Finally, we come to Professor Pelkmans's third 'volet': the extension of GATT coverage to agriculture and to services. In the body of his paper, he has indicated why he thinks little is likely to happen so far as agriculture is concerned. In this section, he has little positive to suggest (other than the more stringent control of export subsidies on agricultural products, which he included in his discussion of subsidies). Although he has lumped agriculture and services together in his third volet, they seem to me to be problems of rather different order. Agriculture has always been regarded as covered, at least in principle, by the GATT; had it not been, there would have been no need for a US waiver. The difficulty with agriculture has been the unwillingness of key governments *either* to accept for most agricultural products the rules they have accepted, more or less, for manufactures, *or* to make any significant effort to work out modified rules that would take account of some of the particular problems in this field. In short, agriculture, like other difficult problems – textiles, trade with less developed countries, some aspects of article 24 trade – has been 'handled' by removing it from the basic rule-system of the GATT. At least part of the reason for resort

to this system-weakening practice of simply 'excepting' difficult problems has been the fact that the GATT process has been too 'legalistic';
unless the matter could be regulated by precisely drafted, enforceable,
substantive rules, the GATT has not been well equipped – either in
terms of staff or in terms of the attitudes and habits of its member
governments – to see whether there were other ways of making progress.

So far as services are concerned, we are, at least in some respects, in
a new area, which poses new conceptual problems that have still to be
further explored and resolved. Again, Professor Pelkmans draws on
Community experience to make some suggestions worth pursuing. But
I note that he has doubts – which I share – whether enough in the way
of the guiding principles that should govern trade in services can be
agreed upon to make much of this area 'governable' by a quasi-legal
'codes' approach. Again, we come back to the need for a different kind
of GATT: one in which the discipline of the substantive rules in the
General Agreement and the Codes is supplemented by much more in
the way of consultation, policy discussion, negotiation on complaints,
and constant surveillance of trade policies broadly defined.

The rather Delphic comment at the very end of his paper hints at
another change that will be needed, if the GATT is to develop into the
kind of international trade organization that now seems to me to be
desirable. As it extends its range and as more countries become more
involved in its work, there will have to be more resort to restricted-
member groups, and for some purposes it seems likely that countries
will have to be grouped in constituencies in much the same way as they
are today in the Executive Board of the International Monetary Fund.
Sometimes the highly developed countries will need to go further in
accepting rules to 'manage their interdependence' than most states
need to do. Frequently policy-oriented issues will not lend themselves
to fruitful discussion in large groups. More use of limited-member
groupings and of group representation for some purposes are, however, only likely to be acceptable if adequate arrangements are made
for ensuring that countries not participating in any particular activity
are kept informed of what is happening and given adequate opportunities to be heard, if they are affected in any way, and if it is clear that the
consequence will be an increased willingness to discuss and resolve difficulties within the framework of the GATT, rather than by negotiations among a limited number of countries outside the GATT.

A GATT capable of playing the broader, policy-oriented role sketched
out above would be a very different organization from the GATT we
have known in the past. I suspect that Professor Pelkmans would agree
with me that it is the kind of GATT we need, despite the fact that his
specific suggestions for reform appear to be much more modest. I agree

with him that the willingness of the protagonists in the 'bickering bigemony' to accept more international discipline is an essential condition of adequate reform. But their agreement would no longer – by itself – be a sufficient condition. Not only Japan, but a number of major-NICs must, at a minimum, also be ready to accept the consequences of an improved system. Unfortunately, I also share Professor Pelkmans's pessimism; for I see few signs that the necessary conditions exist for the kinds of reform either of us has in mind.

NOTE

1 For a more extended presentation of my views on needed reforms, see Miriam Camps and David Diebold Jr, *The New Multilateralism: Can the World Trading System be Saved?* (Council on Foreign Relations, New York, 1983).

Comment 2

WOLFGANG HAGER

Pelkmans emphasizes constants in his rich and stimulating analysis. In addition, his primary interest is in 'law and order', as potentially represented by GATT. This is a fruitful approach, which teaches us much about the evolution of the current system. The analysis might be usefully complemented, however, by an assessment of new structural elements in the contemporary world economy which are liable to alter the way the EC and the US interact with each other and with GATT.

In one perspective, Western Europe and the US share a common characteristic of being high-cost producers. These costs, which, broadly, are composed of high wages, including social security charges, and regulations, which limit the 'efficient' exploitation of human and natural resources, are the results of socio-political bargains struck during the initial post-war decades, when Europe and the US had a virtual monopoly over the production of most tradables. In the one case where that monopoly was broken, textiles, they allied themselves against the rest of the world in the Multi-Fibre Agreement (MFA). As Pelkmans makes clear, the MFA not only violated GATT, but, adding insult to injury, uses its bureaucratic resources to manage the arrangement.

With the underlying economic circumstances of textiles generalized by the growing ability of the newly industrialized countries (NICs) to produce most tradables (including such services as banking or air and maritime transport), one might have expected similar concerted attacks on GATT principles. Instead there have been parallel rather than concerted responses to these and other adjustment problems, which use GATT no less cynically: by either ignoring it or exploiting it for narrow mercantilist purposes.

GATT is ignored in the VER (voluntary export restraints) and
OMAs (orderly marketing agreements) concluded by both the EC and
the US, and are aimed as much at raising prices as defending market
shares. The aim is to generate profits for such sectors as steel and the
motor industry, whose previous erosion under conditions of free international competition threatened to deprive firms of the means to
modernize. Textiles, now an above-average capital-intensive industry, are an early example of protectionist rents being used for this
purpose. GATT and classical economics would have allowed the alternative of cost-cutting (which in practice requires capital) or elimination. This is no longer accepted.

Here we have a second major innovation in the world political
economy: the United States is joining the ranks of the rest of the world
trading community in adopting implicit sectoral production targets.
These are not laid down in any national plan, nor do they form part of
a coherent industrial policy, but they are revealed by diffuse political
processes when the targets are threatened. They are no less real for
that.

Just as one era in world trade drew to a close when the US refused to
be the world's residual balance-of-payments adjuster (Nixon shocks),
so the remnants of GATT orthodoxy are threatened by Comecon-type
developments in West–West trade. For when *all* nations have implicit
production targets in key sectors, the market as arbiter of market
shares can no longer work and is replaced by deals among governments. Pelkmans mentions the negotiated coexistence in agriculture
between the EC and US, which has proved remarkably stable.

In the industrial area, there is bound to be more flexibility and variety
in the means with which implicit production targets are defended.
Local content requirements, familiar from the arms trade, are becoming no less important in civilian areas dominated by procurement
and/or public licensing. Respect for national (high-)price levels is being
asked for, and granted, by Eastern Europe and Japan for many products, often under the seemingly orthodox guise of anti-dumping suits
(or threats thereof). Another favourite route is industrial subsidies
– financial protectionism. The Chrysler rescue marks a historic
turning-point as far as the US is concerned in this regard.

Pelkmans, to my mind, underestimates this issue by reducing his
treatment – taking his cue from the American debate – to (Japanese)
industrial targeting, that is, the offensive mode. His suggestion that
'crucial instruments' for this purpose should be curtailed conflicts with
his own assessment earlier in the same paragraph, which implied
highly country-specific, but diffuse mechanisms of industry-promotion
and -defence. Any GATT effort would 'catch' highly visible, arms-
length government–industry links, of the British type, leaving 'Ger-

many Inc.' or 'France Inc.' undisturbed. American subsidies via generously costed defence contracts would also escape scrutiny.

The problems of North–South adjustment and industrial policy merge in the third major development of recent years: technological mercantilism. This has two sources. One is the wish by Japan, the US and Europe to re-establish their once-universal industrial monopoly by specializing in high-tech areas where they would be safe from new producers. Since the total market for such products is rather small, relative to the productive potential (now overwhelmingly employed in producing 'everyone's goods') of the advanced countries, these attempts at specialization must lead to trade conflicts with 'managed', negotiated settlements. Mutual, quasi-bartered access of the US and Japanese telecommunications markets is one emerging example; complex local content/industrial co-operation deals among European and American firms is another.

The other source of technological mercantilism is that the promise of growth, in each of the advanced countries, is increasingly seen as linked to the speed with which the potential offered by the third industrial revolution – the chip and the gene – is seized. The promise of growth – via maximizing international market shares in new products and services, with their positive feedbacks in terms of cost-reducing economies of scale and rapid capital rejuvenation – is matched by an existential fear, particularly present in Europe, of becoming a second-rate technoeconomic power. All this militates against a GATT-conform game that allows the market to allocate who produces what in the world economy.

Interestingly enough, the European Community faces internally some of the same dilemmas of reconciling fair-trade rules with the member states' mercantilism as does the GATT system. Its ability to deal with this problem puts it into conflict with GATT. Pelkmans notes one aspect of this, that is, competition over 'judicial review' of trade-distorting practices.

Behind this lies a deeper problem. If the Community is to realize its ambition to create a true internal market, by enforcing present rules against subsidies, by depriving technical standards of their role as non-tariff barriers, and by opening national procurement markets, it must provide some substitute for the lost comforts of national home markets. This means, in part, external protection (not necessary in the 1960s because no effective outside competition existed) and, in part, Community substitutes for the diverse government–industry links that constitute the hard core of a 'home market'. In short, there must emerge a sort of economic Euro-nationalism, which is much more difficult to contain in a complementary, GATT-ruled, Atlantic context than earlier tariff-based manifestations of Community specificity.

The only GATT reform that would fully respond to the changed context of the world economy is one that would allow sectoral bargaining to a much larger degree than at present (as, for example, in the shipbuilding committee of the OECD), and jettisoning of an ideological baggage that tries to give legal expression to neo-classical assumptions about economic welfare grafted onto an increasingly non-classical world. That is not a likely prospect. GATT will therefore go the way of another idealistic and stubbornly unrealistic Geneva institution, the League of Nations, its irrelevance disguised by glowing re-affirmations of its principles in international conferences.

Comment 3

JOHN PINDER

Much of the Euro-American bickering that Pelkmans reviews is doubtless short-sighted, narrow-minded low politics. But it also reflects a fundamental flaw in the contemporary political economy: the geographical disjuncture between its economic and its political aspects. It is certainly not news, perhaps it is even banal, to affirm that specialization and scale have extended economic interdependence wider and wider across the world of the twentieth century, while politics remains cast in the nineteenth-century mould of the independent nation-state. But such is the hold of the nation-state on the intellect as well as on politics that this uncomfortable fact is only too often swept under the carpet. It may be useful here to step back from the imbroglios of current trade policy and consider the implications for the reform of GATT of this divorce between economic reason and *raison d'état*.

Pelkmans judges that 'countries rightly refuse to submit their socio-economic construct and traditions as such to intergovernmental scrutiny'. Certainly, any far-reaching policy integration can be undertaken only among countries with similar socio-economic systems. But if countries with similar systems refuse to countenance policy integration, they are likely to make the modern economy unmanageable. For market integration will have placed its management beyond the reach of the national governments, which are refusing to accept a wider international management.

The open trading that is the purpose of GATT can be prejudiced by inadequate integration of macroeconomic policies. Pelkmans mentions the protectionist pressures provoked by overvaluation of the dollar. One could add undervaluation of the yen and high American interest rates. Thus the chapters on money, exchange rates and policy coordination have a powerful significance for trade policy and GATT. The relevance to my argument lies in any movement towards monetary integration in the EC and coordination of macroeconomic policies among the principal industrialized economies.

More directly, open trading can be undermined by incompatible industrial policies. Pelkmans observes that the dismantling of adjustment assistance may have aggravated the 'US propensity to resort to border protection'; and he suggests that 'restructuring plans' should be made a condition of protection against the NICs. One may equally suppose that more effective adjustment assistance would reduce the EC's propensity for border protection and that the Europeans and Americans might do well to give greater weight to restructuring plans when negotiating with each other about, for example, steel.

Apart from protection, subsidies have been the principal instrument of industrial policy; Pelkmans recommends that the examples of EC Commission surveillance and judicial review 'be used more extensively' in developing GATT's implementation of its subsidy code. He also draws attention to the EC's treaty provisions for dealing with domestic regulations that restrict trade. Despite dissatisfaction at the EC's failure to free its internal market of such barriers, Pelkmans is surely right to use it as an example for a wider trading system of which the EC, the US and, to a lesser extent, Japan are the principal foci. For market interdependence in this wider system is reaching the stage at which such interdependence established the need for policy integration within Western Europe; and the political authorities that govern these principal foci may have to choose, during the coming period, between policy integration and market disintegration.

Pelkmans proposes that governments attempt to get through this dilemma by a variety of agreements within GATT, 'with a small core of (mostly) OECD countries moving farthest'. The question raised by my comment is how far they will have to move in order to achieve an adequate collective management of their interdependent economies. The answer I would suggest is that they will have to go much farther than most of the current thinking about reform of the international trading system contemplates: that the sort of industrial policy integration and monetary policy co-operation that has been pioneered in the Community will be a more suitable model than any other for the relationship between the EC, the US and some other industrialized countries in the future. The political implications of this may be radical. But if we do not want an intensifying failure and eventual breakdown of our economic system, these political implications will sooner or later have to be faced.

Comment 4

FRANK WOLTER*

I

My comments on Professor Pelkmans's paper will concentrate on three points. First, I shall address the alleged predominance of the United States and the European Community in the GATT. Second, I shall take issue with Pelkmans's proposition that the United States and the European Community jointly hardly need the GATT. Third, I shall discuss some aspects of Pelkmans's considerations referring to the GATT-reform debate.

II

Pelkmans bases his notion of a 'bigemony' of the United States and the European Community over activities in the GATT, first on the relative importance of these regions in world trade, and second, on the perception that 'when they strongly disagree, nothing happens'. On both accounts, Pelkmans's position appears to me to be too simplistic.

It is no secret that the world market shares of the 122 countries currently applying GATT differ widely.[1] Clearly, the European Community is the world's largest exporter. But the United States, though ranking second (in fact, first if the EC member states are counted individually), is far less outstanding in this respect. For example, compare the following 1983 world market shares: 10.8 per cent for the

* This comment strictly reflects my personal views. It should in no way be taken to implicate the GATT Secretariat.

United States; 8.1 per cent for Japan; 4.0 per cent for Korea, Hong Kong and Taiwan as a group; 3.9 per cent for ASEAN; 4.0 per cent for Canada. The United States' role as an exporter becomes even less conspicuous when looked at in dynamic terms. For example, in 1963 the United States still captured 14.9 per cent of the world market; Japan 3.6 per cent; the three Asian newly industrialized countries 0.8 per cent; ASEAN 2.7 per cent. In other words, the world market shares of the European Community and any of the non-US regions mentioned add up to magnitudes that are as impressive as the aggregate EC–US figures given in the paper.

Similarly, the proposition that strong disagreement between the European Community and the United States puts GATT into inaction is nothing very specific. As Pelkmans correctly points out, GATT essentially works on the basis of consensus. Thus, 'nothing happens' as well when other contracting parties strongly disagree on a specific issue of their particular concern: say, on a proposed dispute settlement. Likewise, a new round of trade negotiations could hardly be launched if, for example, Japan or a group of the larger developing countries strongly disagreed. To this must be added the fact that the interests of the contracting parties cut across simplistic lines such as EC–US or North–South. GATT has many more shades than the paper suggests. However, I am in full agreement with Pelkmans to the extent that the paper implies that responsibility for the trading system as a whole goes with size.

III

The idea that the European Community and the United States jointly hardly need GATT reflects a misperception of the nature and the functions of a multilateral trading system. First, this notion creates the impression that GATT is something distinctly apart from the European Community and the United States, so to speak an entirely separate third party. No: GATT is them, and others. Therefore they have the capacity to work *from within* to improve the functioning of the system.

Second, it must be clarified why they do, or do not, need the system. I should like to suggest, first and foremost, for the prosperity of their own economies. I think Jacques Pelkmans would agree. Now, what does the system offer, that a joint European Community– United States exercise alone could not achieve?

One possibility would be an EC–US agreement to apply all GATT rules (or a similar set of rules) strictly on an *unconditional* most-favoured-nation (MFN) basis. This might not be too bad. However, the United States and the European Community, as well as other countries could only gain if they did it in the multilateral framework. In fact, it would strengthen the system (Japan and other countries would probably join them immediately).

Alternatively, they would conclude, either individually or jointly, a series of bilateral or trilateral *conditional* MFN treaties. In this case, they, and the world economy at large, would be back in a 1930s-type situation with all its economic inefficiencies (distorted price system, excessive uncertainty surrounding trade-related investment, etc.) and rising political tensions.

Third, a transatlantic trade arrangement is clearly inferior to the present system in its role as backbone for national governments to resist the pressures of special-interest groups. In a multilateral trading system with non-discrimination as the guiding principle, restrictive trade measures must be applied to all trading partners across the board. In such a setting, retaliation is more likely, the potential damage from retaliation is much greater and therefore its threat much more forceful than in a bilateral setting.

It is, of course, true that even the present system, with all its checks and balances, has not prevented the world economy from relapsing into protectionism. This brings me to my third comment: the GATT-reform issue.

IV

There can be little quarrel about the notion that the present state of the international trading system justifies serious concern.[2] Pelkmans infers from this diagnosis that GATT needs to be reformed. In analysing the scope for reform, Pelkmans identifies constraints in the form of constants in trade policy-making on both sides of the Atlantic that are not fully mutually compatible. But the author is not agnostic: there remains room for improvement in a variety of fields.

I agree with a number of propositions Pelkmans makes in this context. For example, efforts to establish extensive legal procedures in trade matters at the international level may be too ambitious. I can also see constructive elements in the discussion of the trade-in-services issue. On the other hand, however, I have strong reservations about the proposal to interpret article 19 of GATT in a way that allows for selective (that is, discriminatory) protection. The fact that, as Pelkmans observes, this would only legalize the current practice of many trading nations (voluntary export restraint agreements, orderly marketing arrangements) can be hardly accepted as an argument. There is no sense in legalizing drunken driving just because many people do it. Similarly, there is no hope of restoring the health of the trading system by legalizing the very cause of its present weakness: the trend towards discrimination.

This is not the place to engage in an essay on the reasons for the pro-liferation of discrimination. Loopholes in GATT, producer biases in trade policy decision-making and the rule of political precedent, nationally and internationally, have all played their role. Nor is this the place to develop how non-discrimination can be restored as the guiding principle of trade policy in the major trading nations. Suffice it to state here that the rules should be extended into new areas (for example, ser-vices). The most important current task, however, the strengthening of the system, can be achieved without reform of the system. A new bind-ing commitment of the major trading nations to the backbone of the multilateral trading system, non-discrimination, would go a long way towards resolving most of the system's present defects.[3] On the basis of such a restoration, and perhaps on this basis only, a fruitful evolution of the international trading system is conceivable, including a possible extension of the system beyond its present limits.

V

There are a number of smaller points where I find myself in disagree-ment with Pelkmans. These include the following.

1) Tariff rates are not yet down, as Pelkmans states, to uninter-estingly low levels. For quite a number of commodities, among them many products of particular export interest for developing countries, nominal tariff rates, not to speak of effective tariff rates, have remained significant.[4]

2) The United States did indeed pioneer voluntary export restraint agreements (VERs) but in 1935, not in 1957.[5] Also, VERs are not outside GATT; they are illegal (article 13).

3) It is not only 'exceptionally hard to prove the "inequity" of the market share' in a particular agricultural market. It is impos-sible.

Finally, I should like to confess my envy for economists who are able to calculate the degree of the US-dollar overvaluation.

NOTES

1   There are 90 contracting parties; one country provisionally acceded; 31 countries are applying the GATT de facto.

2   To agree that the multilateral trading system is in trouble, and that it must be
    strengthened, should not deflect attention from the fact that the system has remained
    in better shape than here and there perceived. So far, the multilateral trading
    system has proved resilient enough to prevent the disastrous policy reaction to
    global economic difficulties such as that experienced during the 1930s. That this
    would be the case is not self-evident in view of the series of heavy shocks the bulk of
    the world economy's individual countries has had to absorb, one way or another,
    over the last ten years or so. Second, even today the major part of international
    trade (as covered by the GATT) is carried out in conformity with the rules laid
    down in the General Agreement. As this is the normal state of affairs, this fact gets
    much less publicity, quite naturally, than violations of the international trading
    rules. Third, recent developments in international trade policy include bright spots
    such as some advance implementation of the Tokyo Round tariff cuts, some
    movements towards bringing services into the GATT and agriculture more closely
    under the disciplines of normal trading rules, or successful dispute settlements (in
    fact, since 1952 all but one of about 50 findings by GATT panels have been
    accepted, albeit in a few cases with qualifications on the part of the contracting
    parties).
3   For a comprehensive treatment see Jan Tumlir, 'GATT rules and the Community
    law', Paper prepared for Arbeitskreis Europäische Integration e.V., Tagung
    'Europäische Gemeinschaft und GATT', Bielefeld, 6–8 September 1984.
4   For example, post-Tokyo Round average tariff levels for clothing are 12.5 per cent
    (simple average) or 22.5 per cent (average weighted by MFN imports) in the United
    States, 12.5 or 13.5 per cent in the EC, and 30.5 or 37 per cent in Austria.
5   Cotton cloth vis-à-vis Japan; more formal agreements between the United States
    and Japan, including hosiery, velveteen and corduroy came into effect in 1937. See
    GATT (1984), Textiles and Clothing in the World Economy p. 63.

The Extraterritoriality Issue in the Transatlantic Context: A Question of Law or Diplomacy?*

PAUL DEMARET

INTRODUCTION

In this paper, the words 'legislation' or 'law' are to be construed in their widest sense. They are intended to include legislation in its technical context, executive decrees, court judgements, and decisions of administrative authorities.

This initial definition is of importance, as the question of extraterritoriality[1] concerns a state's general power to make and create 'laws'. The problem of extraterritoriality generally arises whenever a state organ – whether legislative, governmental, judicial or administrative – enjoins an individual to carry out (or refrain from) a certain course of action, such conduct to be enacted either entirely or partially within the territory of another state. It is rare, especially where the measure in question is only of direct relevance to a dispute between individuals, for its extraterritorial character to provoke any adverse reaction on the part of the foreign power on whose territory the conduct is to be wholly or partially carried out. It is a different matter, however, when the measure is concerned with questions of 'public law' (in its continental legal sense).[2] In these instances, a state often feels that it is more directly involved.[3]

Historically, the problem of extraterritoriality first arose in the context of criminal law.[4] It was often asked whether a state could punish ordinary crimes or those acts that were aimed against its security or credit, where one or all of the constituent elements of the act in ques-

* This paper was originally presented in French. The author wishes to express his gratitude to Andrew Renshaw, LL.B, student at the College of Europe, who prepared the translation.

tion occurred on another state's territory, and yet not contravene public international law. This type of situation (notably in those cases where one state, intervening on behalf of the accused, contested the other state's right to punish the crime) could lead to disagreements between the two states. But such disputes were not necessarily taken up by governments and resolved at that level, especially where the accused was a national of the state applying its law or where the act in question was viewed with equal reprobation by the state on whose territory it had been committed (whether only partially or entirely).

The increasingly frequent extraterritorial application of economic legislation, breach of which is punishable in the criminal, civil or administrative courts, has given rise to disagreements between states on an almost regular basis, each state invoking its own sovereignty to justify its actions or to protest against those of others. Two major themes characterize recent years. On the one hand, the problem of extraterritorial jurisdiction in the field of economic legislation has not just been limited to antitrust law. On the other, although the United States, the world's leading economic power, has been the butt of most criticism, the European Community has also received its share of adverse comment.

Obviously, this proliferation of extraterritorial problems in the field of economic legislation is merely a reflection of the increasingly international flavour of economic life. It is interesting to note in this regard that, whether culprit or victim, one of the figures constantly on the scene is the multinational company. By granting extraterritorial effect to a national law, public authorities are often merely attempting to get to grips with a multinational company (in essence highly mobile) and make it comply with the state's legislation or even, in some instances, to use it for its own foreign policy objectives.

Three areas will be dealt with in this paper. First of all, we shall examine the facts, that is to say those pieces of legislation – both of the US and of the European Community – which can be qualified as extraterritorial, as well as the controversies to which they have given rise. Secondly, we shall analyse the problem of the extraterritoriality of laws from the standpoint of public international law. Finally, we shall ask whether the way to resolve or prevent conflicts between states in the area of extraterritoriality is to be found in the legal or the diplomatic sphere.

LAWS WITH EXTRATERRITORIAL EFFECT

This is not the place to describe the various twists that have taken place in the disputes between both sides of the Atlantic case law over extraterritorial jurisdiction. Our task is rather to identify the major points of friction and to single out their cause. This will help us in our search for answers.

There are three areas of disagreement that have arisen between the United States and those states that today make up the EC. The first comprises those laws whose extraterritorial application is inspired by the desire of a state, or group of states, to ensure the coherence and efficiency of its (their) internal policy and by the reactions or threat of adverse legislative reactions of other states. In a second category are to be found those legislative measures which are tailor made for a certain situation, and whose extraterritorial operation is motivated by foreign policy considerations. The problems surrounding the American states' use of the unitary tax system are dealt with in a final section. Although it contains some analogies with the question of extraterritorial jurisdiction, this area is in fact distinct in many ways. Here, the heart of the controversy is to be found in the extension of US tax federalism in the realm of US international relations.

The Extraterritorial Dimension given to Certain Internal Policies

US law   The legislation by which the US has put its competition policy into practice has, since the Second World War, often been extended extraterritorially.[5] Amongst others, the cases that ought to be mentioned are the *Alcoa*,[6] *ICI*,[7] *Swiss Watchmakers*[8] and, more recently, the *Uranium Cartel*[9] and *Laker* cases.[10] Other legislation has also been applied extraterritorially: for example, the federal laws pertaining to securities, whose aim is to protect investors and to sanction fraudulent dealings (especially 'insider trading');[11] reference should also be made to legislation in the areas of taxation,[12] narcotics,[13] boycott and corrupt practices.[14]

Antitrust policy is thus not the only legislative policy to which the American authorities have given an extraterritorial dimension with the aim of achieving greater coherence and efficiency. If we give it a somewhat prominent position in this paper, it is because as the legislation has gradually been put into practice over a period of time, it has supplied us with a catalogue of the different stages where there is a likelihood that the problem of extraterritorial jurisdiction may arise. Three stages can be discerned: the decision by the legislature or the courts to apply the statute in question to a situation involving an international aspect; the order given by a state authority to a party to carry out an act outside its territory; an order given by a state authority, either to a party or to a witness, to produce documents situated abroad.

1) In 1945, in the *Alcoa* case, Judge Learned Hand declared that the Sherman Act governed the conduct of foreign companies, situated outside the US, in so far as their behaviour produced an 'effect' within the

US, such effect being in fact intended by the foreign company in question. This 'effects doctrine' caused a great deal of criticism outside the US,[15] especially, it should be added, prior to the development of the EC's competition policy. This can be relatively easily explained. A wide interpretation of the term 'effect' would bring many agreements or practices, which had either few or no links with the US market, into the scope of US law, even where such agreements or practices were perfectly licit outside the US. Furthermore, the consequences of violating US antitrust law are very serious. A company found guilty of such infringement is liable to criminal sanction or the payment of treble damages. The effects doctrine has in fact not often been pushed to its furthest limits.

A recent jurisprudential trend, following in the wake of the *Timberlane* case,[16] suggests a rather more sensitive approach by US courts to the international implications of their decisions. However, the judgements given in 1980 by the Court of Appeals for the 7th Circuit in the *Uranium* affair[17] and in 1984 by the Court of Appeals for the District of Columbia in the *Laker* case are not in keeping with this line of cases.[18]

2) The decisions by which US courts sometimes order foreign dependants to carry out certain courses of action within their state of origin, with the aim of re-establishing competition in the US import trade, have resulted in rather more concrete reactions on the part of foreign states, who consider that their sovereignty has been assailed. The *ICI*[19] and *Swiss Watchmakers*[20] cases are well known in this respect. In the former, an English court forbade the execution of Judge Ryan's order by ICI,[21] whereas in the latter the Swiss government had to use its influence with the US to obtain a modification of the court's decision. For some, those orders that are to be executed abroad are an infringement of public international law, even where they are coupled with 'saving clauses'. This point will be returned to later.

3) Today, in the area of antitrust law, the major bone of contention between the US and the European states lies in those cases where an American or foreign firm is ordered to produce documents situated outside the territory of the US. Such orders, which can be backed up with sanctions, are given either by the Justice Department, the Federal Trade Commission (FTC), a grand jury or by a federal judge in the form of a pre-trial discovery order.[22] These orders can be addressed to anyone who falls within the *jurisdictio in personam* of the appropriate judicial or administrative authority.[23] Almost any foreign firm which does business with the US either directly or through its subsidiary will satisfy this (last) condition.[24]

Such orders to produce documents have often resulted in hostile reactions on the part of those states within whose territory the documents are to be found. They are the major cause of the adoption of 'blocking statutes' by a number of European states, as well as Canada and Australia, prohibiting, in particular, the passing of economic information to foreign authorities.[25]

Several reasons can be called on to explain this negative reaction on the part of the Europeans. The most important resides in the fact that a different philosophy underlies the way in which a case proceeds and the method in which evidence is adduced. The 'discovery' allowed by US law appears positively exorbitant in the eyes of many Europeans, especially when applied outside the US and within the territory of those states where other laws of procedure are in force. The very idea of 'discovery' in such a form runs counter to the tradition of secrecy in business and banking matters: a tradition well established by law, and an accepted feature of normal 'honest' business life in many countries. Moreover, that a court order of such breadth, coupled with a provision of such coercive force, should be directed at a foreign firm that has not even been summoned before the court as defendant to a civil action or as accused in a criminal one, and may well in fact never be, is seen as shocking. This attitude on the part of the Europeans is well illustrated by the judgment of the House of Lords in *Rio Tinto–Westinghouse*, where the Law Lords refused to give effect to rogatory letters sent to them by an American court.[26]

Orders to produce documents situated abroad are not confined to antitrust law. They are also regularly made in cases invoking the application of fiscal legislation and legislation pertaining to securities. The recipients of such orders are often either the foreign branches of American banks or foreign banks themselves.

European law – Competition law. Generally speaking, the application of European *competition* law has not resulted in the same reaction on the part of the third states as those experienced by the United States in applying its competition law.[27]

1) A concrete analysis of the compass of articles 85 and 86 shows that the European Community authorities have not overstepped the bounds given to US competition law by Judge Hand in the *Alcoa* decision, but have rather remained within those limits. No real difficulties arise when article 85 is applied to firms established outside the EC, but who conclude agreements that are to be executed within the EC under the form of a price increase or division of the market. The same goes for article 86 when it is extended to those foreign companies that hold a dominant position on the territory of the Community and abuse that position either by taking control of a company established within the EC or by refusing to sell to a client in the Community.

A difficult case came to light, however, in the *ICI* affair.[28] ICI, a company established in the United Kingdom (at that time outside the EC), increased the sale price of certain dyestuffs in accordance with a concerted practice agreed upon by various producers in the European Community. ICI did not sell directly in the EC, but sold the products to its subsidiaries established in the EC and who then resold the dyestuffs at a price incorporating the rise decided upon by ICI. As a matter of contract law, the sale therefore took place in the United Kingdom. Advocate General Mayras considered that article 85 applied to ICI by virtue of the effects doctrine as set forth in section 18 of the Restatement (Second) of Foreign Relations Law of the US. However, the Court of Justice did not refer to the effects doctrine to justify the application of article 85. Instead it held that ICI had executed the litigious practice within the EEC by making use of its power to control its subsidiaries. The Court ascribed the conduct of the subsidiaries based within the EC to the parent company by invoking the concept of the single economic entity. This concept has been used in other cases.

2) As yet the Commission of the European Community has never ordered firms established in third countries to carry out actions whose performance would take place entirely outside the territory of the EC. It has always limited itself to directing such companies to modify their conduct or practice within the EC, for example, by limiting their participation in certain European firms[29] or by ceasing to refuse to sell to a client based in the EC.[30]

3) The consideration and investigation of cases by the Commission has not, with the exception of one case, led to open conflict with third states. In order to deal tactfully with the susceptibility of these states, the Commission tries to give a fairly informal tone to its requests for information (although these are in fact based on article 11 of Regulation 17), which it sends to foreign companies or else addresses to their subsidiaries, branches or representatives based in the EC.[31]

The only instance of a real conflict breaking out between the Community authorities and the authorities of a third state is the *Hoffmann–Laroche (Vitamins)* case.[32] In this affair, Mr Adams, an ex-employee of the above-mentioned Swiss company, was given a prison sentence in Switzerland for having passed information to the Commission (who had invited him to go to Brussels), the information being in fact protected by Swiss legislation relating to business secrecy. In order to justify the application of Swiss criminal law, the Federal Tribunal stressed the fact that Mr Adams had organized his trip to Brussels from Switzerland.[33] It should be noted that, in addition to inciting Mr Adams to infringe Swiss law by countenancing this investigatory step, which it could not itself accomplish in Switzerland, the Commission also neglected to use the procedure envisaged for this type of case by the EC/Switzerland Free Trade Agreement.[34]

The Vredeling Draft Directive. In reality, it is the *proposition* for the so-called '*Vredeling*' Directive (rather than the application of articles 85 and 86), which forms the basis for the reproach directed at the Commission, that it wants improperly to extend the application of Community law beyond the frontiers of the EC. This proposition, which was modified in 1983, after discussions with the European Parliament, is designed to ensure that workers employed in the subsidiaries and branches of multinational firms are adequately supplied with information.[35] Even if the proposition is adopted by the Council of Ministers, which does not seem altogether certain, given the opposition to it from some member states, it then has to be incorporated by the member states into their respective national legal systems. The 'Vredeling' proposition (even as adapted) remains a text whose precise limits are difficult to determine in several respects. We shall limit ourselves here to those aspects which can be qualified as extraterritorial. They appear when the 'parent company' is established outside the Community.

The parent company must supply information to its subsidiaries based in the EC who, in their turn, are required to pass on the information to the workers they employ. The latter then have a period of 30 days in which to put forward an opinion. First of all, the parent company must supply information, on an annual basis, about the past and future activities of the whole of the group of companies which it controls, as well as a report on the production sector and geographic zone of the subsidiary in question. Thereafter the parent company must inform its subsidiaries and, through them, consult its workers before taking:

> a decision concerning the whole or a major part of the parent undertaking or of a subsidiary in the Community which is liable to have serious consequences for the interests of the employees of its subsidiaries in the Community.

The parent company must wait for the period during which the workforce can deliver its opinion to expire, before executing its decision. The penalties for non-respect of these obligations are to be fixed by each member state. However, the draft directive provides that the subsidiary companies based in the EC will be held responsible for their parent company's duties, where the latter's decision-making centre is situated outside the Community, unless the firm's management has named an agent who is accountable and based within the EC.

The draft as it stands in its 1983 version authorizes non-disclosure of information

> which could substantially damage the undertaking's interests or lead to the failure of its plans.

For example, this provision can be involved whenever foreign legislation prohibits the communication of economic information. As such it plays the role of 'a saving clause'. In theory, this ought to shield the 1983 draft from the sometimes strong criticisms which were directed at the initial draft by certain American business groups.[36]

There is one fundamental idea underlying the draft: that is, that parent and subsidiaries form one economic entity. The parent company acts as the entity's head, its arms being the subsidiaries. If this line of thought is followed, it is perfectly legitimate to ascribe the behaviour of the parent company to its subsidiaries without being unduly worried by the internal relations between parent and subsidiaries. As we have already seen, the Court of Justice drew on this same idea in the *ICI* case,[37] only in that instance it was to attribute the conduct of subsidiaries to their parent based in the EC and thereby justify the application of article 85 to the parent company.

Being able to ascribe the conduct of a parent company to those of its subsidiaries based in the EC will mean that there is no need for sanctions to be imposed against a parent company situated outside the EC that does not respect its obligations. But the question still remains whether the Commission ought not to have gone on to the logical conclusion of its reasoning. If the multinational group really does constitute an economic entity, why impose obligations on the parent company, instead of simply imposing them directly on those subsidiaries established within the EC?

Blocking statutes. Over the last few years, a number of states have adopted legislation with the specific aim of combating decisions emanating from American administrative or judicial authorities that order their nationals or their residents to pass on information of an economic nature or insist on the discovering of documents situated abroad.[38] Some states have not felt the need to adopt such legislation on an *ad hoc* basis, as they already have legislation which is wide enough to forbid both the passing on of information and the 'discovery' of documents (for example, article 273 of the Swiss penal code relative to business secrecy). It is not the purpose of this paper to analyse the detail and varying scope of this type of legislation, which ranges from automatic application to selective use under the control of an administrative authority.[39] However, it should be noted that the *Protection of*

Trading Interests Act adopted by the United Kingdom in 1980[40] is not
merely designed to tackle the effects of American 'discovery' procedure. The Act also gives (*inter alia*) the British government the power
to prevent a British firm from complying with foreign economic legislation whose extraterritorial application would harm the commercial
interests of the United Kingdom.[41] Furthermore, under certain conditions, the Act allows British companies that have paid judgements for
treble damages in the USA, to recover, in British courts, two-thirds of
the successful plaintiff's damages, that is, the latter in effect is only able
to keep compensatory damages ('clawback provision').

The US did protest when some of the above-mentioned statutes were
adopted, for there can be no doubt that they do limit the extraterritorial
efficacy of American legislation. They may have an extraterritorial
scope themselves in so far as they empower national authorities to en-
join their nationals from carrying certain acts abroad. In the United
States, this type of legislation has sometimes been considered as
damaging to American sovereignty. But even in the United States,
similar Bills have been introduced with a view to creating obstacles to
the demands in the field of information contained in the Vredeling proposition and to other draft directives drawn up by the Commission of
the European Community relative to company groupings.[42]

Certainly the motivation of some pressure groups who canvassed in
favour of the adoption of the 'blocking statutes' should be criticized.
However, that is hardly the essential point. What is more important is
to note that these statutes represent a set-back for diplomacy and the
emergence of a more warlike approach in transatlantic economic relations.[43]

At first sight, the above-mentioned legislation would appear to catch
companies in Morton's Fork, subject as they are to two contradictory
sets of obligations, both of which can be enforced by criminal sanctions. However, in certain cases, blocking statutes can be used as a
defence by companies, and thereby justify the impossibility of their
complying with orders addressed to them by the American authorities.
Analysis of the effect of these statutes on American courts has become
an area of legal studies in itself.[44] These studies tend to show that
American courts do not automatically accept the defences afforded by
such blocking statutes.

Legislative Measures whose Extraterritorial Operation is Motivated by
Foreign Policy Considerations

The use of economic warfare for political ends during peacetime is not
a practice whose use is confined to the US. Economic sanctions were
imposed by the European Community against Argentina at the time of

the Falklands crisis.[45] However, unlike those sanctions imposed by the US at the time of the Iranian hostage crisis and over the Siberian pipeline, these sanctions did not have any extraterritorial characteristics.

The freezing of Iranian assets decided upon by President Carter in 1979 by virtue of the *International Emergency Economic Powers Act* also covered the branches and subsidiaries of American banks established outside the US. This measure was quickly restricted to transactions in dollars. Adopted as it was for security, foreign policy and economic reasons, it did not lead to many cries of protest from the European states. This relative silence can be explained by several factors: a feeling of sympathy *vis-à-vis* the aim pursued, the fact that only Iranian interests were directly involved, and the possible application of article VIII section 2 (b) of the IMF statutes.[46]

None of these factors was present in the Siberian pipeline affair.[47] For reasons of pure foreign policy, namely a desire to influence both the behaviour of the Soviet Union towards its satellite states, and the attitude of her European allies towards the Soviet Union, the American government instituted, in 1981 and 1982, an economic embargo by virtue of the *Export Administration Act*, an Act whose extraterritorial operation still astonishes many. The measures adopted had two extraterritorial aspects. On the one hand, any person subject to the '*jurisdictio*' of the US, no matter where in the world, was prohibited from exporting petroleum or gas equipment to the USSR. Persons subject to the *jurisdictio* of the US included not only individuals and American companies, but also any company controlled by American interests. On the other hand, the US prohibited foreign companies established outside the US and not controlled by its interests from exporting petroleum or gas equipment obtained with American technical help, where the foreign company was either licensed by an American company or where the foreign company had contracted to be governed by American export-control regulations. It can therefore be said that in some ways the measures adopted by President Reagan on the basis of the 1979 Export Administration Act applied retroactively to contracts concluded prior to 1981/2. It is important to note one further element: the products and technical expertise in question were not considered to have any military or strategic importance. Non-compliance with the embargo could lead to various sanctions, the most important being the prohibition of access by the guilty firm to products and technical expertise of American origin.

As a result of these measures, several European governments felt obliged to intervene in order to solve the problem of performance of pre-existing supply contracts, made by companies established on their territories (whether controlled by national or American interests), and in some way linked to the construction of the pipelines. They have ordered these firms, sometimes grounding their reasons on a blocking statute, to perform their contracts. These same firms were at the same time made the object of sanctions on the part of the American authorities.[48]

A note of protest was sent by the European Community to the United States alleging the illegality, by public international law standards, of the bases of extraterritorial jurisdiction invoked by the US: namely, the nationality of the firms' shareholders and the nationality (if it can be so called) of technological goods or information. After a few months the embargo was called off, under circumstances on which the American government did not throw much light.

The American measures shall be examined below from the perspective of public international law. Suffice it to point out here that, fortunately, they proved to be a failure on both political and diplomatic fronts. They constituted a clumsy means of influencing the commercial and foreign policies of the European states. Even if they had been confined to American subsidiaries based in Europe, these measures would still have remained highly questionable in the sense that they involved the mobilization of firms, in peacetime, to further the foreign policy aims of the state on whose territory they operated. To believe that the social reality of a company is limited to the shareholders who control its capital is both an error of judgement and a political miscalculation.

The pipeline affair has not left US economic interests unscathed either. The security of contracts signed by American firms has been put in doubt. The United States' request that American investments should not be subject to discriminatory treatment on the territory of third states also stands less chance of being granted so long as the US stresses, by its measures, the American 'nationality' of its subsidiaries based abroad.[49]

Unitary Taxation or the Extension of Federalism into the Sphere of US International Relations

The term 'unitary taxation' is used to define the particular method by which numerous American states calculate the basis for taxation of branches or companies which operate on their territory. Initially only applied to American interstate trade, this method has since been extended by a dozen or so states to cover their foreign trade as well. The unitary taxation method is fundamentally different from the 'arm's length' system used both by the US to calculate federal tax and by the other member states of the OECD.[50]

Let us imagine a group of companies set up in various states. If the second system were to be applied, then a state would simply tax the profits of the company based on its territory ('separate accounting').

The state could only take into consideration the company's links with other companies of the same group based in different states when it came to calculating the 'transfer pricing' system used between the member companies of the group. It would proceed as if these dealings had taken place at 'arm's length'. The correctives used by the various states are not necessarily identical, hence the 'arm's length' system does not prevent cases of 'double taxation'. Given its highly technical nature, this system requires a certain amount of administrative machinery to operate it. Moreover it is sometimes criticized, as, for many products or services, the reference to 'market price' is unrealistic, owing to the non-existence of an independent market. Whatever its merits, however this system remains of general application in international relations.

In order to simplify and facilitate administration, a number of American states now practise the unitary tax system. The unitary tax system ignores the way in which our economic grouping legally organizes itself in terms of geographical location. The state levying the tax takes into account the mass of income earned by the 'unitary business', some of whose activities are carried out on its territory. An apportionment formula is then applied to these profits, in order to calculate the fraction that can be ascribed to those activities organized by the economic entity on the territory of the state in question.

The notion of 'unitary business' is essentially an economic one. It does not necessarily cover the totality of companies subject to the same controlling body, but rather all those linked by the same economic objectives, as would be the case with companies related through vertical or horizontal integration. On the other hand, actual transactions are not required between these companies. It is sufficient to prove that these businesses all form part of a single economic organization.

The apportionment formula used by American states to calculate that portion of the unitary business's profit ascribable to its territory is based on three equal elements: assets, sales and payroll of the unitary business. California, for example, compares the figures for those assets, sales and payroll of the unitary business inside California with those of businesses outside. The index so obtained is used to calculate the basis for taxation in California.

The unitary taxation system is both simple and rational, at least when one considers the world to be one homogeneous economic area where each dollar invested, spent or earned contributes equally to the profits of the entire economic entity. Its administration lies, to a large extent, on the shoulders of the taxpayer, for example a subsidiary, who must supply the accounts of the entire group of companies, no matter where they are based, and interpret them according to the accounting practices of the state in question.

Multinational companies, especially those whose management is established outside the US, have criticized the fact that this system has been extended on a global level. These criticisms are based on two major points. First, a considerable administrative burden is placed on their American subsidiary and, indirectly, on company groupings based outside the US. Secondly, given the relatively high level of American prices and wages, the unitary taxation system has a tendency systematically to inflate that portion of profit attributable to American states, compared with that attributed to the rest of the world. In effect, the system taxes profits which have already been partially taxed abroad.

It is these two elements which have led some people to say that unitary taxation has extraterritorial effects. This remark is understandable when seen from an economic point of view. From a legal perspective, however, the observation is not correct. Only those companies that carry out activities on an American state's territory are directly taxed by that state. No duty or obligation whatsoever is explicitly imposed on companies based outside the US.

The Supreme Court held the system of unitary taxation to be compatible with the Constitution in so far as the 'due process' and 'commerce' clauses were concerned in intra-American state relations.[51] In its 1983 judgement *Container Corporation of America* v. *Franchise Tax Board*,[52] the Court held further that the system was also constitutional when applied on a world-wide basis. A majority of the Supreme Court judged that such use neither violated the Constitution's 'foreign clause', nor the principle that the US must speak with one voice in international affairs. As the minority opinion suggests, this is something which appears somewhat astonishing.

The Supreme Court decided that the unitary taxation method is both reasonable and just, and that it does not automatically result in double-taxation. To choose the separate accounting method rather than the unitary taxation system would not help prevent cases of double-taxation from arising. On an abstract level, the Court's reasoning is correct. However, we do live in a world with a past and in which the American states are not the only states that exist. In fact, unitary taxation will regularly lead to double-taxation, since, on the one hand, all foreign states use the separate accounting method and, on the other, prices and wages are relatively higher in the US.

It amazes foreign observers that the Supreme Court should admit that, in international relations, the US and the individual states that make up the federation are so out of step with each other. The federation complied with international fiscal practices, well established both by numerous treaties and model-laws; the American states have deviated from such practices.

In its *Container* judgement, the Court stressed the fact that the management of the multinational company in question was established in the US, and did not make any pronouncements as to what would happen where the taxed company were part of a multinational whose management were established abroad. But it is difficult to see how the Court could distinguish between the two hypotheses without discriminating between the two types of companies on the American market and contravening the "equal protection" clause of the Constitution.

Several European states, notably the United Kingdom, have protested against the use of the unitary tax system. The adoption of federal legislation limiting the use of this method to US frontiers would certainly be desirable in order to supress its extraterritorial *economic* effects.

EXTRATERRITORIALITY, CONFLICTS OF PRESCRIPTIVE JURISDICTION AND PUBLIC INTERNATIONAL LAW

Two questions will be examined, in this section: first, does public international law limit a state's jurisdiction? Second, does public international law provide a rule facilitating the resolution of disputes that arise when two states, both equally competent to act, decide to exercise their respective jurisdiction in opposite ways?

Possible Bases and Limits of a State's Prescriptive Jurisdiction

1) No universal treaty exists to define the jurisdiction states enjoy over each other. This does not mean that no such rules exist under international law. Customary international law can provide such rules, but, by their very nature, they are somewhat difficult to identify. Two elements must be established before a customary law can be said to exist: first, a constant and general use by all, or a group of, states; second, the conviction shared by these states that such use is necessary to the proper functioning of international society. This 'custom' can be made up either by acts of the state (legislation, executive practices, judgements) or by conventions containing identical rules. The existence of such a custom is not put in doubt by contrary practice of just one state. But many problems are encountered when attempts are made to calculate the threshold above or below which such use becomes, or ceases to be, a rule of international law. The existence of a customary rule is never absolutely certain until established as such by an international court. In our sphere, only two principles are universally accepted.

In the first place, every state's exercise of acts of sovereignty is limited to its own territory. On another state's territory, a state cannot, unless by permission, perform any act that usually falls within the preserve of public authorities such as judge, carry out investigations, summon witnesses under threat of penalty, execute coercive measures against persons or property. This rule was confirmed by the famous *Lotus* judgement given in 1927 by the Permanent Court of International Justice.[53]

Secondly, and conversely, the power of a state to make laws (whether legislative, administrative or judicial[54]) is not limited to its territory. This second point was also upheld by the *Lotus* judgement. Consequently, a state can make laws which have extraterritorial effect without infringing international law, provided such power is exercised in a way that no coercive measure is applied that may interfere with the exercise of the local territorial jurisdiction. But, there is nothing to prevent a state from enacting coercive measures applicable in its own territories, in order to ensure respect for a law with extraterritorial effect.

Does a state have unlimited prescriptive extraterritorial jurisdiction, or is it in fact fettered in some way? In practice, as this paper has shown, this point is the very crux of the matter, yet equally it is from this moment that the realm of doubt and controversy is entered.[55]

In the *Lotus* case again, the Permanent Court of International Justice declared that:

> Far from laying down a general prohibition to the effect that States may not extend the application of their laws and the jurisdiction of their courts to persons, property and acts outside their territory, it leaves them in this aspect a wide measure of discretion which is only limited in certain cases by prohibitive rules; as regards other cases, every State remains free to adopt the principles which it regards as best and most suitable.[56]

If this judgement is followed, then a state that adopts laws with extraterritorial effect need not justify its basis in international law. It is up to the state that objects to another state's exercise of extraterritorial jurisdiction, to show a 'prohibitive rule'. The court did not give any concrete examples of such rules, but implied that they are rare.

If the *Lotus* judgement is still good (international) law, it follows that the state that adopts legislation with extraterritorial effect need not justify its jurisdiction by citing one of the usual grounds given, namely the territoriality 'claim' (in so far as expanded by the effects doctrine), the nationality claim, the passive personality claim, the security or protection claim and the universality claim.[57]

Some authors share this view.[58] Others, after citing the *Lotus* judgement, do not attempt to identify any of the possible prohibitive rules mentioned by the court, but rather proceed in the opposite direction.

One by one the possible grounds for extraterritorial jurisdiction are examined and definitions as to their limits suggested.[59] Another author, Mann, considers that, in reality, only one ground is necessary, that is the existence of sufficient contact between the state and the situation which the law in question envisages.[60]

It is obviously artificial to try to categorize extraterritorial laws (both past and future) into a few small classes and condemn *a priori* those that do not fit into any such class, or at least only fit in with difficulty. It is more profitable to stick to the *Lotus* judgement and try to determine in each case whether a prohibitive rule exists or not. Such a rule can be said to arise where most states react adversely when faced with a dispute over extraterritorial jurisdiction. Such would probably be the case where the sufficient contact required by Mann does not, in fact, exist. In practice, however, it would be very difficult to analyse, in an abstract fashion, each state's attitude towards the existence (or otherwise) of another state's right to exercise such jurisdiction. To take a concrete example, even if the nationality claim were to be regarded as a link sufficient to justify a state's jurisdiction, it would still be an infringement of public international law for a state to order one of its citizens to commit an act, during peacetime, directed against the security of another state.

2) Let us pass on from the problems surrounding the precise limits governing a state's law-making power and assume that a state is in fact competent to promulgate laws that have extraterritorial effect. If such were the case, then logic dictates that a state should, at the same time, be allowed to require a legal person to comply with this type of law and, in the face of non-compliance, to impose the requisite mode of conduct upon that person. The fact that such conduct is to be performed outside the territory of the above-mentioned state hardly seems relevant. Provided the provision in question does not exceed that which is indispensable to ensure compliance with such a law (whose extraterritorial application is, in itself, permissible), then that provision will not be deemed to infringe international law. The only restriction would be that the state claiming the right to extraterritorial jurisdiction could not do so by exercising its power in a physical sense in the territory of another state. The performance of such acts of sovereignty is indeed contrary to international law.[61] However, there is nothing to prevent a state from attempting to ensure compliance with its 'extraterritorial laws' through the application of coercive measures within its own territory.

A state deemed to have the power to promulgate a law must also be deemed to have the power to pass measures designed to ascertain whether or not such a law has been infringed, even where the measures in question have extraterritorial effect. But once again, the state must refrain from performing acts of sovereignty within the territory of other states.

Public international law does not compel a state to respect, nor, *a fortiori*, apply, those provisions enacted by other states that are deemed to have valid extraterritorial effects. The only consequence, in international law, of such validity, is to extricate the state which passed the measure from international responsibility.

Conflicts between two States' Prescriptive Jurisdiction

1) Nobody would deny that it is possible for two states to be in a position to exercise their jurisdiction legitimately over the same person and under the same set of circumstances. Even those who think that one should categorize the various clauses of competence would admit that numerous examples of concurrent jurisdiction exist. The very fact that some states invoke territorial jurisdiction, whereas others rely on nationality proves the point. Furthermore, concurrent jurisdiction would often exist even where states were only to invoke territorial jurisdiction. For an example of where an individual falls into the scope of two different states' sets of legislation, one only has to think of the case where a person either commits an offence within the territories of both states, or else commits the offence wholly within the territory of one state, yet it produces its effects in the territory of the other. As we know, in the field of international economic relations such instances are common indeed.

Laws enacted by states enjoying concurrent jurisdiction will inevitably conflict with each other. Unfortunately, even if public international law were to distinguish between the various bases of jurisdiction, it certainly does not supply us with a hierarchy of such bases, nor does it supply us with a framework by which such conflicts can be resolved. Provided it has the jurisdiction so to do, a state is not prohibited *per se* from ordering an individual to adopt a certain mode of conduct in the territory of another state, even when such conduct would be illegal there. On the other hand, a state with the necessary jurisdiction can prevent an individual behaving in the manner prescribed by the other, equally competent, state.

2) This situation is quite unsatisfactory and it is the reason why the Restatement (Second) suggests that when a disagreement is in the offing, the states in question should have recourse to a 'balancing test', before deciding to exercise their jurisdiction.[62] The latest draft Restatement goes further. It advocates the use of a 'balancing test' to decide whether a state actually enjoys such jurisdiction.[63]

Several authors consider that where the exercise of extraterritorial jurisdiction is injurious to another state, then such exercise is contrary to international law. Consequently, if the behaviour presented by legislation with extraterritorial effect represents an interference with the policies and organization of a third state, then the exercise of that jurisdiction should be contracted. This really only amounts to a vague rule of thumb. Even if it were more substantiated, the criterion would still not be terribly helpful. Where state A prescribes a certain mode of conduct to a firm that is likely to cause grave economic injury in state B, this may result from behaviour initiated in state B which is just as harmful from its point of view. For an example take the case of international cartels.

By way of conclusion, even if it does seem both timely and desirable that a state should exercise its jurisdiction in such a way as to diminish the risk of disagreements with other states (especially when the fairness of such a course of action towards an individual is considered – after all, the whole point of the law is to try to govern that individual's conduct), there is as yet no rule of public international law which forces it so to do. In practice, when conflicts arise, the state, on whose territory the course of action is supposed to take place, will, as we have seen, always have the final word. After all, it is that state, and that state alone, which has sufficient coercive power to ensure that it is its law that wins the day. In this sense then, but only in this sense, can it be said that the territorial principle reigns supreme.

TOWARDS A FRAMEWORK FOR THE RESOLUTION OF DISPUTES BETWEEN STATES IN THE AREA OF EXTRATERRITORIAL JURISDICTION: THE POSSIBILITIES

1) Does customary international law provide any useful hints as to how the matters in issue between both sides of the Atlantic are to be solved? The preceding arguments tend to prejudge the answer, namely, at its present level of development international law provides very few hints. Nevertheless, some do exist.

States cannot carry out acts of sovereignty on the territory of other states. This rule gave an American court the opportunity to quash a subpoena addressed by the Federal Trade Commission to a French firm based in France,[64] something which ought to lead to a less aggressive position on the part of the American authorities in this area.

Given that a state has extraterritorial jurisdiction, there is nothing illegal *per se* in a court ordering (as was done in the US *ICI* case) that a measure should be performed in another state, whether at the level of the judicial proceedings themselves or at the later 'remedies' stage, provided that the measure so ordered is in proportion to the course of action. Such was the case of Judge Ryan's order in *ICI*.[65] However, the state in whose territory the measure is to be performed remains free to oppose it.[66]

On the other hand, a state authority cannot order the performance of a measure abroad without having first decided whether it does in fact have the necessary jurisdiction (from the standpoint of international law) to apply its substantial law to the litigation in question. As Judge Wilkey in *FTC* v. *Saint Gobain* recognized,[67] several American judgements seem to have transgressed this particular precept.

As to the enumeration of the bases and limits of a state's law-making power, public international law is of little help. However, judging by state practice, it would seem that the enlargement of the territorial principle by the effects doctrine is, both in fact and international law, perfectly legitimate. Furthermore, such extension is in many cases vital to the efficacy of economic legislation.

A problem, however, has been highlighted by the particularly wide conception of extraterritorial jurisdiction adopted by the US during the pipeline affair. (The US, it will be remembered, pushed the idea of 'nationality' to its furthermost extremes.) Even though the extremely adverse reactions on the part of the Europeans would lead one to believe that a law of prohibition existed (or rather was created), a reading of the *Lotus* judgement shows that such an extension should not be condemned *a priori*. If the strict classification of jurisdictional bases is applied, then the scales are definitely tipped against such an extension.

The pipeline affair is noteworthy on two counts. It shows that the discussion as to the enumeration of jurisdictional bases has in part drawn a veil over the true problem: namely, the actual contents of the legislation adopted by the US. It is this that is unacceptable to the Europeans. The legislation would have remained unacceptable, even if all the firms in the EC covered thereby had (in the company law sense) American nationality. The pipeline affair also shows that research in international law should now start its explorations in two directions. In the first place, research is needed to discover and determine those extraterritorial laws whose *content* is unacceptable from the perspective of international law. Secondly, there is a need to identify and enumerate those cases where the nationality of shareholders and company managers can be used as a launching pad for the exercise of a state's law-making powers extraterritorially. It is interesting to note in this respect that in all the above-mentioned extraterritorial issues one element continually recurs. Both the European and US authorities pay scant attention to the legal personality of the companies during their examination of the multinational or economic entity of which they form a part.

As noted above, the unitary tax system does not raise the problem of extraterritoriality in its classic form, but covers rather another question of international law. Given the widespread use achieved both in time and in space by the so-called 'arm's length' method of taxation, could it not be said that the US are contravening a customary practice of international law by allowing the federal states to apply the unitary tax system to foreign trade?

2) International law does not regulate the disputes caused by the existence of concurrent jurisdiction. Would it be possible for national laws themselves to evolve in such a way as to contribute towards a body of rules, aimed at solving these conflicts, or, even better, to avoid completely the causes of such disputes?

In the US, the balancing-test idea – an idea born in the area of private international law – is seen in a rather favourable light.[68] Two levels should be distinguished. First, as far as the court called to apply antitrust legislation with extraterritorial effect is concerned, the balancing test has the advantage of introducing the 'international' element in an explicit manner, something which the effects doctrine does not do. Whether a judge is in fact well qualified to determine what importance to give to the interests of his own country, let alone the interests of foreign state, is another question. It would not seem to be necessarily desirable to suggest that foreign states should appear before a court to express their views. The judgement on the 7th Circuit in the *Uranium* case is quite revealing in this respect.[69] The proper interlocutor for a government is normally another government, rather than a judicial authority.

It is certainly desirable that, rather than just being applicable at the court level, the balancing test should also be considered by the legislative and executive prior to adopting legislation with extraterritorial effect. Wherever a measure is clearly of extraterritorial application, then the national judge must apply it as such. However, there is nothing to compel the legislative or executive to adopt such a measure. A 'balancing test' was in fact incorporated in the Export Administration Act (1979). Unfortunately it was never used.

On the European side, a change of attitude towards the extraterritorial application of American legislation of fairly permanent character (notably the antitrust and fiscal legislation) by some member states would certainly help clear the atmosphere. The neutral observer would be shocked to note that states, themselves endowed with competition rules and who also apply a policy penalizing tax evasion, do not show much enthusiasm for the application of the same policies when pursued more vigourously by the US.

3) Conflicts between states over questions of extraterritorial jurisdiction will never be solved by the evolution of customary international law, nor by the spontaneous evolution of internal laws. There is a need for greater communication between states, who should attempt to transfer disputes from the judicial to the governmental plane, where solutions are easier to find.[70] Governments speak to each other as equals and are able to express and evaluate their respective interests. When a state appears before another's court, then, as we have already seen, it often perceives any extraterritorial judgement that may be made to be an attack on its sovereignty. This psychological element, which is particularly evident in the relations between the European states and the major power (the US), should not be underestimated.

Communications between states could take the institutionalized form of agreements, opening out into the setting up of formal procedures.[71] Such agreements already exist between the US and some other industrialized states. However, they are not of much use except where each state's legislative policy is similar on the substantive plane. The Swiss Federal Court's judgement in the *Santa Fe* case (concerning insider trading) is significant in this respect.[72] In the short term, the most useful initiative would be for the US, the EC and its member states to work out a convention on the means of proof allowed in cases of infringement of economic legislation on their respective territories.

Law or diplomacy? The answer is both law and diplomacy. In the short term, the diplomats must take over from the US courts and European legislators, who have sometimes treated the question of extraterritorial jurisdiction more like a table tennis or even boxing match. In the longer term, however, the way forward to the peaceful solution of these disputes will be through the coordination or harmonization of the economic and procedural legislation of the US and the European states.

While awaiting these developments, there is one final request: that is, that states apply their respective laws . . . diplomatically.

NOTES

1 The extraterritoriality issue has been the subject of many articles, books and conferences since the Second World War. A full treatment of the problem of extraterritoriality in the transatlantic context is provided, in concise form, by Rosenthal and Knighton, *National Laws and International Commerce* (Routledge & Kegan Paul, London, Boston and Henley, 1982). This book, whose authorship bridges the Atlantic, offers a balanced approach to the issues and is intended for non-lawyers. Two recent conferences also deserve mention, as they cover most aspects of our problems and present various perspectives: the Conference sponsored by the International Law Association, Extraterritorial Application of Laws and Responses

Thereto, London, 11-12 May 1983, and the Conference on Extraterritoriality for the Businessman and the Practicing Lawyer, held at the Georgetown Law Center in June 1983. The Georgetown papers were published in *Law and Policy in International Business* (vol. 15, 1983, pp. 1095-1221), together with an extensive bibliography.

2 Whether or not the often-rigid separation maintained between private and public international law is justified is discussed by Lowenfeld, 'Public law in the international arena: conflict of laws, international law and some suggestions for their interaction', *Recueil des cours*, vol. 163(II) (1979), p. 315.

3 For a scholarly discussion of jurisdiction under private and international public law, see Mayer, 'Droit international privé et droit international public sous l'angle de la notion de compétence', *Revue Critique de Droit International Privé* (1979), pp. 1-29, 349-88 and 537-83. The third part of Mayer's article is relevant to the subject of this paper.

4 See the cases cited by O'Connel, *International Law*, vol. 2, 2nd edn, (1970), 823-31 and Akehurst, 'Jurisdiction in international law', *British Yearbook of International Law*, vol. 46 (1972-3), pp. 145, 152-69.

5 On the extraterritorial application of US antitrust laws, see generally Fugate, *Foreign Commerce and the Antitrust Laws*, 3rd edn, (1982); Hawk, *United States Antitrust Laws and Multinational Business*, (1981); Atwood and Brewster, *Antitrust and American Business Abroad*, 2 vols, 2nd edn (1981); Rahl (ed.), *Common Market and American Antitrust: Overlap and Conflict* (1970). For a very recent and thoughtful survey, see Meessen, 'Antitrust jurisdiction under customary international law', *American Journal of International Law*, vol. 78 (1984), p. 783.

6 *United States* v. *Aluminium Co. of America*, 148 F. 2d 416 (2d Cir. 1945).

7 *United States* v. *Imperial Chemical Industries, Ltd*, 105 F. Supp. 215 (S.D.N.Y. 1952).

8 *United States* v. *Watchmakers of Switzerland Information Center, Inc.*, 133 F. Supp. 40 (S.D.N.Y. 1955).

9 *In re Westinghouse Electric Corp. Uranium Contracts Litigation*, 563 F. 2d 992 (10th Cir. 1977); *In re Uranium Antitrust Litigation*, 617 F. 2d 1248 (7th Cir. 1980). On the origin and operation of the cartel itself, see Rothwell, 'Market coordination by the uranium oxide industry'. *The Antitrust Bulletin*, vol. XXV (1980), p. 233.·

10 *Laker Airways Ltd* v. *Sabena*, 731 F. 2d 909 (D.C. Cir. 1984).

11 See Norton, 'Extraterritorial jurisdiction of US antitrust and securities laws, *International and Comparative Law Quarterly*, vol. 28 (1979), pp. 575, 584-7 and 590-4.

12 See, for example, *United States* v. *Vetco, Inc.* 644 F. 2d 1324 (9th Cir. 1981), *cert. den.* 454 *U.S.* 1098 (1981) and *United States* v. *Bank of Nova Scotia* 691 F. 2d 1384 (11th Cir. 1982), *cert. den.* 454 U.S. 1084 (1983).

13 See Note, 'Trends in extraterritorial narcotics control: slamming the stable door after the horse has bolted', *New York University Journal of International Law and Politics*, vol. 16 (1984), pp. 353, 374-90.

14 See Marcuss, 'Extraterritoriality: US antiboycott law and the Foreign Corrupt Practices Act, *Law and Policy in International Business*, vol. 15 (1983), p. 1135.

15 See Jennings, 'Extraterritorial jurisdiction and the United States antitrust laws', *British Yearbook of International Law*, vol. 33 (1957), pp. 146, 164 ff. Mann. 'The doctrine of jurisdiction in international law', *Recueil des cours*, vol. 3 (1964), pp. 9, 100 ff.

16 *Timberlane Lumber Co.* v. *Bank of America* 549 F. 2d 597 (9th Cir. 1976), where the court decided that an 'interest balancing test' was to be used before exercising US jurisdiction. See also *Mannington Mills, Inc.* v. *Congoleam Corp.* 595 F. 2d 1287 (3d Cir. 1979).

17 See note 9 above.

18 See note 10 above.

19 See note 7 above.

20 See note 8 above.

21 *British Nylon Spinners, Ltd* v. *Imperial Chemical Industries, Ltd* (1952), 2 *All E.R.* 780 (C.A.).

22 As for foreign discovery under US law, see Rosenthal and Yale-Loehr, 'Two cheers for the ALI restatement's provisions on foreign discovery', *New York University Journal of International Law and Politics*, vol. 16 (1984), p. 1075; Note, 'Extraterritorial discovery: an analysis based on good faith', *Columbia Law Review*, vol. 83 (1983), p. 1320; Rahl, 'Enforcement and discovery conflicts: a view from the United States', Paper presented at the Fordham Conference on International Antitrust (1978); Onkelinkx, 'Conflict on international jurisdiction: ordering the production of documents in violation of the law of the situs', *Northwestern University Law Review*, vol. 64 (1969), p. 487.

23 A court or an agency is competent to adjudicate if it possesses jurisdiction over the subject matter of the action and over the person of the defendant, provided that the latter receives proper notice; see, for example, *Federal Trade Commission* v. *Compagnie de Sain-Gobain-Pont-à-Mousson* 632 *F. 2d* 1300, at 1318 and sq. (D.C. Cir. 1980). The due-process clause of the Constitution is not satisfied if the defendant lacks sufficient 'minimum' contacts with the forum.

24 See Rahl, 'Enforcement and discovery conflicts', pp. 2–4.

25 See notes 38–41 below.

26 *Rio Tinto Zinc* v. *Westinghouse Elec. Corp.* (1978) 2 *W.L.R.* 81 (H.L.).

27 On the application of articles 85 and 86 of the EEC Treaty to situations which are at least in part international, see Harding, 'Jurisdiction in EEC competition law: some recent developments', *Journal of World Trade Law* (1977), p. 422; Bischoff and Kovar, 'L'application du droit communautaire de la concurrence aux entreprises établies à l'extérieur de la Communauté', Clunet (1975), p. 671; Jacquemin, 'Application to foreign firms of European rules on competition', *Antitrust Bulletin*, vol. XIX (1974), p. 157; Goldman, Les effets extraterritoriaux de la politique de la concurrence', *Revue du Marché Commun* (1972), p. 612.

28 *Imperial Chemical Industries and others* v. *Commission* 14 July, 1972, *Recueil* 1972, 619; [1972] *C.M.L.R.* 557.

29 See *Re Agreements between Philip Morris, Inc. and Rembrandt Group Ltd* (1984) 2 *C.M.L.R.* 40. This case is now before the Court of Justice.

30 See the Commission's decision in the *Commercial Solvents* case, 14 December 1972, *O.J.E.C.* L 299/51/1972, affirmed by the Court of Justice, 6 March 1974, *Recueil* 1974, 223.

31 It is worth noting that the Commission, as a matter of routine, sends EC officials abroad with the purpose of gathering information necessary to anti-dumping proceedings. This is done with the acquiescence of the foreign countries whose exports are under investigation, which probably explains why this has not led to public protestations on the part of those countries.

32 Commission, 9 June, 1976, *O.J.E.C.* L 223/27/1976, Court of Justice, 13 February 1979, *Recueil* 1979, 461.

33 *Stanley Adams* v. *Staatsanwaltschaft des Kantons Basel-Stadt*, Swiss Federal Tribunal, 3 May 1978, [1978] 3 *C.M.L.R.* 480.

34 See articles 23 and 27 section 2 of the Free Trade Agreement between Switzerland and the EC. On the *Adams* affair, see J. Werner, editorial, *Revue Suisse du Droit International de la Concurrence* (1981), p. 3 (who argues that the practices of Hoffmann-Laroche did not affect trade between Switzerland and the EC) and the documents reproduced *ibid.*, pp. 39–80.

35 For the text of the draft directive, see *O.J.E.C.* C 217/3/1983. For an analysis of its content, see Pipkorn, 'The draft directive on procedures for informing and consulting employees', 20 *C.M.L.Rev.* 725 (1983).

36 See Editorial Comment, 'A turnabout in extraterritoriality', *American Journal of*

International Law vol. 76 (1982), p. 591; Gill, 'The director's dilemma', paper presented at the International Law Association in London in 1983.

37 See note 28 above.

38 Among those countries are Australia, Canada, France, the United Kingdom.

39 For such a review see April, 'Responses to extraterritorial exercises of jurisdiction', paper presented at the International Law Association Conference, in London in 1983.

40. On this statute, see A. V. Lowe, 'Blocking extraterritorial jurisdiction: the British Protection of Trading Interests Act', *American Journal of International Law*, vol. 75 (1981), p. 257; Blythe, 'The extraterritorial impact of the antitrust laws: protecting British trading interests', *American Journal of Comparative Law*, vol. XXXI (1983), p. 99; Lowenfeld, Sovereignty, jurisdiction and reasonableness: a reply to A. V. Lowe', *American Journal of International Law*, vol. 75 (1981), p. 629.

41 The statute was applied in the *Laker* case, see Recent Developments, 14 *Georgia Journal of International and Comparative Law*, vol. 14 (1984), p. 181 and invoked before British courts; see *British Airways Board* v. *Laker Airways Ltd* (1983) 3 *All E.R.* 375 (C.A.), reversed by (1984) *All E.R.* 413 (H.L.).

42. These Bills are mentioned in the references cited above; see note 36.

43. See Sinclair, 'Responses, to extraterritorial exercises of jurisdiction. The diplomatic response', paper presented at the International Law Association Conference, held in London in 1983.

44 See Cohen-Tanugi, 'Les juridictions américaines face aux lois étrangères interdisant la communication de renseignements économiques', *Revue Critique de Droit International Privé* (1983), p. 213; Joelson, 'International antitrust: problems and defenses', *Law and Policy in International Business*, vol. 15 (1983), p. 1121.

45 On the question of economic sanctions, see the papers and case-studies presented at the Conference, organized by the Belgian Society for International Law, entitled: 'Les moyens de pression économique et le droit international', Brussels, 26–27 October 1984.

46 See Edwards, 'Extraterritorial application of the US Iranian assets control regulations', *American Journal of International Law*, vol. 75 (1981), p. 70; Gianviti, 'Le blocage des avoirs iraniens par les Etats-Unis', *Revue Critique de Droit International Privé* (1980), p. 279.

47 On the Siberian pipeline dispute, see for example, Audit, 'Extra-territorialité et commerce international. L'affaire du gazoduc sibérien', *Revue Critique de Droit International Privé* (1983), p. 401; A. V. Lowe, 'Public international law and the conflict of laws: the European response to the United States export administration regulations', *International and Comparative Law Quarterly*, vol. 33 (1984), p. 515; Zaucha, 'The Soviet pipeline sanctions: the extraterritorial application of US export controls', *Law and Policy in International Business*, vol. 15 (1983), p. 1169; Note, 'Extraterritorial application of the Export Administration Act of 1979 under international and American law', *Michigan Law Review*, vol. 81 (1983), p. 1308.

48 See Atwood, 'The Export Administration Act and the Dresser Industries case, *Law and Policy in International Business*, vol. 15 (1983), p. 1157.

49 Americans took quite a different view when the 'nationality' of foreign-controlled subsidiaries established in the United States was in issue, see *Sumitomo Shoji America, Inc.* v. *Avagliono* 102 *S.Ct.* 2374 (1982). These were considered to be 'American' corporations for the purpose of applying American law.

50 On unitary taxation, see Redmond, 'The unitary system of taxation. Identification of the source of income', *Bulletin for international fiscal documentation* (1981), p. 99.

51 See *Moorman MFG. Co.* v. *Bair* 437 *U.S.* 267 (1978); *Exxon Corp.* v. *Wisconsin Dept. of Revenue* 447, *U.S.* 207 (1980); *Mobil Oil Corp.* v. *Commissioner of Taxes of Vermont* 445 *U.S.* 425 (1980).

52   103 *S.Ct.* 2933 (1983); 22 *International Legal Materials* 855 (1983).

53   P.C.I.J., Series A, No 10, p. 11.

54   See above, p. 124.

55   See Weil, 'International law limitations on state jurisdiction', paper presented at the International Law Association Conference, held in London in 1983.

56   Cited in note 53 above; see p. 19.

57   These are the various principles which are sometimes invoked to ground a state's criminal jurisdiction, see O'Connel, *International Law*, vol. 2, pp. 823–31; Jennings, 'Extraterritorial jurisdiction', pp. 148–61.

58   See, for example, Weil 'International Law Limitations'.

59   See for instance Jennings, 'Extraterritorial jurisdiction'.

60   Cited in note 15 above.

61   In other words, the correct and meaningful distinction is between a state's *prescriptive jurisdiction*, understood in a *broad sense* (covering the power to make statutes, executive regulations, judgements and administrative orders) and a state's *coercive jurisdiction* (covering the power to execute *physical or material acts of sovereignty*), and not, as many authors suggest, between prescriptive jurisdiction in a restricted sense (covering legislative jurisdiction, i.e. the power to make general rules) and enforcement jurisdiction (which is meant to cover both judicial or administrative orders applying general rules to particular cases and acts of coercion needed to implement those orders). International law does not limit prescriptive jurisdiction (in its broad sense). But it does limit a state's coercive power to its territory.

62   *Restatement (Second) of the United States Foreign Relations Law*, Section 40.

63   Section 403. The proposed change is criticized by the US Department of State, see Robinson, 'Conflicts of jurisdiction and the draft restatement', *Law and Policy in International Business*, vol. 15 (1983), p. 1147.

64   See note 23 above.

65   See note 7 above.

66   As was the case in the *Nylon Spinners* case, see note 21 above.

67   See note 23 above.

68   See the cases cited in note 16 above and the views of Rosenthal and Knighton, in *National Laws and International Commerce*, pp. 26 ff; as well as those of Shenefield, 'Extraterritoriality in antitrust', *Law and Policy in International Business*, vol. 15 (1983), pp. 1109, at 1113 ff. However, there are exceptions, see the cases cited in notes 9 and 10 above and the not so 'cheerful' opinion of Maier, 'Interest balancing and extraterritorial jurisdiction', *American Journal of Comparative Law*, vol. XXI (1983), p. 579.

69   See note 9 above.

70   In this respect, the strict separation between the executive and the judicial branches of the US federal government can make it difficult to operate such a shift. For example, antitrust cases are not only brought by the US government, but also by private parties. In the latter case, the US government may be powerless to intervene.

71   See Note, 'A comparative analysis of the efficacy of bilateral agreements in resolving disputes between sovereigns arising from extraterritorial application of antitrust law: the Australian agreement', *Georgia Journal of International and Comparative Law Quarterly*, vol. 13 (1983), p. 49.

72   Reproduced in *International Legal Materials*, vol. XXII (1983), p. 785. But since that decision, the Swiss government has announced its intention to submit to parliament a Bill making insider trading a crime, see *International Herald Tribune*, 25 October 1984.

Comment 1

DOUGLAS E. ROSENTHAL

Paul Demaret has done a characteristically first-class piece of work. I disagree with only two points in his paper, and both are issues on which people can reasonably disagree.

First, I believe that the central problem is not clashing views about the legitimacy of extraterritorial enforcement jurisdiction. Rather, the core issue is the legitimacy of unilateral action by one state as to matters in which other states have direct sovereign interests, where unilateral action necessarily requires the undermining or erosion of the other state's effective implementation of its national laws and policies within its own territory.

Much extraterritorial law and policy is applied today by consent of nations; usually multilaterally, sometimes bilaterally. For example, Professor Demaret's paper discusses discovery as sometimes causing a major problem in private international civil litigation. But the discovery that goes on in trade proceedings under the GATT all the time, and which is multilaterally agreed to (or at least tolerated), is more intrusive and often has fewer limitations than the rules of discovery in civil litigation in the United States. American enforcement officials swoop into factories in Japan, Belgium and the Federal Republic of Germany almost every month, poring through masses of confidential data and engaging in enforcement jurisdiction within the territories of those nations. They do so because nations recognize that the alternative to allowing this to continue is having US trade law enforcers make conclusive presumptions concerning liability that would be very damaging to effective exportation to the United States. The problem is not extraterritorial law enforcement *per se*; it is

unilateral extraterritorial enforcement in circumstances that impair
the ability of a foreign state to govern its own people in its own territory.

Secondly, I disagree with those who think that the problem of such
unilateral assertions of conflicting jurisdiction is essentially a political
and diplomatic issue and that international law provides little help in
finding proper limits to such assertions. It is obvious that the importance of political and economic factors must be taken into account in explaining problems like this. None the less, there is an important role
here for international law as well.

I think the extent to which political and economic factors are important, particularly as to the intrusive application of US law and policy, is
reflected in the various political institutions of competence responsible
for each one of the three areas of disagreement identified by Professor
Demaret, that is: extraterritorial application to ensure the coherence
and efficiency of a state's national policy; extraterritorial export,
technology control and other laws motivated by foreign policy considerations; and state unitary tax systems. The extraterritorial enforcement of US national laws is primarily the responsibility of the federal
judicial branch. Enforcement of trade control laws for foreign policy
purposes is primarily within the competence of the executive branch.
The engine that drives the issue of unitary taxation is the revenue
demands of the states within our federal system. There is no one agency,
no one branch of the US government with whom one could work out a
diplomatic resolution of all of these problems. Perhaps one could convince the executive branch to adopt a much more consensus-oriented
multilateral approach to export controls. As for unitary taxation, the
US executive branch basically supports the European position, but is
unable to impose its views either on some of the unitary tax states or on
Congress, which is made up of representatives from those states who
are very sensitive to the states' perceived political interests.

It is unfashionable in the United States to believe that international
law can really play a useful role in resolving sovereign conflicts. I
would argue that that lack of fashion is indeed one of the problems in
the United States: there is not sufficient respect for the relevance of
international law in dealing with international political and economic
problems. I believe that there are four emerging principles of international law, which are so self-evidently sensible, and which have some
foundation in international law, that one can support their good sense
and validity both as legal and as political matters. It ought to be possible,
ultimately, to try to establish them by multilateral agreement in the
OECD and the GATT, as well as in other multilateral fora. If we could
obtain agreement on these four principles, the problem would be without
doubt substantially reduced.

The first principle is that one would not adjudicate in the courts of any one nation any conduct which a foreign sovereign government has taken direct explicit responsibility for causing. This is a principle short of foreign compulsion. If a foreign government is willing to state that it assumes responsibility for private conduct that takes place significantly within its territory, that assertion should be sufficient to preclude adjudication in the courts of another nation. This first principle could have prevented a US court adjudicating a case such as the antitrust prosecution of the Swiss watchmakers' cartel,[1] in which the Swiss government ratified the activities of the Swiss watch industry in Switzerland, but did not compel collusive conduct.

The second principle is that the corporate nationality or single economic entity basis for jurisdiction should never overrule a contrary law or policy of the incorporating or host jurisdiction of the subsidiary. It is wrong to say that there is an integrated corporate enterprise over which jurisdiction can always be imposed, so that one can exercise control over foreign subsidiaries merely because one has control over the parent. If the effect of asserting those controls is to undermine the sovereign laws of a nation in which the parent or the subsidiary is domiciled, or was chartered, then that law should not be enforced.

The third principle is an obligation to seek, and to seek earnestly and with patience, bilateral and multilateral solutions to international problems before taking unilateral action. For example, the US Securities and Exchange Commission (SEC) has invited comments on an enforcement staff proposal to apply a waiver by conduct presumption so that the SEC and the US courts could assert jurisdiction over any foreigner who places a trade on a US securities exchange from a foreign location.[2] The SEC enforcement staff's proposed rule states that if a foreigner initiates a trade abroad, it can be presumed as a matter of law that he or she waives any possible claims to not being subject to the jurisdiction of US insider trading laws and of US courts in which those laws can be enforced. Whatever the merits or demerits of the underlying concern with the insider trading, it is absolutely wrong for the United States or any other nation unilaterally to impose such a rule, until there has been some effort to work out multilateral agreements on the nature and extent of the problem of insider trading and the needs and opportunities for a joint approach to resolving the problem. The SEC's request for comments on the proposed rule shows commendable sensitivity to the views of others.

The fourth principle is one that we all have learned in our religious and educational upbringing, the golden rule: Do not do to others what you would not want them to do to you. For example, if the regulations that the United States applied to European firms in the Soviet pipeline case had been applied against US corporations that were subsidiaries or licensees of, say, French parent enterprises, the US would have found such laws intolerable. Or consider the US reaction, if France had export-control regulations that made it illegal for the American Motors plant in Indiana to fulfil a contract to deliver 10 000 cars to Chile, because French policy prohibited, on foreign policy grounds, exports by foreign subsidiaries of French parent corporations to Chile. The American government, the United Auto Workers Union and the people of Indiana would surely reject the validity of French law in this situation.

These four principles are reasonable ones that the nations of the Western alliance ought to be able to accept. I recognize that there is a great disparity between accepting these as useful propositions and having them formally adopted as binding rules of international law. But the former is at least a start.

NOTES

1 *United States* v. *Watchmakers of Switzerland Information Center, Inc.*, 133 F. Supp. 40 (S.D.N.Y. 1955), 1963 Trade Cas. (CCH) 70,600 (S.D. N.Y. 1962), *judgment modified*, 1965 Trade Cas. (CCH) 71,352 (S.D. N;Y. 1965).
2 Securities Exchange Act Rel. No. 21186, File No. S7-27-84 (30 July 1984).

Comment 2

GARY K. BERTSCH

US efforts to apply American export controls extraterritorially have been highly controversial at home and abroad. Recent American efforts grew out of the Reagan Administration's concerns that the Europeans were not taking its warnings about the strategic implications of East–West trade and technology transfer seriously. It is important to re-examine some of the recent episodes and the political reactions they generated. Concerning the question of East–West energy co-operation, for example, particular quarters in the Reagan Administration – particularly the Department of Defense – were deeply concerned about the question of excessive Western dependence on Soviet energy resources. At issue was the Urengoi gas pipeline, which would deliver natural gas from the Soviet Union to Western Europe. At the Ottawa Summit in the summer of 1981, President Reagan had urged the European allies to reassess the advisability and security implications of the pipeline and to consider pursuing energy alternatives. The President declared that he opposed the pipeline in principle, if not in practice. The West Europeans informed President Reagan of their intentions to proceed with the pipeline, the so-called East–West trade deal of the century.

During the summer and autumn of 1981, US officials continued to warn the European allies about the security and economic implications of the pipeline, particularly the issue of West European vulnerability to Soviet gas leverage. In July 1981, high officials in the Department of Defense proposed opposing the pipeline in practice, but at that point they were overruled by the President. Myer Rashish, a State Department official, then led a delegation of US officials to Europe to discuss US proposals for energy alternatives. The mission failed. Although they were always interested in considering energy options, the Europeans remained committed to the Urengoi pipeline project.

In February 1982, Lionel Olmer, Undersecretary of Commerce, disclosed that the US government was now considering extraterritorial sanctions that would both prohibit subsidiaries of US firms from exporting non-US oil and gas equipment and technology to the USSR, and prohibit export to the USSR of products made abroad using technology exported from the United States prior to the imposition of the US controls. The decision to apply these extraterritorial sanctions was left in abeyance, pending a summer mission to Europe to get allied support for tighter credit and financial conditions on East–West trade, and President Reagan's participation in the June 1982 Versailles Summit. Although the mission and Versailles Summit proceeded independently, the US pressed the allies to raise credit rates and tighten financial supports for East–West trade in both. When the allies failed to support the US proposals fully, President Reagan returned from the Summit and announced on 18 June 1982 the extraterritorial extension of the US controls noted above. These controls appeared to be directed more at the US's European allies than at its adversaries.

The President's actions unleashed political storms both at home and within the alliance. Senate Foreign Relations Committee Chairman Charles Percy (R–I11) said it 'is difficult to see how this action will do any more than split the NATO alliance and give the Soviet Union an opening to further divide us'.[1] The US Chamber of Commerce said the 'unprecedented blanket prohibition over US subsidiaries and affiliates and control of previously licensed US technology pose serious questions concerning the present direction of US international economic policy'.[2] George Ball, former Undersecretary of State, called the sanctions a 'great affront' to US allies, saying that the administration's claim that it was blocking the pipeline to pressure the Polish government to ease repressive measures was 'mere shadowplay'.[3]

Congress was soon drawn into the foray as well. After listening to Undersecretaries Olmer and Buckley defend the President's actions, a House subcommittee approved legislation on 4 August 1982 to terminate the Reagan Administration's controls on the export and re-export of US oil and gas technology to the Soviet Union.[4] The House Foreign Affairs Committee said the President's controls add 'substantially to both the perception and the fact that the US controls are more of a sanction upon Europe than upon the Soviet Union'.[5] On 10 August, the Committee voted 22–12 to abolish the President's controls. The House Bill was introduced in the US Senate on 13 August by Senator Paul Tsongas (D–Mass), who said the President's policy 'is driving a wedge between the United States and Western Europe, to what must be the obvious delight of the Kremlin'.[6]

The European allies also registered their strong dissatisfaction with President Reagan's policies. In June 1982, the Foreign Ministers of the European Community threatened court action against the US sanctions and called them 'contrary to the principles of international law, unacceptable to the Community, and unlikely to be recognized in courts in the EC'.[7] In July, the European Community lodged a formal protest calling on the Reagan Administration to reverse its decision. The protest was preceded and followed by more stiff criticism from the EC Foreign Ministers and European heads of state.

Citing 'substantial agreement' among the allies on an economic strategy toward the Soviet Union, President Reagan announced the lifting of the extraterritorial controls on 13 November 1982.[8] Although the President noted that the allies agreed not to engage in trade arrangements that contribute to the military or strategic advantage of the Soviets, or serve preferentially to aid the 'heavily militarized Soviet economy', the so-called agreement was of questionable significance. Within hours the French tried to dissociate themselves from it by saying in a communiqué that France was 'not a party to the agreement' announced in Washington. On the more positive side, the agreement did result in four alliance studies (NATO, OECD, IEA, COCOM) concerning the broader issues of East–West economic relations. Ideally, the agreements in principle that have emerged from these studies will result in agreements in practice minimizing the likelihood of future 'pipeline imbroglios'.

The issue of extraterritoriality and US export controls did not go away with President Reagan's lifting of the oil and gas controls. It remained a topic of domestic and alliance acrimony, and generated further political controversy throughout the 1983–5 period as the US Congress attempted to renew (unsuccessfully through the winter of 1984/5) the Export Administration Act. During this period, the Reagan Administration sought to protect its extraterritorial claim to apply US export controls to US subsidiaries, licensees and other affiliates abroad; it also sought to extend US controls in the form of a US import ban on the products of foreign companies that violated US controls by allowing unauthorized re-export of US origin items, as well as unauthorized exports by US subsidiaries of non-US origin items.

Powerful interests in the private sector, and many of their representatives in the US Congress, vigorously opposed the Reagan initiatives; they feared that such an extension of US export controls extraterritorially would further damage US export performance, as Western companies would avoid reliance on US technologies due to the uncertainties of the often politically motivated US controls. The European allies also expressed their opposition to the ideas of extraterritorial application and import controls. A British policy statement released in 1984 noted that it was 'unacceptable politically for the authorities of one country to extend legislation to companies in the United Kingdom in ways which displace British policy and may harm employment and profitability of British companies'.

EC concern with the proposed Reagan export-control legislation focused on three central issues: extraterritoriality, contract sanctity and import controls. The EC objected to the *extraterritorial* application of US controls because:

1) economically, the controls will damage European interests by reducing trade;
2) politically, extraterritoriality is viewed as US interference in the domestic affairs of sovereign countries; and
3) legally, it is viewed as contrary to international law.

Concerning *contract sanctity*, the EC feels that only the most exceptional circumstances can justify interference with existing contracts. Finally, concerning *import controls* – that is, the barring of foreign companies (that violate US technology controls) from the US market – the EC considers this an arrogant and intolerable extension of exterritoriality, allowing the US to punish allied companies for conduct that is regarded outside US jurisdiction.

These acrimonious and destructive disputes in both the pipeline and the Export Administration Act episodes need not have occurred. They resulted because of the lack of trust and good faith between the United States and its Western allies. As Professor Demaret concludes, intra-alliance communication and consultation, and greater harmonization of national legislation and policy, can do much to avoid future disputes. Although legislative and policy uncertainties still exist, recent signs point to more effective communication and consultation.[9] It is to be hoped that the West has learned some lessons from the recent disputes over the troublesome issue of extraterritoriality and East–West trade.

NOTES

1 *International Trade Reporter: US Export Weekly*, 29 June 1982, p. 454.
2 *International Trade Reporter: US Export Weekly*, 20 July 1982, p. 558.
3 *International Trade Reporter: US Export Weekly*, 10 August 1982, p. 671.
4 *International Trade Reporter: US Export Weekly*, 17 August 1982, pp. 699–700.
5 *International Trade Reporter: US Export Weekly*, 24 August 1982, p. 748.
6 *International Trade Reporter: US Export Weekly*, 17 August 1982, p. 699.

7 *International Trade Reporter: US Export Weekly*, 29 June 1982, p. 454.
8 *International Trade Reporter: US Export Weekly*, 16 November 1982, p. 259.
9 See, for example, 'Britain and US to consult before using trade powers', *Financial Times*, 23 November 1984.

Comment 3

JEAN-CLAUDE SCHOLSEM

1) The lively controversy between the United States and the other industrial countries on the issue of unitary taxation recalls certain aspects of another fiscal quarrel: that which took place during the 1970s, provoked by the development of the VAT systems on the eastern side of the Atlantic. In both cases, one commercial partner was confronted with the international emergence of an unfamiliar taxation mechanism, which appeared to be damaging to its interests.

The rapid diffusion of VAT inside the Common Market and in other European countries provoked overt hostility on the part of the United States. The US was not, of course, concerned with the internal aspects of this particular system of indirect taxation as applied in Europe. What provoked criticism was the international impact of the system, in other words the mechanism of export refunds and taxation of imports (border tax adjustments).

An abundant literature developed rapidly on this subject, similar to that which is now blossoming on the subject of the system of unitary taxation: scientific or academic studies, together with diplomatic and political statements.

This brief reminder of a recent, but already half-forgotten fiscal controversy has no other purpose than to put into context the one we are about to examine: to illustrate how the characteristics of an internal fiscal regime, which are unfamiliar abroad, are liable to create international tensions when that fiscal regime is extended to the international scene.

2) The controversies relating to the international impact of VAT have given way to another controversy, revolving around the international

extension of unitary taxation as practised by a dozen states in the United States, led by California.

Although the actors have changed their roles and the attack now comes not from the United States, but from the other industrialized countries, the two controversies nevertheless bear a certain resemblance. In the present case, the commercial partners of the United States see themselves confronted with the international emergence of a technique that has been used for a very long time in the United States, but is largely unknown to them and seems to them to be unfair and arbitrary.

This technique, described by Professor Demaret in his paper, is designed above all to allocate between the different states of the Federation a realized profit – whether made through branches or by subsidiaries – in several of them. A large number of states have deliberately turned their backs on the international practices of separate accounting, replacing them with an inclusive method of allocating profits. This method seems to go back to early practices of taxing firms at the federal state level and is thus well established in American fiscal traditions.

The Supreme Court decided that, under certain conditions (and it must be said that these are rather loosely defined), these inclusive formulae neither violate the Commerce Clause nor the Due Process Clause of the Constitution. It is interesting to note that the inclusive reference systems or assessment keys used by the different states are not uniform and that, as a result, a certain amount of double-taxation (of the same profit) is tolerated in principle within the overall framework of the taxing of firms by different states, which also shows the degree of fiscal autonomy retained by the states.

3) Against this historical backdrop, it is appropriate to record the problems posed by the international extension of the unitary tax system. As long as the system remained confined to the territory of the United States, it is hard to see what grounds its commercial partners would have had for complaining about it. The problem arises the moment certain federal states extend the regime to foreign subsidiaries of American firms, or, even more so, to the whole of an international group, where a single subsidiary operated in the particular state (world-wide unitary taxation).

The essential criticisms directed against the international application of unitary taxation are:

a) the extraterritorial application of such a tax;
b) the contradiction with the recognized international practice of the separate accounting method.

It is interesting to analyse how the Supreme Court of the United States responded to these criticisms in its decision of 27 June 1983,

Container Corporation of America v. *Franchise Tax Board*. In this case, the essential point was to establish whether it was constitutionally permitted, in view of the application of the inclusive reference systems for the geographical allocation of income or profits, to consolidate the profits of foreign subsidiaries of American firms.

The first objection is that such a system or method equates to extraterritorial taxation. In this respect, a first reaction springs to mind. How could the Supreme Court in effect change its own mind? If unitary taxation does not violate the Due Process Clause and does not end up as or result in extraterritorial taxation inside the United States, how could its extension to the rest of the world possibly have this effect?

The objection of the international community is well known: what is true in a strongly homogeneous economic environment is no longer true within the international framework, which is characterized by a marked heterogeneity of economies. In the latter framework, unitary taxation biases systematically the allocation of world-wide profits in favour of jurisdictions where prices are altogether higher and necessarily taxes profits which are not linked with economic activity in the territory.

This concrete argument did not convince the majority of the Supreme Court judges, but it was very clearly advanced in the minority opinion of three of the judges, one of them being Chief Justice Burger. The majority, on the contrary, when confronted with the very different profit figures for California, calculated using the unitary taxation method rather than that of separate accounting, posed a preliminary question: what is the validity of the latter figures? Who can be certain that they will be more valid than the former ones (those calculated for unitary taxation)?

The Supreme Court displays an astounding scepticism with respect to the traditionally accepted method, and that included acceptance by the United States, of separate accounting. Unitary taxation and separate accounting were referred to equally dismissively. 'We have seen', wrote the Court, 'no evidence demonstrating that the margin of error (systematic or not) in the three factor formula is greater than the margin of error (systematic or not) inherent in the sort of separate accounting urged upon us by the appellant.'

Given the functional integration, the centralization of management and the economies of scale that characterize a 'unitary business', it becomes almost pointless to ask exactly where the profit has been made. According to the Court, 'allocating income among various jurisdictions bears some resemblance to slicing a shadow'. Ever since, in this climate of scepticism, no argument can be derived from the results obtained by the separate accounting method to demonstrate the extraterritorial effect of unitary taxation.

The Court takes pleasure in displaying the theoretical and practical weaknesses of the system of separate accounting, corrected by the concept of arm's length transactions. The case about unitary taxation becomes a case about a rival principle.

Is the separate accounting method able to avoid double-taxation? Not at all: for this it would be necessary that all the countries forming the international community have the same conceptions of the admissible corrections of profits with reference to arm's length pricing. Thus, concludes the Supreme Court, if California had to be responsible for systematically avoiding all international double-taxation, it would be obliged not only to apply the separate accounting system, but also to accept each and every adjustment to profit figures made unilaterally, in the name of the arm's length pricing principle, by other countries: a manifestly absurd solution.

This deprecatory analysis of the separate accounting method naturally leads to the conclusion that unitary taxation does not violate the Foreign Commerce Clause, because international double-taxation is no more avoided with one system than with the other, and that, in the absence of an explicit directive from Congress, the states are not required to align themselves to the fiscal methods used at the federal level.

The minority opinion, on the contrary, holds that there is a fundamental difference between double-taxation caused by differences of assessment using arm's length pricing – which pose problems only at the level of actually affecting taxation, and thus can be more easily eliminated by international negotiations – and the unavoidable and irreducible double-taxation caused by the application of two principles that are so fundamentally different as separate accounting and unitary taxation.

4) The *Container* decision does not end the legal debate and arguments about the system of unitary taxation: it only touches on the problem of its extension to foreign subsidiaries of American parent companies, and explicitly leaves open the question of its application to American subsidiaries of foreign groups. However, it is above all the second question which provokes the irritation of the international community and a number of foreign governments.

On the one hand, it would presumably be extremely difficult for the Supreme Court to distinguish such a case from the *Container* case, since it had adopted and accepted the fundamental logic of unitary taxation, even in an international context. If a distinction has to be made, so as to allow foreign groups to be excluded from the world-wide unitary system, the American groups will not fail to complain that they are being discriminated against. But where exactly is the discrimination?

How does one evaluate or calculate it? Some foreign groups are now advancing precisely these arguments and invoking the fiscal conventions signed by the United States, as well as the Treaties of Friendship, Trade and Commerce. The discrimination rests notably in the fact that the administrative requirements indirectly imposed on the foreign groups are without common measure with respect to those imposed on American groups.

There are other differences in the international extension of unitary taxation, depending upon whether the parent company is American or foreign. In the first place, the risk of foreign reprisals is much greater when the parent company is foreign: these reprisals will clearly be directed against the United States as a whole and will cast a threatening shadow over the unity of the federation in matters of foreign policy, and indeed impediments to the conclusion of international conventions on double-taxation have already resulted from this source. Secondly, the economic hypotheses on which unitary taxation rests seem more fragile when the parent company is foreign. It is actually more plausible to conceive of unquantifiable transfers of value benefit, stemming from organizational unity, from the parent company to the subsidiary rather than vice versa.

It is thus rather difficult to predict the Supreme Court's reaction, were it to be confronted by this second aspect of world-wide unitary taxation. Will the problem be resolved in the meantime by a policy of subtle pressure on the various states so that they abandon the system in exchange for certain guarantees, as a form of administrative assistance with a view to obtaining more from the income or profits of multinational enterprises?[1] Or, if the solution is blocked, will Congress be persuaded to legislate? Or, yet again, will the problem not be resolved, but be left to market forces? In such a case, investors will leave those states that practise world-wide unitary taxation and the legislators of those states will be forced to reconsider their position. Or, alternatively, there will be no such effect, and in consequence the rationality and the equity of the taxation system under criticism will be demonstrated.

The market can also be the judge, but unfortunately it takes longer to pronounce its verdicts than is likely to be acceptable in this particular case.

NOTE

1   See the solutions envisaged in the Report to the World-wide Unitary Taxation Group, prepared by the Treasury Department's Office of Tax Policy, *Bulletin for International Fiscal Documentation*, November 1984, pp. 510–17.

6

Flexible Exchange Rates and National Monetary Policies

NIELS THYGESEN

INTRODUCTION AND SUMMARY

The present paper addresses three topics. First, the experience with flexible exchange rates since 1973 is summarized. It is marked by a high degree of short-run volatility and, more imporant, by large cyclical movements of apparently increasing amplitude. These features are reflected at the time of writing in unprecedented misalignments between the dollar on the one hand, and the yen and the Deutsche Mark (and most other continental currencies) on the other hand, whether one looks at simpler calculations of competitiveness or at more sophisticated measures relating to a sustainable current-account position over the medium term, as proposed by Williamson.[1]

Secondly, the implications of the observed performance of the flexible-rate system are briefly examined. Following the lead of Goldstein[2] and Williamson, a list of potential costs and benefits (except for the implications for the autonomy of national monetary policies, which was the main benefit anticipated at least by European policy-makers) are examined. The balance of costs and benefits in these other respects appears unfavourable.

The final section which, as the title of the paper indicates, is central to the theme, looks at the interaction of national monetary and fiscal policies under floating rates. A number of empirical studies have shown that, prior to 1983, the anticipations of the European countries, and of the Federal Republic of Germany in particular, to achieve a much higher degree of monetary autonomy from the United States than under the Bretton Woods system were not fulfilled; the degree of synchronization of interest rates or of monetary growth rates in the United States and Europe did not markedly change. It is argued, however, that this resulted primarily from deliberate policy reactions in Europe, rather than from economic necessity. The picture is somewhat modified if one looks at the most recent period since the US recovery got under way in early 1983 and, even more so, if one looks at real interest rate differentials. In the latter case, a widening divergence is observable since 1979, when US real rates shot up. The strengthening of the dollar seems mainly attributable to this divergence, and European complaints about limited autonomy should be modified by the recognition that relative monetary policy has become more powerful, because of the exchange-rate depreciation. But the case for taking the strain off this transmission mechanism through better coordination of both fiscal and monetary policies has become very strong, because of the costs of misalignment and the danger of sudden currency reversals, which could bring the continuation of the recovery throughout 1985–6 to an abrupt halt.

DIMENSIONS OF EXCHANGE-RATE FLEXIBILITY: VOLATILITY AND MISALIGNMENT

It is a trivial, but necessary observation that the exchange rates between the world's major currencies – the US dollar, the yen, the pound sterling and the Deutsche Mark (DM) – have become not only flexible, but increasingly volatile and out of line with what economists as well as bankers used to regard as underlying determinants of 'equilibrium exchange rates'. It is remarkable that this latter notion, which played a key role when the size of desirable realignments were discussed towards the end of the Bretton Woods era, and particularly in the preparations for the Smithsonian Agreement of December 1971, has disappeared completely from the official vocabulary and nearly from the academic. The de-emphasis of the concept at the official level was already visible in the Second Amendment to the IMF Articles of Agreement decided upon in Jamaica in 1976, and the IMF has made little effort to revive it in the exercise of surveillance. (See, however, the discussion of misalignment below.)

Figure 6.1 may help to recall the main facts about changes in currency relationships since the Bretton Woods system came under strain in late 1967; the fixed-rate system began to unfold with the 15 per cent sterling devaluation in November of that year, although it only broke down formally when it became clear at the end of February 1973 that the second major dollar devaluation in less than 15 months had failed to calm speculation. The period after the formal end to any intervention

Percentage deviations with respect to dollar parities of October 1967
monthly averages of daily figures*

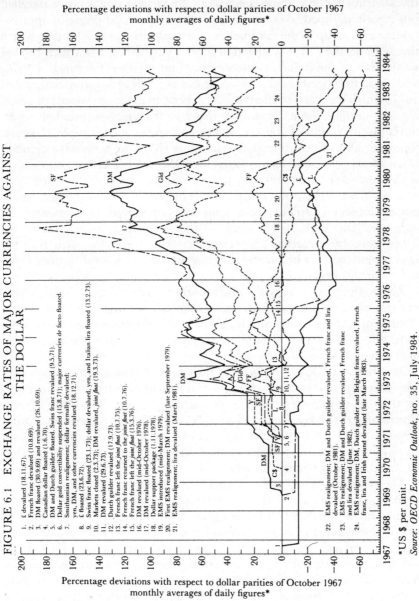

FIGURE 6.1   EXCHANGE RATES OF MAJOR CURRENCIES AGAINST
THE DOLLAR

1. £ devalued (18.11.67).
2. French franc devalued (10.8.69).
3. DM floated (30.9.69) and revalued (26.10.69).
4. Canadian dollar floated (1.6.70).
5. DM and Dutch guilder floated. Swiss franc revalued (9.5.71).
6. Dollar gold convertibility suspended (15.8.71); major currencies de facto floated.
7. Smithsonian realignment; dollar formally devalued;
    yen, DM, and other currencies revalued (18.12.71).
8. £ floated (23.6.72).
9. Swiss franc floated (23.1.73); dollar devalued, yen, and Italian lira floated (13.2.73).
10. Markets closed (2.3.73); DM revalued (19.3.73).
11. DM revalued (29.6.73).
12. Dutch guilder revalued (17.9.73).
13. French franc left the *joint float* (10.7.75).
14. French franc returned to the *joint float* (10.7.76).
15. French franc left the *joint float* (15.3.76).
16. DM revalued (mid-October 1976).
17. DM revalued (mid-October 1978).
18. Dollar support package (1.11.1978).
19. EMS introduced (mid-March 1979).
20. First EMS realignment; DM revalued (late September 1979).
21. EMS realignment; lira devalued (March 1981).

22. EMS realignment; DM and Dutch guilder revalued, French franc and lira
    devalued (October 1981).
23. EMS realignment; DM and Dutch guilder revalued, French franc
    and lira devalued (June 1982).
24. EMS realignment; DM, Dutch guilder and Belgian franc revalued, French
    franc, lira and Irish pound devalued (late March 1983).

*US $ per unit.
Source: OECD Economic Outlook, no. 35, July 1984.

obligations between the four major currencies may be divided roughly
into three phases: an initial period of approximately 2½ years of pronounced cyclical swings of less than a year's duration, as the yen and
the DM fluctuated around a substantially weaker dollar, with parallel,
but greatly damped, movements in sterling; a second phase of approximately 2 years up to the summer or early autumn of 1977, during which
the yen and the DM stabilized around a slow trend towards a further
weakening of the dollar, while sterling first plunged (in most of 1976)
and then stabilized; and a third phase beginning around September
1977, which has been marked by unprecedentedly large swings of growing amplitude. The early part of this recent phase was marked by an
initial appreciation of the non-dollar currencies for a couple of years,
followed, after a year of rapidly changing shifts, by a massive depreciation of the yen and particularly the DM, with sterling following a
separate course of strength up to early 1981. The OECD graph ends
with March 1984, a point of time when the weakening of the non-dollar
currencies seemed to have been temporarily reversed, but between that
date and the end of 1984 all of the three non-dollar currencies
depreciated by a further 15 per cent *vis-à-vis* the dollar, bringing the
DM back to or a bit below the rate negotiated at the Smithsonian Institute nearly thirteen years ago.

Although figure 6.1, with this important proviso, gives a fair initial
impression of the dramatic cyclical swings in exchange rates and clearly
documents the widening amplitude of nominal exchange rates over the
third phase of the period of floating, it still understates the magnitude
of the evolution in two respects.

The first, and least important, respect is that of *short-term volatility*.
The graph traces monthly averages and fails to capture the initial jump
in 1973 in day-to-day changes in exchange rates. The IMF *Annual
Report* has regularly surveyed trends in short-run volatility around
trend movements and found an increase by a factor of between 5 and
10 relative to the quiet periods under the Bretton Woods system, that
is, those without parity changes.

The reason for labelling this qualitative change in the functioning of
exchange markets as being less important is that most of the available
studies of the impact of month-to-month or day-to-day variability of
nominal exchange rates on international trade flows have failed to un-
cover any significant impact on international trade flows.[3] That short-
run volatility, contrary to the intuitions of many economists, seems to
have only a very limited impact on trade is also the main conclusion of
a study by the Group of Thirty.[4] The respondents in the financial and
non-financial sector tend to emphasize the availability of hedging
facilities in various forms and, more generally, seem more concerned
about other uncertainties in the international trading environment

than short-run exchange-rate volatility. Though the available evidence may still be regarded as inconclusive, it is at least clear that short-term nominal – and, since price levels move sluggishly, also real – exchange-rate volatility is a less serious problem than medium-term '*misalignment*'.

Following Williamson, we shall understand this concept to mean 'a persistent departure of the exchange rate from its long-run equilibrium level'. There are various ways of giving concreteness to this notion, ranging from the simplest one of combining relative price trends with the nominal exchange rate into a measure of the real exchange rate, or competitiveness, to the more sophisticated notions developed by Williamson and others to calculate a structure of exchange rates compatible with a sustainable pattern of current account balances for the main countries. Figure 6.2 records the OECD's measures of competitiveness – three different definitions of 'the real effective exchange rate' – for the seven major industrial countries since the start of floating. Relative to both 1975 – the base period in the figure – and 1973, US competitiveness has deteriorated substantially, that is, by 20–30 per cent using the OECD's preferred measure, relative unit labour costs. German and Japanese competitiveness has improved, though by less than the deterioration in the US position, while the United Kingdom has lost competitiveness, despite some reversal of the 'overvaluation' of sterling, which reached a peak in 1981. Similar conclusions are found if one looks at a broader set of relative price indicators, such as the additional ones used by the IMF. Considering that an important reason for the breakup of the Bretton Woods system was that it had led to 'misalignment' exchange rates by pushing the US and UK currencies towards overvaluation *vis-à-vis* the two surplus countries, Japan and Germany, it is a first and striking observation on the working of the floating-rate system that it has permitted misalignments to reach larger proportions than even the sternest critics of the fixed-rate system were pointing to around 1971. (The international organizations considered a devaluation of the US dollar of about 10 per cent consistent with a sustainable current-account position, a view which was accepted by the then US Administration.)

Calculations of the real exchange rate are admittedly crude and unavoidably ambiguous, because of the multiplicity of possible price series and base periods. More fundamentally, there may be solid grounds for arguing that a constant real exchange rate does not represent equilibrium. The discovery of large domestic energy resources pushes up the real exchange rate for sterling compatible with a sustainable current-account position, as does, though less obviously, a high rate of capital formation in the tradable goods sector for the yen; in other cases, non-price factors, such as a structurally unfavourable composition of exports or particularly high energy requirements in the domestic production

FIGURE 6.2   MEASURES OF RELATIVE COMPETITIVE POSITION
(indices in US $ terms: 1975 = 100)

---- Relative unit labour costs in manufacturing
—·— Relative average value of manufactured exports
—— Relative consumer prices
···· Forecasts

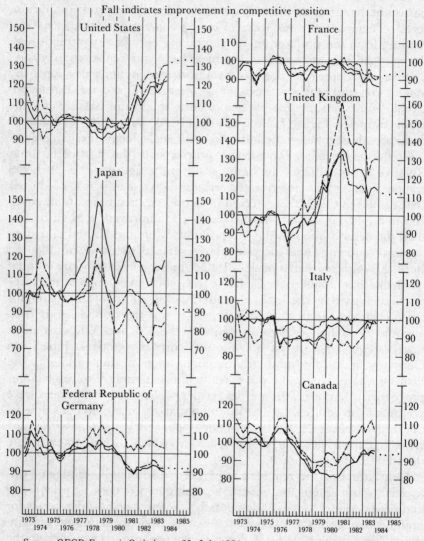

Sources: *OECD Economic Outlook*, no. 35, July 1984.

structure at a time of two oil price rises, may require reflection in a
lower real exchange rate to make the current-account position sustainable. Finally, 'normal' capital flows need to be taken into account in
assessing external equilibrium.

Williamson discusses most of these refinements elaborately in his calculation of misalignments, and hence of equilibrium exchange rates, yet his conclusions are broadly similar to those which surface from the simple figure 6.2. He reaches two general conclusions: maximum departures from the trend in equilibrium exchange rates have become larger under floating for all major currencies (except the French franc) than in the final decade of the fixed-rate system; and the present misalignments are very sizeable. His figures refer to early 1983 and no update is available to my knowledge; a rough application of his method suggests that the overvaluation of the dollar must by the end of 1984 have risen to the 25–30 per cent range, and the undervaluation of the DM and the yen to at least 15 per cent – in short, larger misalignments in the sense of unsustainable current-account positions than at any previous time under floating, and substantially larger than at the end of the fixed-rate system.

Although I find the procedures used by Williamson to obtain estimates of misalignment sound and the estimates themselves plausible, or even on the conservative side, the point is not to endorse particular numbers, but only to underline that the exchange rates prevailing in 1984 between the dollar and other significant currencies were indicative of severe misalignment. It is totally implausible that they could be explained merely by so-called real factors, whether structural or cyclical. In the former category, some observers have put great emphasis on a US lead in high technology, at least *vis-à-vis* Europe; but if one looks more carefully at US investment, only a very minor part can be attributed to high-technology sectors. In the cyclical category, one may point to the relatively much stronger upturn in the US than in either Europe or Japan in 1983–4, bringing the American economy faster and nearer to full-capacity utilization than any major European economy, as a factor justifying some real appreciation of the dollar. But the ultimate test is whether the prospective current-account position of the United States is sustainable, after due – and generous – allowance for these factors. The answer is unambiguously that it is not.

Table 6.1 summarizes recent trends and the 1984–5 prospects for the current accounts of the three main OECD countries, indicating a rapidly growing US deficit and relatively smaller, but historically larger Japanese and German deficits. Though part of these imbalances are due to factors other than movements in exchange rates, notably differentials in the growth rates of domestic demand, most observers would agree that the bulk must, by 1984, be attributed to the cumulative effects of dollar overvaluation and corresponding yen and DM undervaluation. Marris has estimated that, if domestic demand were to develop in parallel in the United States, Western Europe and Japan, thus eliminating the 'growth gap' between the US and the rest of the

TABLE 6.1   CURRENT-ACCOUNT BALANCES, 1981–5 ($ billion)

	1981	1982	1983	1984[a]	1985[a]
United States	4.6	−11.2	−40.8	−86.5	−105
Japan	4.8	6.9	20.8	30.5	36
Germany	−5.8	3.6	3.9	5.75	10
Rest of OECD	−23.4	−28.6	−8.6	−1.25	6.5
Total OECD	−27.0	−29.3	−24.7	−51.75	−52.5

[a] Estimated values.

Source: OECD Economic Outlook, no. 35, July 1984, p. 61.

OECD area, the US current-account deficit would continue to rise rapidly, reaching possibly a level of at least $200 billion by the end of the 1980s – if one could, indeed, imagine foreign financing of this magnitude to be forthcoming.[5]

Some observers console themselves that the present and projected future levels of the US deficit are grossly overstated. The argument is that the sum of the current-account position for the major groups of countries does not add up to zero, as it should, but to a large negative number, at present approximately $100 billion, and that some of this fictitious deficit is due to the United States. Even if one allots a third of this global discrepancy to the US current account – and that is the highest conceivable US share – the fundamental nature of the disequilibrium does not change. Significant reversals of the present exchange-rate misalignments are a necessary ingredient in the international adjustment process over the next few years.

The following two sections will look briefly at the costs and benefits of having put so much of the burden of adjustment on the exchange-rate system.

COSTS AND BENEFITS OF MISALIGNMENT

The problem about assessing the costs and benefits of obvious misalignments in exchange rates of the kind experienced in the recent past is the definition of a reasonable standard of reference. Simply assuming that the alternative would have been continuous adherence to equilibrium exchange rates in the sense defined in the previous section begs the question, because the national policies required to sustain such a constellation would have been substantially different from those actually pursued, hence implying broader revisions of the entire macro-economic scenario. Exchange rates are both a symptom and a cause of tensions between relative policy actions and other differences in national behaviour; they cannot just be assumed to have followed another course. Not least, expectations regarding rates of interest, inflation and exchange rates themselves would be changed by a commitment, explicit or perceived, of the authorities of a country to manage their exchange rate more tightly. European currency experience testifies to the importance of such modifications of both official and private behaviour. The commitment of EMS member countries to keep their 'internal' exchange rates within relatively narrow limits in the short run, and to push realignments into the background as the major instrument to resolve policy divergence has not only modified official behaviour; private agents have taken notice and changed their assessments in a way that was difficult to imagine on the basis of the turbulent phase that intra-European exchange rates went through in the mid-1970s. At the global level – between the dollar and the European currencies – this perception has faded completely, as agents know that the authorities will not take a view as to the appropriate level of the exchange rate, much less defend such a view.

Because the subject is difficult and inherently impossible to quantify, there are few studies available that help to evaluate the costs and benefits of misalignments in any systematic way. The surveys by Goldstein and Williamson suggest that, abstracting initially from the central issue of policy coordination and monetary autonomy, the balance of costs and benefits of unconstrained exchange-rate flexibility is unfavourable, or in other words that there are important net costs to be weighed against the possible benefits to national policy autonomy from allowing the exchange rate to swing widely.

Four elements point in this direction in such a qualitative evaluation: adjustment costs in the tradable-goods sector; a slow-down in the rate of capital formation; pressures for protectionism; and an upward push to the average world rate of inflation. The three first points are closely linked.

Exchange-rate cycles, and the resulting temporary, but not entirely short-lived misalignments to which they seem to lead in practice, impose adjustment costs on the sectors producing tradable goods. Some of these costs are not likely to be reversible. Firms that have been bankrupted or significantly reduced in scale by appreciation that turns out to have been unwarranted in the medium term are unlikely to resume or restore production; symmetrically, firms that have taken investment decisions, encouraged by what they thought was a more permanent improvement in their competitive position, suffer losses as undervaluation of the currency is corrected.

Repeated experiences of this kind will dampen the rate of capital formation in the tradables sector and promote an inward-looking attitude.

Uncertainty about the permanence of changes in competitive positions must tend to slow down international investment in particular, hence impeding welfare gains from specialization. Admittedly, there are no solid empirical studies that permit quantification of these effects. Yet there can be no doubt that real appreciation squeezed profits and investment in countries such as the Federal Republic of Germany and Switzerland in 1977–8, and in the United States recently; the apparent strong US investment performance in the present recovery is heavily concentrated in residential construction and transportation equipment for other non-tradable sectors. The alternative policy of keeping the real exchange rate more stable would obviously imply that more of the burden of adjustment has to be put on the sectors producing non-tradable goods and services – including the public sector.

Misalignment breeds demands for protection. Whatever may be said for the ability of flexible exchange rates to resolve international policy divergences anonymously in the market, the costs to international co-operation and to the domestic political process in countries with over-valued currencies are important. Previous chapters in this book focus on the international trading rules, and in the present context it suffices to say that the acrimony which marks trading relations between the United States and its trading partners, including some major LDC exporters, in 1983–4 might have been far better contained had the mis-alignment of the dollar been less pronounced. Moreover, protective attitudes tend to survive their initial cause; as the experience in Europe demonstrates, even prolonged undervaluation does not reverse industrial support policies that found their justification in earlier periods of poor competitiveness. The international institutional framework is not well equipped to handle the complicated *quid pro quo* between trade and industrial policy, on the one hand, and co-operative exchange-rate management, on the other hand. Even the European Community with a full policy agenda is not efficient in negotiating such packages internally; but it *has* effectively limited real exchange-rate swings.

Asymmetries in the way appreciation and depreciation work their way into the domestic price structures are sufficiently well established to warrant the conclusion that a cycle of undervaluation and its unwinding will push up prices and costs by more than the opposite sequence is able to dampen them. There are signs that real-wage rigidity had diminished in Europe by the early 1980s, relative to the period after the first oil-price shock; in some countries, real wages have declined by 2–3 per cent annually after the second oil-price shock. Appreciation no doubt helped to slow US prices and wages in the recent phase. Recent estimates based on large models of the US economy suggest that a 10 per cent appreciation of the dollar reduces the US price level by nearly 2 per cent. Yet, full symmetry can hardly be said to exist between the inflationary and deflationary impulses inherent in an exchange-rate cycle. In the absence of symmetry, countries may be pushed into policy actions that aggravate international divergence, as when European countries tightened policies to mitigate the inflationary impact of depreciation of their currencies at the bottom of the recession of 1980–1.

Superficial and non-quantitative as this brief survey is, it does point in the direction of net costs to the international system of exchange-rate misalignments. But if countries perceive that, they have gained more freedom in the design and implementation of national policies, and hence in achieving overall economic performance with respect to growth and inflation that may offer sufficient compensation.

THE MYTH OF NATIONAL MONETARY AUTONOMY

Of all the arguments advanced in favour of exchange-rate flexibility prior to the transition to floating in 1973, the expected regain of national monetary autonomy was without doubt the single most important one in the European countries. This was understandable in the light of both practical experience and prevailing theoretical notions.

As regards practical experience, German, Dutch and Swiss policy-makers were distressed by the implications for their domestic monetary policies of the commitment to intervene in exchange markets to keep their currencies within the prescribed band *vis-à-vis* the dollar. The strong impact of changes in US monetary policy on interest rates and money supplies in Europe had drawn severe criticism already in 1969–70, when US monetary tightening and subsequent relaxation had prompted large outflows of capital from Europe in 1969 and subsequent reflows. With cyclical developments slightly out of phase on the two sides of the Atlantic, the Europeans found the gyrations 'imposed' on them incompatible with their own policy aims; and they claimed they lacked the institutional prerequisites for effective sterilization policies, the solution then proposed by US officials. But the European hope in 1971, when the dollar began to float, was still that one more realignment would preserve the system of fixed rates.

Contrary to expectations, the Smithsonian realignment of December 1971, and the widening of the intervention band which accompanied it, did not help significantly. Interventions were occasionally significant in 1972, and in the final months of the fixed-rate system in early 1973 they reached truly unprecedented proportions; the Bundesbank bought more than $8 billion in February–March 1983. It had become axiomatic that in order to regain control of domestic monetary conditions, the intervention obligations *vis-à-vis* the inherently unstable dollar had to be abolished completely.

The feeling that exchange-rate flexibility had to come was shared, though with more misgivings, by the managers of Europe's weaker currencies. The UK government, profoundly affected by its long struggle in the 1960s to maintain the parity of sterling at $2.80, had learned that the November 1967 parity of $2.40 did not fully remove the external straitjacket on domestic policy. By the time of the Smithsonian Agreement, which reversed most of the 1967 devaluation, the UK authorities were already in the midst of an ambitious experiment in expansionary policy, a 'dash for growth', including a remarkable dismantling of existing monetary controls (the Competition and Credit Control Reform of 1971). This quest for monetary autonomy was not compatible with a fixed rate for sterling. Although the UK authorities referred mainly to the pressures on their currency within the joint-margins arrangement in the European Community ('the snake'), which they had joined less than two months earlier, they abandoned all exchange-rate commitments in June 1972. Italy was no more at ease with its commitments, which it initially tried to sustain by extending capital controls and by allowing the rate for financial transactions to float. And France, which had long been the prime advocate of fixed, or at least tightly managed exchange rates, had introduced similar devices in 1971. They were originally intended to dampen inflows of capital and upward pressures on the franc in the period preceding the Smithsonian Agreement, but they soon proved equally applicable in the outward direction. It was not until January 1974, after the first oil-price shock, that the French authorities pulled the franc out of the European currency arrangements; traditional French antipathies against floating had weakened, although they remained stronger than in the Federal Republic of Germany and other major European countries.[6]

Whatever the differences in attitudes and initial concerns within Europe, there was no doubt a widespread consensus that fixed rates had to be abolished and that flexibility would restore a substantial degree of monetary autonomy to Europe as a whole – though not necessarily to individual countries, if some joint management of intra-European currency relationships were to be retained. There was also widespread agreement that the increasingly frequent efforts at crisis management of exchange rates preceding the 1971–3 realignments had put US–European relations under damaging strain, because the respective national interests were clearly perceived so differently on the two sides of the Atlantic. This view was certainly shared by the US government, whose officials had borne the brunt of the very substantial efforts that went into the international monetary negotiations.[7] Most of the US officials tended initially to take a less negative view of the feasibility of a fixed-but-adjustable rate system than most of the Europeans, after the dollar had been devalued and depreciated in the course of 1971–3 by far more than they had themselves thought necessary. They were also more favourable to the notion of maintaining some objective indicators to guide the management of exchange rates, as exemplified in their proposal for a reserve indicator in the Committee of Twenty.[8] But they were at least as unhappy as the Europeans about the tendency for the dying Bretton Woods system to create apparent maximum tension without any lasting achievements.

The official expectation that flexible rates would restore a much greater degree of autonomy and effectiveness to monetary policy, which seemed to have become nearly powerless in the final years of the Bretton Woods system, appeared then to have a strong underpinning in theoretical and empirical economics. In the former area, the influential work of Fleming[9] and Mundell[10] had strikingly modified thinking about the relative impact of fiscal and monetary policy. The effectiveness of monetary policy in affecting domestic output and employment would be greatly increased by adding, in a system of flexible exchange rates, the transmission channel through appreciation and depreciation, following a (relative) tightening of monetary policy in the home country. Conversely, fiscal policy would lose some of its impact, because the changes in the exchange rate induced by modifying tax rates and/or public expenditures tend to offset the initial fiscal thrust, as long as monetary policy is non-accommodating.

Such a reversal in the ranking of the policy instruments seemed of limited consequence, since the monetary authorities were seen at the time as having the main responsibility for the short-term management of demand near production capacity within the constraint of an acceptable long-run inflationary performance of the domestic economy. Although inflation rates were not widely divergent in the main OECD countries in the final years with fixed rates, the notion developed that differences in the structure of labour markets, in competitive practices among firms and in the degree of political tolerance of inflation were becoming sufficiently important to warrant gradual accommodation through changes in the exchange rate. This emerging divergence appeared particularly significant between, on the one hand, the United States after its unprecedented long boom in the 1960s and, on the other hand, the Federal Republic of Germany.

While the officials could find comforting analytical support in their desire for more flexible rates, they also had no difficulties in locating empirical studies that underpinned their view of fixed rates as unsustainable in a world of high capital mobility. For example, the Bundesbank was quick to endorse the results of an important study by two IMF economists, which claimed to show that, on average, as much as 75–80 per cent of domestic policy actions affecting the monetary base in Germany was offset by private external capital flows within a month; in periods of speculation in a DM-appreciation, the offset was more than complete, leading to perverse results in the Bundesbank's stabilization efforts.[11] Though these particular estimates were subsequently shown to have had a pessimistic bias, because they failed to take fully into account the interaction of sterilization and offsetting capital flows, they reinforced the Bundesbank's instinctive and profound aversion to any intervention obligations – an attitude which has surfaced on several later occasions: in the German reluctance to consider a joint European-dollar policy, in the negotiations to replace the snake by the EMS, and in the critical response which any specific proposal to tighten the management of the global exchange-rate system invariably provokes from German officials.

In the light of the apparently well-founded anticipations at the transition to floating, one would expect that it would be easy to demonstrate a clear downward shift in the degree of interdependence of the US and European economies. If the image of US economic performance and policies being imposed on reluctant European partners prior to 1973 were correct, one would expect a significant *decoupling* of several key economic variables. With the exchange rate operating as a shock absorber, permitting the individual countries to retain more of the impact of their domestic policy actions and making each of them more robust *vis-à-vis* external shocks, both inflation rates – for which exchange-rate flexibility was designed to leave more scope for divergence – and the growth rates of output (and, more indirectly, employment) and of the money stock as well as interest rates should, in principle, be more loosely related after the introduction of flexible rates.

Yet most empirical studies show no such erosion of linkages after 1973, but rather, if anything, the opposite. This applies both to studies that focus on the early years of floating,[12] and to more recent work covering a full decade of floating.[13] There has apparently been no loosening of the interdependence between economic trends in the United States and in Europe at least up to 1982. There has been no clear change in the degree of uniformity of annual inflation rates in the United States and the four main European countries; it has remained relatively weak between the US and the FRG, while it is somewhat stronger and has increased a bit between the US and the three other large European countries. The correlation with the US rate of growth of output seems to have risen clearly in all four European countries, according to the two most recent studies.

These results are not, as Swoboda argues, necessarily an indictment of the insulating and autonomy-granting potential of flexible exchange rates. It is quite conceivable that these effects have been swamped in the post-1973 period by the impact of the two severe common shocks that hit the world economy in 1973–4 and in 1979–80, namely the two oil-price increase. The modified exchange-rate regime did not permit any escape from the policy dilemma posed by these shocks – regardless of the degree of (downward) exchange-rate flexibility countries were prepared to see for their currency, they could not avoid a contraction of output and upward pressure on the inflation rate. Arguably, real interdependence might have increased by more, if the fixed-rate system had still been in operation after 1973.

The results for monetary interactions are more striking, however. There is evidence in the recent studies referred to of stronger linkages between growth rates in the national money stocks not only within Europe, which is understandable since EC currency arrangements have imposed constraints on the extent to which policies could diverge within the Community, but also between the United States and the four main European countries. Swoboda finds similar results when looking at interest-rate changes (so-called 'innovations') rather than money-stock growth rates. Short-term monetary interdependence has not evidently diminished in the floating-rate regime, except possibly for countries that have accepted extreme fluctuations in their dollar exchange rate such as Switzerland.

The studies referred to are primitive in the sense that they move straight to correlations between the national variables in question, under each of the two exchange-rate regimes, without permitting an assessment of other changes in the environment than the degree of exchange-rate flexibility. If the post-1973 period was indeed marked by a greater common element in the world economic environment because of the oil shocks, this would in itself go some way toward explaining the tendency to greater parallelism in money growth rates and interest-rate changes. But there is a further explanation, stressed by de Grauwe and Fratianni.

The difference between the pre- and post-1973 periods is one of degree, rather than the dramatic break which conventional terminology suggests. There are two main modifications to be made to the simplified picture. The first is that exchange rates had become less stable in the final years of the Bretton Woods system; a number of important parity changes occurred from 1967 onwards. After early 1973, the main European countries did not abandon their exchange rates fully to market forces; they intervened very substantially to influence rates in a desired direction. Most of the time they did not get any assistance from the US authorities, the main exception being the efforts of the Carter Administration to stem the decline in the dollar in 1978.

But in addition to the continuation of exchange-rate objectives in a broad sense, there was also a more indirect factor at work, namely, the roughly parallel adoption of monetary targets in the United States and the main European countries. Most of the large industrial countries

perceived that they could not use their partly regained monetary autonomy to pursue ambitious expansionary monetary policies in the climate
of the mid-1970s. They deliberately constrained their room for
manoeuvre by announcing targets for the growth rates of one or more
of the main monetary aggregates. These targets were not set solely in
the light of domestic considerations; they were also seen as an indirect
way of stabilizing expectations in the exchange markets, and hence the
exchange rates themselves. Indeed, any observer looking at the targets
set in the initial 1975–8 period would have thought they were a good
recipe for fairly stable exchange rates between the major currencies.
That expectation proved incorrect; roughly parallel growth rates of
observed monetary aggregates and of the targets for them were not a
sufficient condition for stabilizing exchange rates.

After 1979 the Europeans had to undertake their interventions without coordination with the United States, and most of them used up a
substantial part of their dollar reserves in the effort to stem depreciation
(for example, about one-half for the UK, one-third for several other
European countries and 15 per cent for Germany).[14] One may say that
the Europeans initially clearly did not want a fuller decoupling from
US policies, and that hence they managed to combine the disadvantages of strong policy linkages with new ones in the form of misalignments.

A significant phase in this respect was the bottom of the recession,
after the second oil shock, when the Europeans, initially led by some of
the high-inflation countries, but from February 1981 strongly reinforced
by the Federal Republic of Germany, moved to tighten their interest
rates in order to diminish tensions with the United States, where interest rates had moved to far higher levels after the changes introduced
in Federal Reserve policy from late 1979. Despite indications that
efforts to reduce monetary growth sharply in Europe, and in the FRG
in particular, at a time of high and rising unemployment could drastically worsen the recession,[15] the Europeans gave precedence to their
anti-inflationary efforts.

This policy adjustment in Europe was largely unsuccessful in containing the rise in the dollar, which resumed later in the spring of 1981,
this time with an explanation that was less clearly monetary. This was
the first year of Mr Reagan's presidency and the prospect of higher
public expenditures mixed with tax cuts gave rise to higher interest-rate
– and possibly inflationary – expectations.

As this process unfolded, the sense of a policy dilemma became more
acute in Europe. The United States was increasingly following a policy
mix of very expansionary tax and expenditure policies, and relatively
tight monetary policies, which led to high nominal and real interest
rates. This did not greatly worry US public opinion, because some of

the tax changes, notably the Tax Equity and Fiscal Responsibility Act (ERTA) of 1981, tended to raise the expected after-tax return to real investment; the decline in inflation at the same time automatically improved depreciation provisions. From 1982, the brighter outlook for sales helped to spur several categories of investment. Finally, some of the rise in US interest rates could be attributed to financial deregulation, which was popular with the public. The US economy was, in short, well cushioned in both economic and political terms against any reversal of the shift to higher interest rates. The only group that might have mounted an effective resistance would have been the producers of tradables, but they do not carry sufficient weight in the relatively closed US economy to muster widespread sympathy for the squeeze on them through dollar appreciation, which has been the main other financial effect of the policy mix. Real interest rates have been allowed to remain high, and the pressure to change policy significantly is still weak. The Federal Reserve has maintained a fairly rigid stance by sticking to moderate growth rates for the monetary aggregates, though with one important exception between September 1982 and the summer of 1983, when the recovery still was in doubt and high real-dollar interest rates were seen as an additional factor (with the US recession) in aggravating the international debt situation. But after the US economy picked up strongly from early 1983, the Federal Reserve could again pursue fairly tight targets.

Over this period the European countries have to a substantial extent decoupled their interest rates from those in the United States. As figure 6.3 shows, real interest rates in the Federal Republic of Germany have drifted slightly down to historically normal levels, despite a renewed updrift in US rates, and the spread is currently larger than at any time since the start of floating. Other European countries, particularly EMS members, have geared themselves increasingly to German rather than the US rates, and have – despite their complaints to the contrary. Nominal interest differentials within the EMS tend to reflect inflation differentials, but less than fully, since intra-EMS exchange rates have become more stable over 1983–4.

What these different phases in monetary policy indicate is that the extent to which monetary autonomy is exercised in the floating-rate system is primarily a question of the policy responses to the policy mix in the United States. At a time when inflationary fears dominate in policy-making, as they did in 1981, Europeans may choose to align themselves on US monetary policies that in themselves would be regarded as unduly tight in a domestic perspective. It seems appropriate to question whether they might have had a better trade-off by avoiding some of the considerable fiscal contraction which most European countries have been pursuing since 1981, in other words to have

FIGURE 6.3   REAL INTEREST RATES AND REAL $/DM INDEX

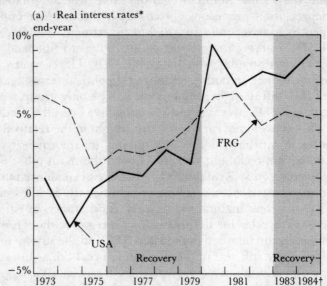

(a) Real interest rates*
end-year

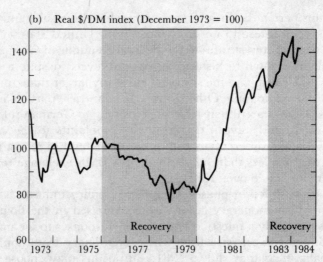

(b)   Real $/DM index (December 1973 = 100)

*Based on commercial bank lending rates to prime borrowers.
†Mid-year.
Sources: (a)   Morgan Guaranty Trust
              (b)   Philips & Drew.

copied elements of US fiscal policy rather than monetary policy.[16] The course of fiscal policy in the US and the rest of the OECD have become steadily more divergent (see figure 6.4); in the light of the primacy given to fiscal contraction – *Konsolidierungspolitik* – in Europe, and with inflation continuing to decelerate, it was, on the other hand, unavoidable that the Europeans would sooner or later turn to some monetary stimulation and use the more powerful transmission of such policies through further exchange-rate depreciation from the already low levels of their currencies. In the first half of 1983, the EMS countries went through one such period of relative monetary expansion; and the further improvement of competitiveness and the decline in interest rates helped to trigger whatever limited expansion we have seen in Europe in 1983–4. Since then policies have again become more cautious, but decoupling has been allowed to proceed further.

The cost of this deliberate choice of macroeconomic policy mix in the United States, as in Europe, has been some further considerable misalignment of exchange rates. The lower panel of figure 6.3 suggests that real rate differentials have up to now been a major determinant of the evolution of the $/DM rate.

In the absence of major shifts in the risk assessments of investing in dollar relative to other currency assets, the key to modifications in the exchange-rate relationship lies in the scope for affecting relative real interest rates. From a European viewpoint, however, it is not a fair criticism of the flexible exchange-rate system that it has removed once more the monetary policy autonomy that was expected of it. The truth is rather that flexible exchange rates have made monetary policy more powerful in demand management and that European countries have exploited this room for manoeuvre by conducting a relatively expansionary policy – relative, at least, to the tight policies pursued over most of the recent period by the Federal Reserve Board.

The basic change in the context within which monetary policy operates now relative to the fixed-rate period therefore lies in the transmission mechanism through the exchange rate and the willingness of countries to tolerate the implications of their own national monetary policies. Constraints of this kind may be sufficiently severe to warrant the conclusion that monetary policy in a more fundamental sense has not become more autonomous under flexible rates than it was under fixed rates.

It may be worth ending this chapter by noting that the fixed-rate arrangements prevailing among the EMS members have not precluded some residual element of monetary autonomy. Once financial markets perceive that the authorities are determined to maintain approximately stable exchange rates and adjust monetary policies in case of ultimate

FIGURE 6.4   DIVERGENT FISCAL POLICIES, 1981–4

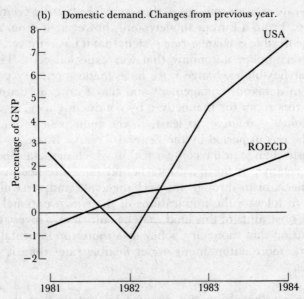

(a)   Fiscal impulse. Cumulative change in structural
budget deficit from 1980.

(b)   Domestic demand. Changes from previous year.

ROECD   The rest of the OECD area (the figures in the
top panel are for the six largest OECD
countries other than the United States.)

Source: OECD Economic Outlook, no. 35, July 1984.

need, there is a certain latitude in the short-run management of monetary trends. But possibly these experiences of the EMS members are not easily generalizable to the world level; after all, fiscal policies have been far more in line among the EMS members than between Europe and the United States. This, in connection with the confidence that exchange-rate policies have inspired, has made possible the limited autonomy that remains even under fixed rates within the EMS.[17]

What can be done, given the two basic conclusions emerging from this paper, namely, that exchange-rate flexibility is excessive between the dollar and the European currencies (plus the yen), but that there is no early prospect for any global arrangement to remove existing misalignments gradually and to stabilize exchange rates around sustainable levels?

There are basically three approaches to this problem – if one agrees that exchange-rate misalignments have entailed more costs than benefits, at least if one looks ahead to the unwinding of present imbalances. The first is to aim for policy coordination in a more fundamental sense in the major countries, that is, for the design of fiscal and monetary policies to keep the international as well as the domestic effects in mind. That would, in a medium-term perspective, be sufficient, but the approach is hardly feasible, given the complexities of domestic policy formulation in the main countries, and notably in the United States. The second is to attack the excessive exchange-rate flexibility at its source – the high degree of capital mobility. Several authors (and quite a few continental European policy-makers) have suggested the introduction of a tax on capital – in practice, probably all – transactions across frontiers in order to dampen capital mobility. Here, both the practical feasibility of the proposal and its theoretical justification are in doubt; one could well imagine very large exchange-rate movements also in a world of low capital mobility.

The third approach is the more interesting and potentially promising: to aim for implicit policy coordination by exploiting fully the information contained in the level of the exchange rate and its movements. This is the topic of Professor McKinnon's proposal in the following chapter; I have little to add to it, except to express the general sympathy that the principle of giving monetary policy a more international orientation and to do so through a fairly simple policy rule related to the exchange rate is fully in line with the arguments in the present chapter. But the present situation is marked by misalignments so severe that it will be very difficult to engage in any constructive dialogue on monetary coordination à la McKinnon. There is no understanding in the United States – and possibly rightly so, given the nervous state of financial markets and of the exchange market prompted by the US fiscal deficit – for a request to ease monetary policy significantly.

Maybe a market process could bring the United States and Europe to a point where monetary coordination became feasible. The scenario I have in mind is the following. Assume a substantial dollar depreciation (at approximately parallel growth rates on the two sides of the Atlantic), but not so far as to remove fully the present overvaluation of the dollar in terms of the European currencies. At some point, the US interest in avoiding additional inflation through allowing the dollar to continue to slide will converge with European interest in avoiding a further loss in competitiveness *vis-à-vis* the United States through continued real appreciation and create the basis for some common action to stabilize exchange rates as a level that is seen by both sides as sustainable.

There is an asymmetry between upward and downward movements in the dollar; the former may be criticized on both sides of the Atlantic, but it is hard to address in a coordinated manner, because it contains compensating features that are attractive to both: inflation fades in the United States, and export-led growth picks up in Europe. The opposite scenario of a depreciating dollar is more likely to be met with joint alarm and a certain willingness to co-operate. That was in evidence in 1978, when the Carter Administration co-operated with Europe in interventions and some reorientation of monetary policy. That occurred, however, at a very low level for the dollar. It is a major task for policymakers in both the United States and Europe to respond jointly the next time while the main exchange rates are closer to a longer-run sustainable level, hence avoiding a new long cycle of initially undervaluation and subsequently renewed overvaluation of the dollar.

NOTES

1   J. Williamson, *The Exchange-Rate System*, Policy Analyses in International Economics, Vol. 5 (Institute for International Economics, Washington, DC, 1983).
2   M. Goldstein, 'Have flexible exchange rates handicapped monetary policy?', *Princeton Special Papers in Economics*, no. 14 (1980).
3   Cf. two rather massive surveys of the literature: International Monetary Fund, 'Exchange rate volatility and world trade', *Occasional Paper*, no. 28 (August 1984); and Federal Reserve Board, 'Effects of exchange rate variability on international trade and other economic variables: a review of the literature', *Staff Studies*, vol. 130 (by V. S. Farrell *et al.*) (1983).
4   Group of Thirty, *Foreign Exchange Markets under Floating Rates* (New York, 1980).
5   S. N. Marris, 'The problem of the dollar', unpublished testimony to the US Congress, Washington, DC, 7 August 1984.
6   This difference in attitude surfaced several times in the 1970s: in the French paternity for the concept of 'fixed-but-adjustable' central rates in the Outline of Reform for the international monetary system in 1974; in the French efforts to give more precision to the obligations to correct disorderly conditions in the exchange market, resulting in the compromise at the 1975 Rambouillet Summit and leading

ultimately to the Second Amendment to the IMF Articles of Agreement embodying IMF 'surveillance' of exchange rates; and in the French interest in strengthening EC currency arrangements through more rules in 1974 (the Fourcade Plan), a common dollar policy in 1975 and the launching of the European Monetary System in 1978–9. Basically, France, has always been more confident than the Federal Republic of Germany that it could manage its domestic monetary conditions in accordance with domestic policy requirements, despite obligations to intervene in the exchange market, a difference in attitude attributable to the more limited international role of the franc relative to the DM, and to the greater readiness of France to restrain capital movements and to use quantitative methods, in particular credit ceilings, in domestic monetary control.

7   Cf. R. Solomon, *The International Monetary System: 1945–76: An Insider's View* (New York, 1977).

8   See Committee of Twenty, *International Monetary Reform* (International Monetary Fund, Washington, DC, 1974).

9   M. Fleming, 'Domestic financial policies under fixed and under floating exchange rates', *IMF Staff Papers* (November 1962).

10   R. A. Mundell, 'The appropriate use of monetary and fiscal policy for internal and external stability', *IMF Staff Papers* (March 1962).

11   Cf. P. J. J. Kouri and M. Porter, 'International capital flows and portfolio equilibrium', *Journal of Political Economy* (May/June 1974).

12   For example, B. Hickman and S. Schleicher, 'The interdependence of national economies and the synchronization of economic fluctuations; evidence from the Link Project', *Weltwirtschaftliches Archiv*, vol. 114 (1978).

13   For example, A. K. Swoboda, 'Exchange rate regimes and US–European policy interdependence', *IMF Staff Papers* (March 1983); P. de Grauwe and M. Fratianni, 'Economic interdependence since the early seventies', *International Economics Research Paper* no. 43 (Center for Economic Studies, Leuven, 1984); and S. Micossi and T. Padoa-Schioppa, 'Short-term interest rate linkages between the United States and Europe', *Temi di discussione*, no. 33 (Banca d'Italia, Rome, 1984).

14   Cf. de Grauwe and Fratianni, 'Economic interdependence'.

15   Cf. J. Artus, 'Effects of US monetary restraint on the DM–$ exchange rate and the German economy', International Monetary Fund, (April 1982).

16   As argued by, for example, Marris, in 'The problem of the dollar', and R. Layard *et al.*, 'The case for unsustainable growth', *CEPS Papers* no. 8/9 (Centre for European Policy Studies, Brussels, 1984).

17   Cf. N. Thygesen, 'Exchange-rate policies and monetary targets in the EMS countries', in R. Masera and R. Triffin (ed.), *Europe's Money* (O.U.P. Oxford, 1984).

Comment 1

STANLEY W. BLACK

The international trade specialists who have been wrestling with enormous trade imbalances will no doubt be happy to hear from Professor Thygesen that international monetary economists have given up on the view that freely floating exchange rates can be relied upon to adjust trade imbalances effectively, because of rational expectations. Of course in Chicago this idea dies hard, as they tend to believe that an *observed* exchange rate is an *equilibrium* exchange rate, rendering the concept of overvaluation nugatory!

Why is it clear that the dollar is overvalued? Surely not simply because the United States current account is in deficit. Rather, it is because the current-account deficit and its underlying cause in the federal government budget deficit are not sustainable in the medium term. We know that the US current account has switched from an approximate balance in 1980 to −2.7 per cent of GNP in 1984, as the federal government deficit has increased from 2.3 per cent of GNP to 4.6 per cent. The current-account deficit is not sustainable because of its sectoral effects on domestic production and employment (if for no other reason), and the government budget deficit because it entails an interest bill that will rise from 75 per cent of the total deficit to 80 per cent over the next few years. Thus we will be borrowing to pay the interest, a condition for which the debtor less developed countries (LDCs) are rightly faulted. This is not sustainable.

If one looks at a graph of the current account and real exchange rate for the United States, the Federal Republic of Germany or Japan since 1973, it looks like the track of a sailing boat with a drunken sailor at the tiller, or more precisely like an autocorrelated random variable. So a natural question is: why accept such large variations in nominal variables which have large real effects? Why not just peg the exchange rate and use monetary policy to guarantee the peg? We know that it can be done, both in theory and (imperfectly) in practice. We have the examples of the Bretton Woods system and the European Monetary System as evidence.

When one takes a detailed look at the fluctuations of the dollar, as Professor Thygesen has done and as I have done in a recent paper,[1] one finds a changing series of causes of the ups and downs of the dollar *vis-à-vis* other currencies. During the period 1973 to early 1974, the dollar moved inversely to the interest-rate differential, apparently in response to the initial conditions in early 1973 of an overvalued dollar, the resumption of intervention by central banks in mid-1973, the oil embargo of late 1973, and the end of the capital controls in early 1974 by the United States and the Federal Republic of Germany. From mid-1974 to the end of 1975, interest-rate differentials seemed to move the trade-weighted exchange rate, but the current account also rose and fell with the dollar. Then, from the beginning of 1976 to late 1978, the exchange rate again moved inversely to the nominal interest-rate differential, as changes in the differential inflation rate appeared to dominate. Since late 1980 the dollar has been strong, due to high real interest rates in the United States, problems with LDC debt leading to capital flight, the relative movements of fiscal policies in the US and other OECD countries (pointed out in Thygesen's figure 6.4), and other factors.

Such a chronology makes it clear that differences in monetary growth rates do not explain all of the exchange-rate fluctuations; rather, the explanation seems to be a mixture of monetary and real factors. If it were only due to monetary factors, then the discipline over monetary policy offered by pegged exchange rates might help to reduce monetary divergences, including reducing the variability of US monetary policy. But this favourable outcome may not necessarily follow, as there is abundant evidence that the monetary discipline of a pegged rate has not been particularly effective on the members of the European Monetary System. Nor would it be effective on the United States, given its strong focus on internal objectives for macroeconomic policy.

Susan Strange's chapter notes that US monetary policy, as reflected in the variability of real interest rates during the 1970s and 1980s, has not provided a steady hand on the tiller of the international monetary system. In fact, it is clear that low real interest rates encouraged less developed countries to borrow too much in the 1970s, while today's high real rates are forcing them to retrench.

I can think of three reasons for keeping a degree of monetary independence between the United States and Europe. First, there is the

difference in openness of the economies, which favours the use of a floating exchange rate for external adjustment by the United States, but
favours pegged exchange rates for individual European countries seeking domestic stability. Second, political differences, both over time and
across countries, lead to differences in willingness to accept fluctuations
in real interest rates and real wage rates. These differences in social
attitudes towards risk lead to differences in the willingness to use
monetary policy for internal objectives. Third is the desire of policy-
makers to keep 'room for manoeuvre' to use monetary and fiscal
policies for domestic purposes, whether socially beneficial or not.

There are also three reasons to repeg exchange rates, or at least to
reduce the magnitude of fluctuations. First, the 'discipline' argument
suggests that it is wise to *reduce* the authorities' 'room for manoeuvre', if
they are inclined to act as the United States did during 1981–4 or
France during 1981–2. Second is the desire to reduce the costs of mis-
aligned exchange rates, as explained by Thygesen's arguments. A
third argument, due to Harrod,[2] has recently been formalized by
Black.[3] Reduced exchange-rate risk might induce greater stabilizing of
private capital flows, because the responsiveness of capital flows to interest differentials varies inversely with both the level of risk aversion
and the degree of perceived exchange-rate risk.

The balance of these arguments can of course lead in either direction. For myself, I tend to agree with Thygesen and McKinnon on the
desirability of reduced exchange-rate flexibility, and I agree with
McKinnon that monetary policy is an important tool for reducing the
variability of exchange rates. Where I disagree with McKinnon is on
his unwillingness to go beyond purely domestic monetary measures to
reduce it. Only if assets denominated in different currencies were
perfect substitutes in private portfolios – that is, if agents were risk
neutral – would there be no additional benefit from using *external* instruments of monetary policy such as central-bank intervention in the
exchange market.

But the desire for monetary autonomy is likely to prevent either a
return to pegged rates or a strong orientation of US monetary policy to
international factors.

NOTES

1   Stanley W. Black, 'Changing causes of exchange rate fluctuations', *Brookings
    Discussion Papers in International Economics*, no. 12 (Brookings Institution,
    Washington, DC, January 1984).
2   Roy F. Harrod, *Reforming the World's Money* (Macmillan, London, 1965)
3   Stanley W. Black, 'The effect of alternative intervention policies on the variability
    of exchange rates: the Harrod effect', in J. S. Bhandari (ed.), *Exchange Rate Manage-
    ment under Uncertainty* (MIT Press, Cambridge, Mass., 1985), pp. 73–82.

Comment 2

PAUL DE GRAUWE

Niels Thygesen's paper is an excellent survey of the issues concerning the scope for national monetary policies in a world of exchange-rate flexibility. There is little I have to quarrel about, so my comments will consist mainly of qualifications.

One qualification I would like to make concerns the nature of monetary interdependence since the inception of floating exchange rates. We observe that the yearly (short-term) growth rates of the money stocks and of the inflation rates of the major countries have been more correlated with each other during the post-1973 period than during the Bretton Woods period. The long-run growth rates of money stocks and of inflation rates, however, have diverged more across countries since 1973 than before that date. Thus the empirical evidence about monetary interdependence during the flexible exchange-rate period seems to be rather subtle. The new exchange-rate regime of the post-1973 period did allow countries to determine their long-run inflation rate more or less independently from the rest of the world, as most economists had predicted. However, countries found it very difficult to control the yearly movements in their price levels, and to shield these from outside shocks. In short, the post-1973 international monetary system was characterized by considerable long-run national monetary independence, but relatively strong short-term dependence of national price levels and money stocks on world monetary conditions.

A second, more essential qualification I would like to make concerns Niels Thygesen's view about the role of the EMS. The question I would like to ask is whether the EMS has allowed its members to achieve a greater amount of financial autonomy *vis-à-vis* the US than

other non-EMS countries in Europe. Here the evidence is clear: since
1979 the level and the variability of nominal and real interest rates has
been as high inside the EMS as outside the EMS in Europe. Particularly
disturbing is the fact that the small EMS countries have fared significantly worse than comparably small European countries outside the
EMS, as far as the level of their interest rates is concerned. Tables
6.2.1 and 6.2.2 illustrate these points.

It is of course true that the EMS has allowed greater exchange-rate
stability within the system, which is a positive achievement of the
system. However, the EMS has not allowed its members to achieve
greater independence from the financial shocks that originated in the
US than other European countries that followed an individual approach
in their exchange-rate management.

The main reasons for this failure to achieve greater monetary independence from the US are two fold. First, there is the role of the Federal
Republic of Germany, which, especially up to 1982, tried – mostly
unsuccessfully – to stem the upward movement of the dollar by selling
large amounts of foreign exchange and by allowing the growth rate of
the German money stock to decline. In so doing, the US deflationary

TABLE 6.2.1   NOMINAL AND REAL INTEREST RATES (GOVERNMENT
BOND YIELDS): AVERAGE DURING 1974-8 AND 1979-83

	Nominal interest rates		Real interest rates	
	(1974–8)	(1979–83)	(1974–8)	(1979–83)
Belgium	8.7	12.1	−0.4	5.1
Netherlands	8.7	9.9	0.7	4.5
Denmark	13.8	17.5	3.4	7.8
Ireland	14.2	15.7	0.0	1.0
FRG	7.7	8.6	2.9	3.8
France	9.5	13.5	−0.8	1.7
Italy	12.6	17.9	−3.8	0.9
Mean	10.7	13.7	0.3	3.5
US	8.1	11.7	0.2	2.8
UK	13.8	13.0	−1.8	1.7
Japan	8.1	8.2	−3.5	4.0
Austria	9.0	9.2	2.4	4.2
Norway	7.5	11.5	−1.5	2.2
Sweden	9.1	12.2	−0.8	2.1
Switzerland	5.2	4.6	0.4	0.1
Mean	8.7	10.1	−0.7	2.4

The real interest rate is defined as the difference between the government bond yield and the
observed rate of inflation. Thus, the real interest-rate concept is an *ex post* (realized) concept.
Source: IMF, *International Financial Statistics*.

TABLE 6.2.2   MEASURES OF VARIABILITY OF NOMINAL AND REAL
INTEREST RATES. (GOVERNMENT BOND YIELDS)

	Standard deviation		Mean absolute change	
	(1974–8)	*(1979–83)*	*(1974–8)*	*(1979–83)*
Nominal interest rates				
Belgium	0.2	1.5	0.5	1.4
Netherlands	0.7	1.1	0.9	1.3
Denmark	0.7	2.4	1.3	2.4
Ireland	2.2	1.4	2.7	1.8
FRG	1.7	1.0	1.2	1.4
France	0.5	2.3	0.9	1.8
Italy	1.7	2.6	1.4	2.0
US	0.3	1.5	0.6	1.5
UK	1.0	1.3	1.4	1.2
Japan	1.2	0.7	1.0	1.0
Austria	0.6	1.9	0.5	1.0
Sweden	0.8	1.1	0.5	0.9
Switzerland	1.4	0.7	1.0	0.7
Real Interest rates				
Belgium	2.9	0.7	2.6	0.8
Netherlands	1.7	0.8	1.5	1.2
Denmark	1.8	1.8	3.7	2.0
Ireland	3.7	2.4	5.5	2.4
FRG	0.5	0.7	1.0	0.9
France	1.5	2.2	1.6	1.3
Italy	3.3	3.4	3.3	3.4
US	1.7	4.3	2.0	2.7
UK	4.4	3.7	5.5	3.8
Japan	5.6	1.6	5.7	1.8
Austria	1.6	0.7	0.9	0.7
Norway	1.6	2.3	1.7	2.5
Sweden	1.0	2.3	1.3	3.1
Switzerland	2.6	1.0	1.5	1.6

Source: IMF, *International Financial Statistics.*

monetary policy was transmitted to the FRG and, given the predominance of that country in the EMS, to the rest of the system.

The second major reason why it proved difficult to insulate the
system from outside disturbances is related to the recurrent lack of
credibility of the existing exchange-rate structure in the system. Thus
outside disturbances easily generate changes in expectations about
these official exchange rates, and force the EMS countries involved to
adjust their monetary policies.

Comment 3

HENK JAGER

Any evaluation of the functioning of competing exchange-rate systems must be based on some criteria. Even if the evaluation is only concerned with the interaction with monetary policy, as in Professor Thygesen's contribution, the need for this choice of criteria remains. In this respect, Thygesen is mainly guided by the autonomy of national monetary policy which fixed and flexible exchange rates allow.

He develops his views in a clear and useful analysis, which starts with a description of the increased exchange-rate volatility. Thereupon, the author continues with a qualitative approach of net costs of unconstrained exchange-rate flexibility. Four sorts of costs are identified: namely, adjustment costs of temporary misalignments; a slow-down in capital formation because of increased uncertainty in the sector of tradables; a rise in protectionism; and an upward push in world inflation. Against these costs Thygesen sets two potential benefits of floating: the fact that a substantial degree of autonomy of monetary policy in Europe was regained; and the restored effectiveness of monetary policy which, according to the author, 'seemed to have become nearly powerless in the final years of the Bretton Woods system'. With respect to the latter benefit Thygesen feels a firm conviction, whereas he has some doubts about the former. This is witnessed by both the title of his final section ('The myth of national monetary autonomy') and the concluding remark that the disadvantages of the transmission mechanism through the exchange rate and constraints on the willingness of countries to tolerate the implications of their own national monetary policies may be sufficiently severe to state that 'monetary policy in a more fundamental sense has not become more autonomous under flexible rates'.

Thygesen's treatment of the benefits of flexible exchange rates is to some extent open for debate. The significance of one of these benefits needs clarification, the significance of the other can be questioned, and at least one new benefit can be added. This viewpoint will be elaborated below. After that, I shall briefly discuss the merits of a quantification of the costs and benefits of different exchange-rate systems, which might eventually lead to the choice of an optimal one.

AUTONOMY

The hesitation Thygesen shows in concluding that there is increased autonomy – that is, being in control of domestic policy-makers – of monetary policy under floating rates is, in my opinion, needless. If a country's monetary authorities do not intervene in the foreign-exchange market, domestic money supply is completely exogenous. The foreign-source component of the monetary base, which is present in the case of fixed exchange rates, is then completely absent. Consequently, floating rates imply a wholly autonomous monetary base. The transition from truly fixed to flexible exchange rates, moreover, disconnects the domestic interest rate and the interest rate abroad. The divergence between the two is determined by the expected rate of change of the domestic currency's value expressed in foreign currencies, enlarged by a possible risk premium. Although these determining factors are by no means autonomous in the sense defined before, they can be influenced by the domestic policy-makers. Therefore, they probably gain their hold over the domestic interest rate too.

Thygesen's hesitation to state that the autonomy has been increased ensues from a somewhat confusing interweaving of this potential benefit with the *costs* of flexible exchange rates. The transition to flexibility does indeed create new channels by which the insulation of the domestic economy for external disturbances may be threatened. But the conduct of monetary policy to reduce these new costs – which are extensively described by Thygesen – must not be mixed up with a loss of autonomy. Not until there is a form of international coordination of national monetary policies in order to repel these violations of insulation, will autonomy decline anew.

EFFECTIVENESS

According to Thygesen, monetary policy has certainly become more powerful in demand management as a consequence of the introduction of floating exchange rates. Surely this thesis can be deduced incontestably from the theory of open economies developed in the 1960s. If the exchange rate is flexible, for example, an expansionary monetary policy both increases domestic demand and leads to an incipient balance-of-payments deficit. In fact, this will not come through, but it will appear as a depreciation which, in turn, causes a continued rise in demand for domestic products.

In the 1970s, however, this theoretical Keynesian framework was subjected to a thorough extension. It has been enriched with an endogenous aggregate supply function; the interdependence between nominal wages and prices, whereby wages are also sensitive for terms-of-trade effects; financial wealth; the explicit recognition of budget constraints; and exchange-rate expectations as well. It appears that, by means of an economic model that is extended in such a realistic way, monetary policy may lose its effectiveness entirely.[1]

As a consequence of the existence of budget restrictions, monetary policy will not only involve a change in the money stock, but this change will have to be accompanied by an equal and opposite change in the liabilities of the private sector. This reveals that an expansionary monetary policy has two equal and opposite impacts upon private financial wealth: a rise as a result of the increased money supply, and a decline of wealth caused by the offsetting increase in liabilities (or a fall in net securities) of the private sector. For that reason, there is no stimulus on domestic output and demand emanating from a growth of private financial wealth.

Due to the expansionary monetary policy, however, an incipient excess money supply and excess demand for securities are created. Unlike the situation in a system of fixed exchange rates, in the event of floating rates these disequilibria will not disappear by means of the purchase of foreign securities alone. Under floating rates, the exchange rate will depreciate with diametrically opposed influences on domestic output and the demand for domestically produced goods. On the one hand, domestic output will decline as a result of the rise in import prices consequent upon the depreciation. This follows from the fact that in the model there is complete price indexation for wages and, in addition, domestic output depends inversely on wages deflated by the price level of only *domestically* produced goods. These are, indeed, not unrealistic assumptions for the 1970s. On the other hand, the demand for domestic output increases by means of the terms-of-trade effect upon demand through both a shift of demand away from imported goods and an enlargement of export demand. This divergence, which occurs between demand for and production of domestic goods, leads to a rise in the price of these goods.

Assume now, provisionally, that the ultimate changes in the exchange rate and the price of domestic output, which are deduced above, are equal. In the case of completely indexed wages, these changes will result in two *equally large*, but oppositely directed effects on domestic output. In contrast, such changes in exchange rate and price of domestic output have a net influence on the demand for this output. The reason is that the rise in the price of domestic output has a terms-of-trade effect as well as a real wealth effect; each of these two effects will diminish demand for domestic output. Equally large effects exist as a result of the depreciation, whereby only the terms-of-trade effect is oppositely directed compared with that generated by the price rise. On balance, therefore, demand for domestic output will be lowered, whereas output itself has not changed. Consequently, equilibrium in the market for domestically produced goods will not be restored by means of *equal* ultimate changes in the exchange rate and the price level of domestic output, but only if the rise in the latter will be smaller than the rate of depreciation. For that reason, the new equilibrium will be characterized by *domestic output* being *lower* than it was before the expansionary monetary policy was conducted.

It can easily be shown that the negative influence of monetary policy on domestic output disappears as soon as the wealth effect on demand for domestic goods is absent. The expected positive relation between an expansionary monetary policy and growth of output only comes into being if, for example, there is no longer any wage compensation for a deterioration of the terms of trade. In view of the complete price indexation of the wage rate in several European countries during the 1970s, a negative or neutral impact of monetary policy upon output was not unrealistic during that period with floating exchange rates.

DEGREES OF FREEDOM

An advantage of the transition to managed floating rates – which Thygesen pretty well neglected – is unquestionably the fact that it augments the degrees of freedom to pursue domestic goals of economic policy. This results from the fact that because of the transition the framework of economic ends and means changed in the following sense.

The exchange rate and the balance of payments were eliminated as goals. After the transition to floating, indeed, the exchange rate is allowed to exceed the intervention points, while the balance-of-payments equilibrium is realized automatically – by means of private market forces alone. So, in principle, the external ends of economic policy disappeared. This implies an increase in the degrees of freedom for economic policy. This development has partially counteracted because the exchange rate's par value was dropped as a policy instrument. In the event of the adjustable peg system of Bretton Woods, the par value could be considered as an instrument, since the monetary authorities could at times change its value, which functioned as a guidance for speculators to a certain extent.[2] Under floating rates, however, the par value is absent.

Of course, the two then external economic goals retain their significance as intermediate variables, with their sometimes disturbing effects on the internal economic goals. With regard to the exchange rate, these effects are described in the section of Thygesen's study entitled 'Costs and benefits of misalignment'. They may even induce the monetary authorities to adopt certain restrictions on exchange-rate variation. But because of the present freedom to choose its own exchange-rate system, a country's room for manoeuvre to pursue domestic goals in economic policy will even in these circumstances remain larger compared with a system of permanently fixed rates or of an adjustable peg.

THE MERITS OF QUANTIFICATION

Finally, I will end with some remarks about the practical merits of quantifying the only qualitative reflections on competing exchange-rate systems. As long as the implications of each of the systems are not quantified, their significance for policy is rather small. With respect to the implications, Thygesen suggests that they are 'difficult and inherently impossible to quantify'. I agree with the first part of this statement, but not with the second. Starting from an econometric model with an endogenous exchange rate, it is possible by means of simulation or optimal control studies to quantify the individual implications, and even – as far as optimal control techniques are applied – to add the quantitative results of these individual implications for each exchange-rate system. Another important difference between these quantification methods is that in an application of optimal control techniques other instruments of economic policy, besides the exchange-rate system, will simultaneously be adapted to the newly created situation too. Thygesen underlines the importance of such a possibility, without however referring to quantification methods, when he states that: 'the national policies required to sustain such a constellation [namely, continuous adherence to equilibrium exchange rates as opposed to misalignment] would have been substantially different from those actually pursued, hence implying broader revisions of the entire macroeconomic scenario'. Optimal control techniques allow these revisions and even give them emphasis.

Although an application of optimal control techniques has a good many limitations, it is interesting in view of the preceding remarks to look at some results of a recent study which contains such an application to exchange-rate systems.[3] An econometric model and a macroeconomic loss function are the essential elements in an optimal control study. In the investigation concerned, they relate to the Netherlands. The model employed is a quarterly linear model estimated for the period 1967(I) –76(IV), using two-stage least squares. In principle, it is a dynamic Keynesian model and stresses the country's external relations. The exchange rate is endogenous, whereby the balance-of-payments identity, with clearly demonstrable portfolio-balance characteristics, determines this rate. By means of this model and a loss function, which is based on revealed preference, optimal Dutch policies are determined for the period 1970–6 under different exchange-rate arrangements.

As appears from the total losses presented in the study referred to, optimal managed floating diminishes the loss compared with the optimal adjustable-peg system, and both these arrangements are to be preferred to optimal free floating. The fact that managed floating is the best arrangement underlines the relevance of the advantage described above. The – at first sight – surprisingly bad result of free-floating rates arises from the impossibility of this system to use the stock of monetary reserves as an instrument of economic policy. Contrary to free floating, both managed floating, and the adjustable-peg system can, at least if desired, partly avoid the opportunity costs of monetary reserves.

The costs specified per target, in the study in question, demonstrate that the advantages of optimal managed floating with regard to the adjustable-peg system lie in a lower inflation rate and a current-account balance that better approaches the desired time-path. On the other hand, the relative drawbacks of managed floating are the volatility of the terms of trade (on the import side), unstable growth of real national product, and a lower average value of this product – although real national product ends up with a higher level in comparison with the result in the adjustable-peg system. Moreover, a considerable advantage of managed floating appears to be that all the instruments of economic policy track their desired time-paths better. Finally, it is worth noting that managed floating, in turn, is surpassed in attractiveness by a crawling-peg system, which uses a formula for parity change.

NOTES

1   This will be illustrated here with an example derived from H. Jager, 'The impact of the exchange rate system on the effectiveness and implementation of stabilization in the Netherlands', *De Economist*, vol. 127(1) (1979), pp. 158–60.

2   Cf. G. Haberler, 'How important is control over international reserves?, in R. A.
    Mundell and J. J. Polak (ed.), *The New International Monetary System* (New York,
    1977), pp. 111–32.
3   H. Jager, 'The optimal exchange-rate system and its significance for economic
    recovery', paper presented at the Conference on Monetary Conditions for Econ-
    omic Recovery, held in Amsterdam, in November 1984.

7

The Case for Internationalizing American Monetary Policy*

RONALD I. MCKINNON

For the 1971–83 period of volatile exchange rates and extensive official intervention (in dollars) by foreign central banks, how did international influences impinge on US prices and GNP? Here I show empirically that the dollar exchange rate turns out to be a robust leading indicator of fluctuations in American GNP and in the dollar prices of internationally tradable goods. As figures 7.1 and 7.2 indicate, the dollar depreciations of 1971–3 and 1977–8, and the great appreciation of 1981–3, did indeed signal the future course of American inflation and deflation. By largely ignoring the dollar exchange rate and money growth in other industrial countries, the US Federal Reserve System (FED) has, over the past fifteen years, thrown away valuable information for ironing out the American business cycle. Then, because the United States is at the centre of the world dollar standard, American cyclical fluctuations feed back into the rest of the world. Thus other central banks issuing convertible currencies – mainly those of Western Europe and Japan – have a vested interest in co-operating with the FED to better stabilize their mutual exchange rates and aggregate money growth.

THE FAILURE OF EMPIRICAL EXCHANGE-RATE MODELS

With floating fiat moneys, everybody knows that governments need not subordinate their monetary policies to maintain short-run exchange-rate

* This paper is adapted from chapter 4 of Ronald I. McKinnon, *An International Standard for Monetary Stabilization* (Institute for International Economics, Washington, DC, 1984).

stability – nor are they likely to converge to the same long-run rate
of price inflation. Moreover, if international capital can move freely,
foreign financial assets are the most conveniently liquid alternative to
holding money or bonds denominated in the domestic currency. Consequently any new information (news) – about future inflation,
political risk, interest rates, or the terms of trade of any one country
– causes the preferences of international investors to shift continually in
order to hedge against future uncertainty.

The resulting volatility, and sustained misalignments, in exchange
rates upsets foreign trade and domestic financial stability. Moreover,
these exchange fluctuations, based on shifting asset preferences, cannot
be predicted on the basis of past information on money growth, price
movements or trade surpluses.[1] Indeed this asset-market approach emphasizes the importance of news changing future expectations[2] such
that the current exchange rate varies randomly.

THE PROPOSAL FOR INTERNATIONAL MONETARY COORDINATION

My starting-point is to reverse the logic of this standard analysis. Accept
the fact that, without international monetary coordination, movements
in exchange rates cannot be successfully predicted. However, because
it does reflect changing future expectations, pressure on the exchange
rate contains valuable information about potential inflation or deflation
to come. These international shifts in portfolio preferences, whether
into (or out of) domestic money *or* bonds, accurately signal when the
effective demand for the domestic money is changing.[3]

Therefore the central bank should continually adjust the domestic
money supply to maintain exchange equilibrium against 'hard' foreign
currencies (those which are convertible and whose own internal purchasing powers are known to be stable). Money growth should be
higher than normal when the domestic currency tends to appreciate,
and vice versa. By following such an exchange-rate rule, the central
bank in any industrial economy (including the United States) can better prevent unexpected inflations or deflations.

What suffices for any small or medium-sized industrial economy,
however, is insufficient for the huge American economy at the centre of
the world dollar standard. Other countries frequently intervene to
(partially) stabilize their dollar exchange rates – and vary their domestic money growth to support these interventions. Besides the average
dollar exchange rate, the Federal Reserve System should be concerned
with growth in the monetary base of the industrial countries as a group
– what I call 'world' money. Coordinating national monetary policies

to achieve fixed exchange rates would make little sense if their collective money supply was growing at 100 per cent per year!

In practice, 'world' money has been heavily influenced by speculation for or against the dollar in the foreign exchanges.[4] World money expanded when the dollar was weak in 1971–3 and again in 1977–8, and then contracted with international demand shifted in favour of dollar assets in 1981–2. The resulting international inflations and deflations fed back into the prices of American tradable goods (as shown below).

The key to stabilizing the American (and the industrial world's) price level is therefore to internationalize US monetary policy. Acting in the best interests of the United States, the Federal Reserve System should see itself as the world's monetary balance wheel by:

1   allowing growth in the US money base to deviate from its norm in order to stabilize the dollar exchange rate with hard-currency trading partners;
2   compensating for excesses or shortfalls in money growth in these same partner countries so as to smooth growth in world money.

Fortunately, these two aims need not conflict, if the other principal central banks, say, the Bundesbank and the Bank of Japan, co-operate with the FED. Indeed, if each of the three central banks agrees to fix its rate of domestic credit expansion, but symmetrically varies the 'foreign' component of the national monetary base to stabilize the dollar/mark or dollar/yen exchange rates, both aims will be automatically satisfied. When one country's money supply is expanding, the other(s) will be contracting in an offsetting fashion.[5]

THE WEAKENING RELATIONSHIP BETWEEN US MONEY AND NOMINAL GNP

Let us put foreign money growth to one side for now, and consider the United States as a 'small' open economy facing a relatively stable outside world. How can changes in the US money supply be disentangled from changes in US money demand in their impact on American nominal GNP?

Consider the money-supply side first because it is directly observable. Table 7.1 provides annual percentage growth rates of US M1 – coin and currency and checking deposits – for 1956 to 1983 as prepared by the Federal Reserve Bank of St Louis.[6] Except possibly for 1983 itself, American money growth has been considerably smoother than that of other countries since 1970, and even smoother (albeit

TABLE 7.1 MONEY GROWTH IN DOMESTIC CURRENCIES, 11 INDUSTRIAL COUNTRIES
(percentage change in annual average of M1)

	Belgium	Canada	France	Federal Republic of Germany	Italy	Japan	Netherlands	Sweden	Switzerland	United Kingdom	United States	World average	Rest of world[a]
(Weights: GNP 1964)	(0.0132)	(0.0394)	(0.0778)	(0.0892)	(0.0494)	(0.0681)	(0.0144)	(0.0167)	(0.0113)	(0.0796)	(0.5408)		
1956	2.9	-1.2	10.3	7.2	8.5	16.4	-3.7	7.4	6.0	1.0	1.1	3.78	6.94
1957	-0.1	4.0	8.6	12.1	6.3	4.1	-2.0	3.4	1.8	2.7	-0.6	2.43	6.01
1958	5.8	12.8	6.4	13.1	9.9	12.8	11.9	1.6	9.2	3.0	4.3	6.47	9.04
1959	3.2	-3.2	11.4	11.8	14.0	16.5	4.5	18.0	6.1	4.6	0.1	4.53	9.74
1960	1.9	5.1	13.0	6.8	13.5	19.1	6.7	-1.2	10.2	-0.8	-0.4	3.72	8.58
1961	7.7	12.4	15.5	14.8	15.7	19.0	7.7	10.7	8.1	3.2	2.9	7.39	12.68
1962	7.2	3.3	18.1	6.6	18.6	17.1	7.5	5.6	16.6	4.4	2.1	6.18	10.99
1963	9.8	5.9	16.7	7.4	16.9	26.3	9.8	8.1	8.9	0.3	2.8	6.86	11.65
1964	5.6	5.1	10.3	8.3	6.7	16.8	8.5	7.7	0.2	5.0	4.1	6.16	8.59
1965	7.4	6.3	9.0	8.9	13.4	16.8	10.9	6.4	12.8	2.7	4.3	6.59	9.30
1966	6.7	7.0	8.9	4.5	15.1	16.3	7.2	9.9	3.1	2.6	4.6	6.31	8.33
1967	4.7	9.5	6.2	3.3	13.6	13.4	7.0	9.8	6.0	3.2	3.9	5.49	7.37
1968	6.8	4.4	5.5	7.6	13.4	14.6	8.8	-1.8	11.5	6.0	7.0	7.51	8.12
1969	2.3	6.9	6.1	8.2	15.0	18.4	9.4	2.0	9.5	0.4	5.9	7.00	8.30
1970	-2.5	2.4	-1.3	6.4	21.7	18.3	10.6	7.3	9.8	6.4	3.8	5.80	8.15
(Weights: GNP 1977)	(0.0172)	(0.0487)	(0.0885)	(0.1122)	(0.0471)	(0.1404)	(0.0228)	(0.0195)	(0.0148)	(0.0572)	(0.4316)		
1971	10.3	12.7	13.7	12.0	22.9	25.5	16.7	9.0	18.2	11.8	6.8	12.45	16.74
1972	15.0	14.3	13.0	13.6	18.0	22.0	17.7	11.8	13.4	13.1	7.1	12.21	16.10
1973	9.8	14.5	9.9	5.8	21.1	26.2	7.4	9.6	-1.0	8.6	7.3	11.06	13.91
1974	6.8	9.3	12.6	6.0	16.6	13.1	3.1	16.3	-1.7	4.8	5.0	7.78	9.88
1975	12.4	13.8	9.9	13.8	8.3	10.3	18.7	15.2	2.4	15.6	4.7	8.83	11.96
1976	9.6	8.0	15.0	10.4	20.5	14.2	11.8	14.0	7.3	13.8	5.7	9.91	13.10
1977	8.0	8.4	7.5	8.3	19.8	7.0	14.3	8.3	4.7	14.4	7.6	8.72	9.57
1978	6.7	10.0	11.2	13.4	23.7	10.8	5.3	13.6	12.7	20.1	8.2	10.99	13.11
1979	3.5	6.9	12.2	7.4	23.9	9.9	2.7	12.7	7.8	11.5	7.7	9.23	10.39
1980	-0.2	6.3	8.0	2.4	15.9	0.8	4.2	21.1	-5.4	4.9	6.2	5.53	5.01
1981	3.6	4.3	12.3	1.2	11.1	3.7	2.6	12.0	-0.9	10.0	7.2	6.50	5.95
1982	3.4	2.0	14.9	3.5	9.9	7.1	4.9	9.8	3.1	8.3	6.5	6.96	7.31
1983	5.0	10.2	12.1	10.3	17.3	3.0	10.6	11.4[b]	7.6	13.4	11.1	10.1	9.48

[a] United States excluded. [b] Preliminary data. Source: Federal Reserve Bank of St Louis, 'International Economic Conditions', June and August 1983.

higher) than US money growth back in the 1950s and 1960s, when ex-change rates were fixed. Floating rates seem to have given the United States more monetary autonomy on the supply side, as conventional theory suggests.

Table 7.2 displays annual growth in *nominal* US GNP from 1958 to 1983. Since 1971, growth in nominal GNP has been generally higher: greater price inflation more than offset lower real growth. However, I shall not try to distinguish fluctuations in real output from changes in the GNP price deflator. The model presented here only purports to 'ex-plain' fluctuations in nominal GNP.

Consider now a single regression equation linking nominal American GNP – as denoted by Y^{US} – to current and lagged values of American M1 – denoted by M^{US}.

$$\dot{Y}^{US} = C + a\dot{M}^{US} + a_{-1}\dot{M}^{US}_{-1} + a_{-2}\dot{M}^{US}_{-2} + u. \tag{1}$$

The dot over each variable represents percentage rates of change; no subscript indicates that the variable is current, whereas $\dot{M}_{-1}$ is money growth with a one-year lag, $\dot{M}_{-2}$ has a two-year lag, and so on. C is just a constant (which could be related to the trend in velocity), and the a coefficients measure the strength of each of the lagged money-supply variables. The sum of the a coefficients measures the overall impact of money-supply changes on nominal GNP.[7] Equation (1) is one representation of 'domestic monetarism': the widely held view that instability in GNP is primarily due to fluctuations in the supply of money under the presumption that the demand for domestic money is relatively stable.

The random variable or 'disturbance', u, signifies that equation (1) is just a statistical relationship where the independent variables in the right-hand side need not fully explain all the variance in the dependent variable on the left-hand side. Table 7.3 summarizes the results from fitting equation (1) by the method of ordinary least squares for two economically different time intervals: the 1958–69 period of fixed ex-change rates, and the 1972–83 period of dirty floating. This partitioning of the data can be further justified statistically. As measured by a con-ventional F-test, the regression coefficients in the earlier period differ significantly from the later period. (These regression results are reported more fully in tables 7.A.1 and 7.A.2 of the appendix.)

By common convention, $\bar{R}^2$ measures the percentage of variance explained in the left-hand variable of fitted regression equations such as (1). For 1958–69, US money growth explains 63 per cent of the variance in American GNP growth as measured by the $\bar{R}^2$ shown in table 7.3. Then $\bar{R}^2$ falls to 0.33 in 1972–82. (Remember, the maximum value for $\bar{R}^2$ is 1.0.)

TABLE 7.2   GROWTH IN NOMINAL INCOME, 11 INDUSTRIAL COUNTRIES (percentage change in annual GNPs)

	Belgium	Canada	France	Federal Republic of Germany	Italy	Japan	Netherlands	Sweden	Switzerland	United Kingdom	United States	World average	Rest of world[a]
Weights: GNP 1964	(0.0132)	(0.0394)	(0.0778)	(0.0892)	(0.0494)	(0.0681)	(0.0144)	(0.0167)	(0.0113)	(0.0796)	(0.5408)		
1958	0.8	3.8	14.9	7.2	7.4	4.0	1.6	5.6	2.8	4.3	1.3	3.79	6.73
1959	3.1	6.0	9.8	8.8	6.3	12.2	7.0	6.4	6.4	5.1	8.5	8.25	7.95
1960	6.5	4.1	11.0	18.6	15.7	19.8	11.2	8.9	10.1	5.9	3.8	7.83	12.59
1961	5.9	3.4	9.0	10.00	11.2	23.5	4.9	8.8	12.3	6.8	3.6	6.80	10.57
1962	6.9	8.3	11.8	8.3	12.3	10.9	7.1	8.5	10.9	5.0	7.7	8.36	9.13
1963	7.4	7.1	12.1	6.0	14.5	15.4	8.9	7.2	9.6	6.4	5.6	7.51	9.77
1964	11.8	9.4	10.9	9.8	9.5	18.1	17.6	11.5	10.9	9.2	6.9	8.98	11.44
1965	9.1	10.1	8.5	9.2	7.6	12.9	11.5	10.0	7.2	7.5	8.4	8.81	9.29
1966	7.4	11.7	7.4	6.4	8.4	16.2	8.6	8.8	7.7	6.7	9.4	9.20	8.96
1967	7.1	7.4	8.0	1.3	10.2	17.2	10.0	8.5	7.6	5.6	5.8	6.75	7.88
1968	7.1	9.3	8.7	8.4	8.4	18.5	10.4	6.1	7.4	8.0	9.2	9.51	9.87
1969	10.9	10.0	14.0	11.7	10.4	17.7	13.4	8.6	8.5	7.5	8.1	9.80	11.80
1970	11.4	7.4	11.7	13.6	12.5	17.9	12.3	12.0	11.8	9.7	5.2	8.50	12.38
Weights GNP 1977	(0.0172)	(0.0487)	(0.0885)	(0.1122)	(0.0471)	(0.1404)	(0.0228)	(0.0195)	(0.0148)	(0.0572)	(0.4316)		
1971	9.3	10.2	11.5	11.3	8.9	10.1	13.0	8.5	13.4	12.3	8.6	9.86	10.81
1972	12.0	11.4	12.4	9.4	9.7	14.6	13.4	9.5	13.1	10.7	10.1	11.08	11.82
1973	13.3	17.4	13.6	11.2	19.5	21.8	14.9	11.3	11.6	15.1	11.8	14.20	16.03
1974	17.4	19.4	14.7	7.3	23.4	19.1	13.2	13.1	8.9	13.8	8.1	12.12	15.17
1975	10.6	12.1	13.6	4.9	13.2	10.4	9.0	17.4	-1.3	26.2	8.0	10.08	11.67
1976	13.7	15.5	15.5	8.7	24.9	12.1	15.0	12.9	1.8	18.8	10.9	12.61	13.91
1977	8.0	9.3	12.3	6.7	21.3	11.3	14.5	8.5	3.2	15.4	11.7	11.45	11.34
1978	7.4	10.3	13.6	7.5	16.9	9.9	7.7	11.4	3.7	14.6	12.8	11.50	10.82
1979	6.2	13.7	13.9	8.3	21.3	8.0	5.9	12.1	4.9	16.6	11.7	11.63	11.36
1980	6.4	10.6	13.0	6.7	25.1	7.3	5.8	13.4	7.1	17.1	8.9	10.01	10.93
1981	3.4	13.3	11.9	4.0	17.6	6.5	4.3	8.3	9.7	10.4	11.6	9.82	8.61
1982	7.7	5.3	14.6	3.6	16.8	5.1	4.6	8.3	5.7	9.1	4.1	6.28	7.94
1983	6.3	9.0	11.0	4.5	13.7	3.7	2.5	11.6	2.6	8.7	7.7[b]	7.33	7.05

[a] United States excluded.   [b] Preliminary data.   Source: Federal Reserve Bank of St Louis, 'International Economic Conditions', June and August 1983.

TABLE 7.3   REGRESSIONS FOR US NOMINAL GNP:[a] PERCENTAGE
OF VARIANCE EXPLAINED ($0 < R^2 < 1$)

Explanatory variables (percentage change)	1958–69	1972–82	1972–83
US money supply only			
Lagged by calendar years	0.63	0.33	0.00[b]
6- and 18-month lags	0.80	0.50	0.02[b]
US money supply and dollar exchange rate[c]			
Lagged by calendar years	n.a.	0.89	0.57[b]
6- and 18-month lags[d]	n.a.	0.86	0.78[b]

n.a. Not applicable for the 1950s and 1960s, when the dollar exchange rate did not fluctuate significantly.
[a] Annual percentage changes in American gross national product as presented in table 7.A.2.
[b] Based on preliminary 1983 data.
[c] Based on IMF dollar exchange rate trade weighted against 17 industrial countries – see lower panel of figure 7.1.
[d] Money supply lagged 6 and 18 months, with the exchange rate on a one-year lag.
Source: US GNP taken from IMF, International Financial Statistics, 1982 Yearbook. M1 data from Federal Reserve Bank of St Louis, 'International Economic Conditions', June and August 1983. These are the best fits – highest $\bar{R}^2$ – for each lag structure. The best fit is with the exchange rate lagged only one year, and the money supply lagged at most two years.

When nominal GNP and nominal money growth for 1983 are incorporated, the explanatory power of equation (1) disappears altogether for the 1972–83 period. $\bar{R}^2$ is not significantly different from zero in the regression of GNP on money for 1972–83 – as shown in table 7.3. This decline in explanatory power of US M1 accords with the general view of financial commentators: the (lagged) velocity of money in recent years has become increasingly unstable – especially in comparison to the 1950s and 1960s.

Some readers might be (rightly) suspicious of the arbitrary lag structure employed for the money-supply variables in equation (1). In table 7.A.2 of the appendix, the analysis is repeated using 6-month and 18-month lags for the money-supply variables (instead of one- and two-year lags). Although qualitatively the same, the results are even stronger, as shown in the upper panel of table 7.3. The attempt to explain fluctuations in nominal US GNP by US money alone works well in the 1950s and 1960s, when exchange rates were fixed, but becomes progressively weaker in the period of floating exchange rates. In the early 1980s, this decline in the statistical power of a pure money-supply equation is particularly sharp.

What was the proximate cause of the deterioration in statistical fit in the early 1980s? The comparatively low annual growth in nominal GNP in 1982 and 1983 – of 4.1 per cent and 7.7 per cent, respectively (table 7.2) – occurred despite the fact that money growth did not fall in 1982 or 1983 below its norms for the 1970s. Indeed, the 11.1 per cent growth in M^{US} from 1982 to 1983 was very robust by the standards of the 1970s (table 7.1). The domestic monetarist model would have predicted higher growth in nominal GNP than what was actually observed.

My simple single equation estimating procedure, based on 11 or 12 annual observations, need not be the best measure of the impact of US money on US nominal GNP. It is unduly sensitive to the addition of one more observation: witness the sharp further decline in the goodness of fit when the preliminary 1983 observation was added. Elaborate multi-equation statistical models based on quarterly or monthly observations – taking into account levels as well as rates of growth in the variables – might give a better fit. Nevertheless, domestic money growth *by itself* no longer seems adequate to explain cyclical fluctuations in nominal GNP growth.[8] In a financial sense, the open American economy of the 1970s and 1980s appears quite different from its more insular counterpart of the 1950s and 1960s.

THE DOLLAR EXCHANGE RATE AND AMERICAN NOMINAL GNP

Alternatively, suppose that shifts in the (indirect) demand for US money have become more important in the 1970s and 1980s compared to the two preceding decades. Under floating exchange rates, international investors continually move from financial assets denominated in one currency to those denominated in another. Although remaining very important, the effects of money-supply changes by themselves could then be obscured – as reflected in the poor statistical fit for equation (1).

Consider amending our basic regression equation to include the dollar exchange rate as an additional explanatory variable incorporating 'news' that reflects these demand shifts.[9]

$$\dot{Y}^{US} = C + a\dot{M}^{US} + a_{-1}\dot{M}^{US}_{-1} + b\dot{E} + b_{-1}\dot{E}_{-1} + u \qquad (2)$$

$\dot{E}$ is the annual percentage change in the International Monetary Fund's measure of the dollar exchange rate – trade-weighted against 17 other industrial countries as shown in the lower panel of figure 7.1. Because E is measured in foreign-currency units per dollar, $\dot{E}$ being positive reflects dollar appreciation – and vice versa. The a coefficients still represent the impact of money-supply changes on nominal GNP, whereas the b coefficients reflect the impact of fluctuations in the exchange rate. Equation (2) thereby permits supply-side and demand-side fluctuations to be distinguished from one another.

FIGURE 7.1   MOVEMENTS IN THE DOLLAR EXCHANGE RATE
(plotted from quarterly averages, 1975 = 100)

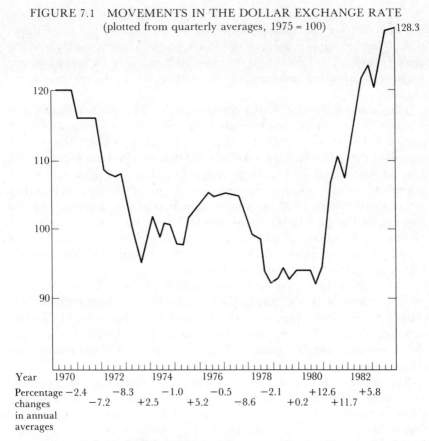

Year	1970		1972		1974		1976		1978		1980		1982	
Percentage changes in annual averages	−2.4		−8.3 −7.2		−1.0 +2.5		−0.5 +5.2		−2.1 −8.6		+12.6 +0.2		+5.8 +11.7	

Average trade-weighted value of the dollar measured against 17 currencies of the major industrial trading partners.

Source: IMF, *International Financial Statistics*, various issues: line amx for the United States.

From fitting equation (2) for the period of floating from 1972 to 1983, changes in the dollar exchange rate appear to have a major impact on GNP growth within a year or so. That is, the b_{-1} coefficient in equation (2) is negative and highly significant at the 95 per cent level of confidence or better.[10] Taking our lowest numerical estimate of b_{-1} = −0.26 to illustrate, if the dollar exchange rate appreciates by 10 per cent this year, growth in nominal GNP slows down by 2.6 percentage points next year – for any given time path in the US money supply.

Consider the same important phenomenon from a slightly different viewpoint. $\bar{R}^2$ increases as one moves from fitting equation (1) with the money supply only, to equation (2), where the exchange rate is also included as an explanatory variable. The relevant comparisons are set out in table 7.3. In the last two columns for 1972–82 and for 1972–83, one can see the sharp increase in $\bar{R}^2$ in moving from the upper panel (money supply only) to the lower panel (money supply and exchange rate). The proportion of total GNP variance explained by our regression equation increases sharply when the exchange rate is included.

This statistical result is at least consistent with the hypothesis that fluctuations are dominated by shifts in the effective demand for US money.[11] In the early 1980s, for example, the appreciating dollar clearly signalled that the international (indirect) demand for base money in the United States had unexpectedly risen. The stance of monetary policy was unduly tight, although money growth in 1980–2 was no less than usual – and from 1982 to 1983 was considerably higher than the average of the past dozen years (table 7.1). Thus the exchange rate picked up the great deflation of the early 1980s, just as it had earlier signalled the two great inflations of the 1970s. And this shows up as a higher $\bar{R}^2$ in the lower panel of table 7.3.

Although the exchange rate is a good indicator of deflation (or inflation) to come, it is also partly the instrument by which deflation (or inflation) is effected. The increased demand for dollar assets in the early 1980s drove the dollar up in the foreign exchanges and directly depressed the American tradable goods industries. Exports fell and imports increased.

But dollar appreciation also signalled to Americans that expected price inflation would be even lower than they had previously thought. Consequently, US portfolio preferences shifted away from goods and real estate and back into financial (dollar) assets. This signalling effect from dollar appreciation contributed to an additional deflationary impact within the American economy – even in those sectors not directly touched by foreign trade.

The statistical significance of the money-supply variables is enhanced once the exchange rate is included in the regression. In equation (2) money growth has a positive effect on GNP in the near term – within a year or so – but has a more negative effect when longer lags are taken into account (appendix tables 7.A.1 and 7.A.2). This part of my analysis fits with the conventional monetarist wisdom that control over the domestic money supply remains important.

If the exchange rate alone is used to explain American nominal GNP, the statistical fit is very poor. Without the money supply as a complementary explanatory variable, the impact of the exchange rate on nominal GNP is obscured. This tends to confirm the monetary approach in which the exchange rate reflects shifts in effective money demand, rather than the narrower interpretation: that it is some exogenous non-monetary force acting only on imports and exports.

In short, in order to measure either supply-side or demand-side monetary influences properly, separate indicators (explanatory variables) for each need to be incorporated into the statistical estimating procedure.

However, our econometric procedure is confined to measuring *changes* in the dollar exchange rate from one year to the next, as shown in figure 7.1. *Sustained* overvaluation or undervaluation of the dollar – measured from some purchasing power parity – is not captured.

Only when floating is 'clean', moreover, can the dollar exchange rate fully reflect changes in US money demand arising from disturbances in the international bond market. Massive interventions by foreign central banks somewhat dampened those fluctuations actually observed. Hence, by no means all relevant information on shifting international currency preferences is captured by our exchange-rate series. Much scope remains for refining the econometrics beyond the simple technique embedded in equation (2).

MONETARY REPERCUSSIONS IN OTHER INDUSTRIAL COUNTRIES

Let us now drop our simplifying assumption that the United States is a 'small' open economy. Because it is the centre of the world dollar standard, shifts in the demand for dollar assets have a substantial impact on money growth in other industrial countries – Japan, Canada and those of Western Europe. And from our principle of indirect currency substitution, we suspect that these currencies are somewhat substitutable with each other in determining inflation or deflation in the world at large.

The money supplies, whose rates of change appear in table 7.1, are defined narrowly to include currency and checking accounts in the M1 category for each of the 11 countries. Precisely which of these convertible currencies are the strongest substitutes for each other, and which should enter with the heaviest weights in any index of world money, is not addressed. The international moneyness of, say, the German mark is not distinguished from that of the Italian lira. Nevertheless, table 7.1 includes the principal moneys that are used to invoice world trade and to denominate internationally liquid wealth in the Euromarkets. In short, we are interested in a narrow definition of money in the spectrum of financial assets, but one which has effective potential as an international medium of exchange and standard of value.[12]

In table 7.1 'world' money growth, the aggregate for these 11 industrial economies as a group, is compiled as the weighted sum of percentage growth rates in national moneys *without* adjusting for exchange-rate fluctuations. From 1956 to 1970, the fixed weights are relative GNPs in the year 1964 for which the US enters with a weight of 0.5408. From 1971 to 1982, the United States receives a lower weight of 0.4316, based on GNPs in 1977. The right-hand column shows money growth in the rest of the world (ROW, ten industrial countries with the United States excluded) also on the basis of these fixed GNP weights.

Why do other industrial countries individually have wider fluctuations in money growth than the United States since floating began? Foreign central banks (weakly) pursued exchange-rate targets while the FED did not. The impact of such interventions on their domestic monetary bases often could not be sterilized, causing the erratic patterns seen in table 7.1. For example, the variable pattern of M1 growth in the Federal Republic of Germany and Switzerland in recent years belies their contention that they are following the principle of constant growth in domestic money.

Consider now aggregate money growth for these industrial countries as a group as shown in table 7.1. During the 1950s and 1960s, world money growth (inclusive of the United States) was smoother than American money growth itself. Fluctuations in national money-growth rates tended to offset each other under the fixed exchange-rate regime.

After 1970, however, table 7.1 shows that world money growth becomes more episodic and cyclical. Modest fluctuations in American money growth were *magnified* by monetary fluctuations in ROW. This greater instability in world money growth is related to the breakdown of the fixed exchange-rate regime. Any (modest) acceleration of American money growth heightens expectations of higher US inflation. International investors then are more apt to switch out of dollars in the absence of any firm dollar exchange parities. Foreign central banks are unwilling to let the resulting dollar appreciation go too far; they eventually intervene to buy dollars and sell their own currencies, causing their domestic money supplies to increase. Since 1970, the three great swings in the dollar exchange rate (figure 7.1) were accompanied by major changes in world money growth (table 7.1).

Even if American money growth were stable, political events could cause a flight from (or into) dollars with similar consequences. In retrospect, one can hardly distinguish shifts in US money growth, initiating a flight from dollars, from 'pure' demand shifts in portfolio preferences against dollar bonds due to some exogenous political or economic news. 'Non-monetary' disturbances were present in each of the three major changes in international portfolio preferences for dollar assets. Let us discuss each in turn.

The Dollar Depreciation of 1971–3

Although American money growth increased from its average of the 1960s, the breakdown of the Bretton Woods system of dollar parities was engineered by the American government's trying to force a dollar devaluation. In August 1971, President Nixon permanently closed the US Treasury's gold window to foreign central banks and imposed a temporary import surcharge until dolar parities were finally realigned in the Smithsonian Agreement of December 1971. In response to threatened devaluation throughout 1971, international investors moved out of dollar assets. The Smithsonian dollar parities broke down in late 1972 and early 1973. Nevertheless, the vain attempt of foreign central banks to maintain these dollar exchange parities – leading to their sharp 1971–2 build-up of dollar exchange reserves – led to the explosive growth in ROW money shown in table 7.1.

The Dollar Depreciation of 1977–8

Again, mild expansion in the rate of US money growth (table 7.1) was accompanied by attempts – beginning in early 1977 – of US officials (including the Treasury secretary) to 'talk' the dollar down. This news interacted with uncertainty about the appointment of a new chairman for the Federal Reserve Board of Governors, and what the future course of American monetary policy might be. The result was akin to an inflation scare that induced international investors to shift out of dollar assets into European currencies and the Japanese yen. The resulting dollar depreciation – almost 35 per cent against yen and marks over two years (figure 7.2) – again induced foreign central banks to intervene to buy dollars. Table 7.1 shows another increase in world money growth in 1978 – although not as massive as in 1971–3. Despite the absence of official dollar parities, the behaviour of foreign central banks was qualitatively the same in the second period as the first. Instability in world money growth, emanating from the United States, was magnified.

The Dollar Appreciation of 1981–2

In October 1979, the Federal Reserve system abandoned short-term interest rates as a monetary indicator, which indeed had contributed to the loss of monetary control in the two earlier episodes. With the avowed aim of disinflating the American economy, the FED adopted a stricter monetarist growth rule. From table 7.1, one can see the modest decline in annual US money growth from about 7.6 per cent over 1977–9 to

FIGURE 7.2   MOVEMENTS IN EXCHANGE RATES

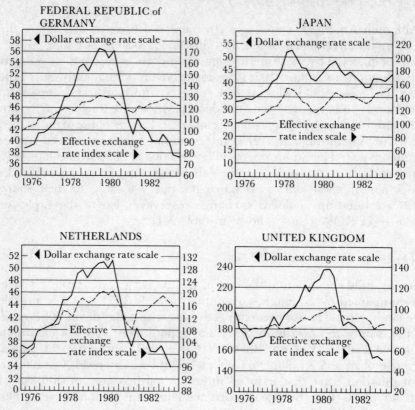

Source: Federal Reserve Bank of St Louis, 'International Economic Conditions', January 1984.

about 6.5 per cent in 1980–2.[13] Throughout late 1979 and the first two-thirds of 1980, however, the market remained unconvinced that the Fed would stick with its disinflation. Then a series of 'accidental' political shocks occurred, which dramatically changed international portfolio preferences toward dollars.

1) By mid-1980, the anticipated election of a more conservative American president. Although the FED's disinflation policy remained unchanged, people began to believe that it would be brought to a successful conclusion.
2) Political turmoil in Europe in 1980–1: the threat of Russian military intervention in Poland, a socialist government in France imposing a wealth tax and tighter exchange controls, and financial crises in several European countries.

3) An unbalanced financial liberalization in Japan: by the end of 1980 exchange controls on international capital flows had been removed while the Bank of Japan continued managing some yen interest rates at below market levels – much as the American government had regulated US bank deposits in the 1970s.

4) By 1982, a huge US fiscal deficit emerged – not financed by additional money issue – which caused high real rates of interest in the United States.

The upshot of these accidental political events was asharp increase in the demand for dollar assets, a great appreciation of the dollar with exchange rate 'overshooting', and – beginning in 1980 – the precipitate fall in ROW money growth (shown in table 7.1) as foreign central banks tried to prevent an undue depreciation of their currencies. What began as disinflation in the United States turned into the worldwide economic slump of 1981–2. In effect, there had been a big increase in the derived demand for US base money which – being on a monetarist rule – the FED did not then accommodate. (Subsequently, FED policy become much more expansionary from mid-1982 throughout 1983.)

THE INTERNATIONAL MONEY MULTIPLIER

Suppose each of our 11 countries' money growth was independently determined as under a 'clean' float. Then the statistical law of large numbers would suggest that proportional variance in world money should – on average – be *less* than that for important individual countries. How then can one succinctly characterize why the supply of 'world' money (inclusive of US M1) has been *more* unstable than money growth in the centre country itself?

The interventions of foreign central banks were *passively sterilized* by the FED, that is, they did not have any effect on the US money supply. Under the institutions of the world dollar standard, foreign interventions in the exchange markets did not directly touch the American monetary base. If the Deutsche mark came under sudden downward pressure, the Bundesbank would draw down its reserves of US Treasury bonds (table 7.1) to repurchase DM base money. The German money supply would contract – as it did in 1981 (table 7.1) – but the American money supply would not expand in an offsetting fashion. Only the stock of US Treasury bonds owned by the private sector would increase – not the American monetary base itself.[14] This asymmetrical arrangement made it particularly easy for the FED to ignore the foreign exchanges in order to focus on domestic monetary indicators such as US interest rates or growth in US M1.

Under such a regime of passive sterilization by the centre country, any *autonomous* money growth by the United States – say, by a domestic open market operation – will force an *even greater expansion in world money* if other countries intervene to forestall their currencies from appreciating unduly.[15] Through this international money multiplier, therefore, the relatively mild fluctuations in US money growth further aggravated the variance in world money – even when international portfolio preferences remained stable on the demand side.[16]

Both these demand-side and supply-side disturbances in world money were correlated with observed movements in the dollar exchange rate. When the dollar was weak, foreign money usually grew above its norm and vice versa. Consequently, in our regression equation (2), part of the strong impact of the dollar exchange rate on US nominal GNP reflected repercussions from fluctuations in the rest of the world's money supply.[17] This is an important channel through which the US business cycle becomes worldwide – with unfortunate reinforcing feedback effects on the American economy itself.

To be sure, exchange-rate changes may insulate other industrial countries from international cycles of economic activity. For example, the undervalued yen in 1981–2 helped the Japanese avoid as sharp a setback in industrial output as occurred in the United States. By allowing its currency to appreciate sharply in 1978–9, the Federal Republic of Germany managed to avoid high American-level price inflation in 1979–80 (see table 7.4). But on balance, the world is thrown into depression when the dollar becomes strong and growth in (world money) contracts, and the global economy experiences an inflationary boom when the dollar becomes weak and world money increases. However, the distribution of this world-wide inflationary (deflationary) pressure depends on the relative over- and undervaluation of each industrial country's exchange rate.

Imagine a two-stage inflation process in a world where national moneys are somewhat substitutable in demand for each other. First, growth in the aggregate money stock determines the overall inflationary pressure in the system. Secondly, countries whose currencies are relatively overvalued will experience little price inflation compared to those that are undervalued.

THE INTERNATIONAL BURDEN OF DOLLAR INDEBTEDNESS

There is another important channel by which fluctuations in the dollar exchange rate – magnified by monetary fluctuations in other industrial countries – exacerbate the international business cycle. In the Third

TABLE 7.4 PRICE INFLATION IN TRADABLE GOODS, 11 INDUSTRIAL COUNTRIES (percentage change in annual averages of WPIs)

	Belgium	Canada	France	Federal Republic of Germany	Italy	Japan	Netherlands	Sweden	Switzerland	United Kingdom	United States	World average	Rest of world[a]
(Weights: GNP 1964)	(0.0132)	(0.0394)	(0.0778)	(0.0892)	(0.0494)	(0.0681)	(0.0144)	(0.0167)	(0.0113)	(0.0796)	(0.5408)		
1958	−4.4	0.4	5.1	−0.5	−1.7	−6.5	−1.3	4.3	−3.2	0.8	1.5	0.68	−0.30
1959	−0.3	0.8	7.2	−0.8	−2.9	0.9	0.2	0.9	−1.6	0.3	0.2	0.57	1.54
1960	1.2	0.2	3.5	1.3	0.8	1.1	0.0	4.1	0.6	1.3	0.2	0.81	1.54
1961	−0.2	0.2	3.0	1.5	0.0	1.1	−0.2	2.2	0.2	2.6	−0.4	0.47	1.50
1962	0.8	1.1	0.6	0.9	3.2	−1.6	0.3	4.7	3.3	2.3	0.2	0.64	1.16
1963	2.5	1.3	2.9	0.5	5.3	1.6	2.4	2.9	3.9	1.0	−0.4	0.72	2.03
1964	4.7	0.9	3.5	1.0	3.0	0.4	6.1	3.4	1.3	3.1	0.2	1.15	2.27
1965	1.1	1.3	0.7	2.5	1.8	0.7	3.0	5.2	0.6	3.5	2.0	1.98	1.95
1966	2.1	2.9	2.8	1.7	1.5	2.4	5.0	6.4	1.9	2.9	3.4	3.02	2.57
1967	−0.9	1.9	−0.9	−1.0	−0.2	1.7	1.0	4.3	0.1	3.1	0.2	0.45	0.75
1968	0.2	2.2	−1.7	−0.7	0.6	1.0	1.9	2.0	0.1	4.1	2.4	1.68	0.83
1969	5.0	3.7	10.7	1.9	3.6	2.0	−2.5	3.5	2.8	3.7	3.9	3.99	4.09
1970	4.7	2.4	7.5	5.0	7.4	3.7	4.6	6.8	4.2	7.1	3.6	4.54	5.65
(Weights: GNP 1977)	(0.0172)	(0.0487)	(0.0885)	(0.1122)	(0.0471)	(0.1404)	(0.0228)	(0.0195)	(0.0148)	(0.0572)	(0.4316)		
1971	−0.5	2.0	2.1	4.3	3.3	−0.8	4.5	3.2	2.1	9.1	3.3	2.94	2.67
1972	4.0	4.3	4.7	2.5	4.1	0.8	5.1	4.6	3.6	5.3	4.4	3.74	3.24
1973	12.4	11.2	14.7	6.6	17.2	15.8	6.9	10.3	10.7	7.4	13.1	12.42	11.91
1974	16.8	19.1	29.1	13.5	40.8	31.4	9.6	25.3	16.2	22.6	18.8	22.00	24.43
1975	1.2	11.2	−5.7	4.6	8.5	3.0	6.7	6.4	−2.3	22.2	9.3	6.93	5.12
1976	7.1	5.1	7.4	3.7	23.8	5.0	7.8	9.0	−0.7	17.3	4.6	6.58	8.09
1977	2.4	7.9	5.6	2.7	16.6	1.9	5.8	9.2	0.3	19.8	6.1	6.35	6.55
1978	−1.9	9.3	4.3	1.2	8.4	−2.5	1.3	7.6	−3.4	9.1	7.8	4.99	2.86
1979	6.3	14.4	13.3	4.8	15.5	7.3	2.7	12.5	3.8	12.2	12.5	10.73	9.39
1980	5.8	13.5	8.8	7.5	20.1	17.8	8.2	13.9	5.1	16.3	14.0	13.33	12.82
1981	8.2	10.1	11.0	7.7	16.6	1.7	9.2	11.6	5.8	10.6	9.0	8.50	8.13
1982	7.7	6.0	11.1	5.8	13.9	1.8	6.6	12.6	2.6	8.6	2.1	4.80	6.85
1983	5.2	3.5	11.0	1.5	10.5	−2.2	1.8	11.2	0.5	5.5	1.3[b]	2.73	3.82

[a] United States excluded. [b] Preliminary data.
Source: IMF, International Financial Statistics, 1982 Yearbook and August 1983, line 63; wholesale price indices including finished goods and primary products.

World, import expenditures by both governments and private entities are severely constrained by their heavy foreign indebtedness in dollars. Consequently, when the dollar appreciates against European or Japanese currencies where LDCs sell their exports, and appreciates against the prices of internationally tradable goods – particularly price-sensitive primary commodities – their debt-service payments in dollars become much harder to meet. LDCs are, therefore, forced to curtail expenditures in world markets in general and for American goods in particular.

The reverse was generally true in the 1970s with dollar depreciation and unexpected inflation in the dollar prices of internationally tradable goods. The wealth or 'budget' constraint on LDC spending in the world economy was (artificially) relaxed, and reinforced the inflationary boom.[18]

But what about dollar creditors in the industrial world? Shouldn't they experience an offsetting improvement in their wealth position and undertake increased expenditures when the dollar appreciates? Generally speaking, no.

First, in so far as dollar creditors reside in the private sector of the United States, their wealth as measured in dollars (their operational numeraire) does not increase when the dollar appreciates against other currencies. Americans didn't feel wealthier in the sense of wanting to increase their expenditures for commodities.

Secondly, Steven Ambler has shown that the private sectors of other industrial countries are, on balance, neither significant dollar creditors nor dollar debtors.[19] However, *governments* in other industrial countries are big dollar creditors because of their holdings of US Treasury bonds and bills. But these creditor governments don't typically adjust their current spending for goods and services to changes in their net international asset position – as long as their exchange reserves are above some minimal level of adequacy.

Consequently, when the dollar appreciates, no positive wealth effect in the industrial countries, including the United States, offsets the increased burden of dollar indebtedness in LDCs. The international demand for goods and services falls. Some of the feedback effects on the United States of this debt-burden effect are also picked up in the regression coefficient for the dollar exchange rate in equation (2).

In contrast, suppose one ignored the operations of the dollar standard, and built a model of the world economy that treated the United States symmetrically with other countries or blocs of similar size. Then, if the dollar unexpectedly became overvalued and the currency of the other bloc became undervalued, there would be no presumption of *net* inflationary or deflationary pressure in the world overall. Deflationary pressure in the United States would be balanced by inflationary pressure elsewhere. But this is a world for the academic journals, not the one in which we live.

PRICE INFLATION IN TRADABLE GOODS

Equations (1) and (2) focused on an explanation of domestic nominal GNP in the United States without trying to build a more complex model that would distinguish real output from price-level changes. And that important distinction would be even harder to make for the world economy at large.

However, the hard currency prices of internationally tradable goods are interesting in their own right. Understanding the process of international price inflation is important if any central bank is to stabilize successfully the purchasing power of its own money.

In table 7.4, broad wholesale price indices (WPIs), inclusive of finished goods and primary products, are a good approximation to tradable goods' prices in the domestic currencies of each of our 11 industrial economies. Let us focus just on two broad measures:

1) the American wholesale price index, because so much of world trade is invoiced in dollars;
2) a 'world' wholesale price index over our 11 currencies that encompass all the significant monies used for invoicing international trade.

Table 7.4 shows percentage growth rates in both the American and world WPIs, which are constructed using the same fixed GNP weights as our monetary series in table 7.1. This is clearly shown in figure 7.3.

From the right-hand columns of table 7.4, the great volatility of tradable goods prices in the 1970s and 1980s – compared to the tranquility of the 1950s and 1960s – is immediately evident. Without any formal statistical regression analysis, moreover, the sharp changes in 'world' money growth shown in table 7.1 obviously *preceded* the great increases and decreases in the rate of international price inflation shown in table 7.4. In 1971–3 and 1977–8 the two explosions in world money (combined with dollar depreciation) were followed by high world-wide price inflation in 1973–4 and again in 1979–80. Subsequently, the dollar appreciation and the monetary slowdown of 1980–2 were followed by a sharp decline in commodity price inflation in 1982–3. These correlations between world money and American prices are clearly shown in figure 7.3.

Might not the two world-wide price inflations be better explained as oil shocks, courtesy of the Organization of Petroleum Exporting

FIGURE 7.3   WORLD MONEY SUPPLY AND US WHOLESALE PRICES

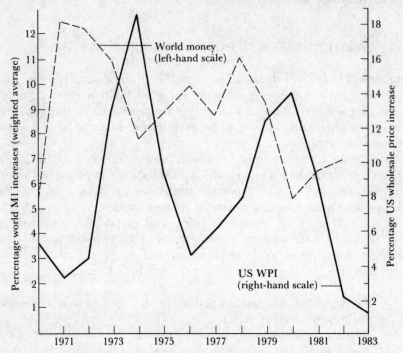

Sources: Federal Reserve Bank of St Louis, 'International Economic Conditions',
            June and August 1983.
            IMF, *International Financial Statistics, 1982 Yearbook* and August 1983, line 63.

Countries (OPEC), rather than as monetary disturbances? I believe not.
World money increased in 1971–2 and early 1973, prior to the Arab–
Israeli war in late 1973 that triggered the first oil shock; and increased
again in 1977–8 well before the Iranian revolution in 1979, which caused
the second oil shock. Because of these prior losses of monetary control,
the world was in for two big price inflations whether or not there were
specific disturbances in the market for oil. Indeed, OPEC was surprised
by bigger price increases than even it anticipated from the production
cutbacks in 1973–4 and again in 1979. Of course, OPEC made the two
price inflations somewhat bigger than they otherwise would have been.

More than most people realize, however, cyclical fluctuations in the
price of oil are endogenously determined by world-wide monetary fluctuations. Under pressure of the great world deflation of 1982–3, OPEC
was forced to cut the price of oil from about \$34 to \$29 per barrel in
early 1983. Most cartels in primary products tend to unravel when
deflations occur. In practice, of course, 'endogenous' fluctuations in oil
prices can't be distinguished from those that are 'exogenous'. Con-

sequently, the price of oil has been left out of my formal statistical analysis to follow.[20]

To explain inflation in the dollar prices of internationally tradable goods as shown in table 7.4, consider the following statistical format:

$$\dot{P}^{US} = C + a\dot{M}^W + a_{-1}\dot{M}^W_{-1} + a_{-2}\dot{M}^W_{-2} + b_{-1}\dot{E}_{-1} + u \qquad (3)$$

Equation (3) shows how the regression was run to get the result portrayed in the lowest panel of table 7.5 and in appendix table 7.A.3. $\dot{P}^{US}$ is percentage growth in the US WPI, $\dot{M}^W$ is percentage growth in 'world' money as it appears in table 7.1, and $\dot{E}$ is still the percentage change in the effective exchange rate. For the 1972–82 period, table 7.5 tells us that the $\bar{R}^2$ was 0.93. That is, world money and the dollar exchange rate succeeded in explaining 93 per cent of the variance in American tradable goods prices over 1972–82. By itself, world money still explained 82 per cent of the variance in US wholesale (producer) prices.[21]

Putting the concept of world money to one side, including the dollar exchange rate, greatly improves how well US money statistically explains American wholesale prices in the following simple regression format:

$$\dot{P}^{US} = C + a_{-1}\dot{M}^{US}_{-1} + a_{-2}\dot{M}^{US}_{-2} + b_{-1}\dot{E}_{-1} + b_{-2}\dot{E}_{-2} + u \qquad (4)$$

In fitting equation (4) for 1972–82, table 7.5 shows that $\bar{R}^2$ increases from 0.26 to 0.74 when the exchange rate is included with US money lagged one way, and from 0.37 to 0.82 with a different lag structure. This importance of the dollar exchange rate remains robust when the preliminary 1983 data are included, or when the important mark/dollar exchange rate (not shown) is substituted for the International Monetary Fund's exchange rate index in the regression equations.

Equation (4) is written to show the somewhat longer lag structure evident in the regression results found in table 7.A.3. Both money-supply and exchange-rate changes take somewhat longer to influence US prices than to influence US nominal GNP. Apparently, American monetary disturbances, on either the supply or demand side, affect output first and then prices with a somewhat longer lag.

For the 1972–82 and 1972–83 periods displayed in the middle panels of table 7.5, the dollar exchange rate picks up some of the influence of fluctuations in the omitted world money variable. Similarly, the strong explanatory power of world money by itself for 1972–83 partly reflects the (omitted) dollar exchange rate. The bottom panel suggests that both are important in determining the American price level.

TABLE 7.5   REGRESSIONS FOR PRICES OF US TRADABLE GOODS:[a]
PERCENTAGE OF VARIANCE EXPLAINED $(0 \leq \bar{R}^2 \leq 1)$

Explanatory variables (percentage change)	1958–69	1972–82	1972–83
US money supply only			
Lagged by calendar years	0.43	0.37	0.50[b]
6- and 18-month lags	0.48	0.26	0.37[b]
'World' money supply only			
Lagged by calendar years	0.00	0.82	0.86
US money supply and dollar exchange rate[c]			
Lagged by calendar years	n.a.	0.82	0.84[b]
6- and 18-month lags[d]	n.a.	0.74	0.73[b]
World money supply and dollar exchange rate			
Lagged by calendar years	n.a.	0.93	0.93

n.a. Not applicable for the 1950s and 1960s when the dollar exchange rate did not fluctuate significantly.
[a] Annual percentage change in US wholesale price index as presented in table 7.4.
[b] Based on preliminary 1983 data.
[c] Based on IMF dollar exchange rate trade-weighted against 17 industrial countries – see lower panel of figure 7.1.
[d] Money supply lagged 6 and 18 months, with the exchange rate lagged not more than two years.
Source: US GNP taken from IMF, International Financial Statistics. 1982 Yearbook. M1 data from the Federal Reserve Bank of St Louis, 'International Economic Conditions', June and August 1983. These are the best fits – highest $\bar{R}^2$ – for each lag structure. The best fit is when the exchange rate and the money supply are lagged at most two years.

In contrast, a purely domestic monetary explanation of cyclical price inflation in American tradable goods is becoming progressively less satisfactory. In the upper panel of table 7.5, the explanatory power of US money by itself falls from an $\bar{R}^2$ of 0.48 in 1958–69 to about 0.37 in 1972–83, by one measure.

But this $\bar{R}^2$ statistic somewhat understates the decline in the predictive power of US money. Because absolute price variance was so much higher in the 1972–83 period, that which is *unexplained* by US money rose sharply in comparison to 1958–69. Tables in the statistical appendix provide the standard error of the regression – a measure of the prediction error involved by using US money (without the exchange rate) to predict US prices. This prediction error rose from 1.1 percentage points in 1958–69 (table 7.A.3) to 3.7 percentage points in 1972–83.

THE RECOGNITION LAG IN AMERICAN
MONETARY POLICY: A CONCLUDING NOTE

What are the policy implications of our statistical analysis? From the 1950s and 1960s to the 1970s and 1980s, the importance of foreign monetary indicators for US monetary policy increased sharply.

In the earlier period, the dollar exchange rate was virtually fixed, and money growth in the rest of the world provided no additional explanation for the US price level. Table 7.5 shows that, in 1958–69, none of the variance was passively determined within the fixed exchange-rate system, and did not reflect major shifts in portfolio preferences for or against dollar assets. Only American monetary policy could independently determine both the American and 'world' price levels.

Consequently, in the 1950s and 1960s, American economists – whether they were Keynesians or monetarists – evolved a 'closed-economy' view of how best to secure domestic monetary control. The peculiar institutions of the world dollar standard, with convincingly fixed exchange rates, made it easy for the United States – the centre country – to vary its domestic money supply while ignoring the foreign exchanges. And, on the whole, this American monetary autonomy was exercised benignly: in the 1950s and throughout most of the 1960s, the dollar prices of international tradable goods remained quite stable (table 7.5).

However, with excessive American monetary (and fiscal) expansion in the late 1960s and early 1970s, the fixed exchange-rate system broke down in 1971–3. Equally important, the effective insulation against foreign monetary disturbances that the United States had enjoyed in the earlier era disappeared in more recent times – as demonstrated above.

Unfortunately, in the 1970s and 1980s, prevailing macroeconomic theory continued on its old track of focusing only on domestic monetary indicators as if the United States were an insular economy. Keynesians favoured interest-rate targets and monetarists favoured stabilizing the growth rate in some purely American monetary aggregate. Because the American government followed prevailing theory(ies) and ignored the foreign exchanges, the American (and world) economy suffered great cyclical instability in the 1970s and 1980s. Unsurprisingly, traditional macroeconomic doctrines fell into disrepute.

STATISTICAL APPENDIX

TABLE 7.A.1   THE DOLLAR EXCHANGE RATE AND GROWTH IN US NOMINAL GNP, 1958-83 (money growth by calendar year)

$\dot{Y}^{US}$	C	$\dot{M}^{US}$	$\dot{M}^{US}_{-1}$	$\dot{M}^{US}_{-2}$	$\bar{R}^2$	SE	DW	Period
	4.05 (3.96)	−0.02 (−0.07)	0.96 (3.98)	−0.11	0.58	1.65	2.64	1958–69
	4.01 (4.69)		0.96 (4.38)	−0.12 (−0.46)	0.63	1.56	2.62	1958–69
	3.92 (0.86)	1.68 (2.62)	−0.77 (−1.19)		0.33	2.07	1.22	1972–82
	1.60 (0.28)	1.93 (2.55)	−1.05 (−1.34)	0.40 (0.69)	0.28	2.50	1.05	1972–82
	8.56 (1.51)	0.26 (0.60)	−0.10 (−0.15)		−0.19	2.72	1.35	1972–83[a]

$\dot{Y}^{US}$	C	$\dot{M}^{US}$	$\dot{M}^{US}_{-1}$	$\dot{E}$	$\dot{E}_{-1}$	$\bar{R}^2$	SE	DW	Period
	6.68 (3.11)	1.91 (6.27)	−1.45 (−4.73)	−0.02 (−0.30)	−0.29 (−4.99)	0.87	0.91	1.49	1972–82
	6.49 (3.38)	1.95 (7.28)	−1.45 (−5.10)		−0.30 (−6.35)	0.89	0.85	1.62	1972–82
	10.30 (2.97)	0.98 (2.74)	−1.10 (−2.02)		−0.35 (−3.94)	0.55	1.68	1.11	1972–83[a]

[a] Preliminary data.

Results of fitting equations (1) and (2). t-statistics for regression coefficients are in parentheses. SE denotes the standard regression error, and DW is the Durbin–Watson statistic. Observations on money and GNP are percentage changes in annual averages. All regressions are ordinary least squares. $\dot{E}$ is concurrent percentage change in dollar exchange rate, and $\dot{E}_{-1}$ is lagged one calendar year (see bottom of figure 7.1). Similarly, percentage growth in nominal GNP is denoted by $\dot{Y}^{US}$, and percentage growth in M1 is denoted by $\dot{M}^{US}$.

Source: US GNP taken from IMF, *International Financial Statistics*. M1 data are from the Federal Reserve Bank of St Louis, 'International Economic Conditions', June and August 1983.

TABLE 7.A.2 THE DOLLAR EXCHANGE RATE AND GROWTH IN US NOMINAL
GNP, 1958-83 (money growth lagged 6 and 18 months)

$\dot{Y}^{US}$	C	$\dot{M}^{US}_{-6m}$	$\dot{M}^{US}_{-18m}$	$\dot{E}$	$\dot{E}_{-1}$	$\bar{R}^2$	SE	DW	Period
	3.80	1.22	−0.35			0.80	1.13	1.37	1958–69
	(6.18)	(6.53)	(−1.73)						
	8.69	1.59	−1.37			0.50	1.78	1.55	1972–82
	(2.51)	(3.20)	(−2.73)						
	9.85	0.70	−0.72			0.02	2.48	1.05	1972–83^a
	(2.05)	(1.25)	(−1.14)						
	13.25	1.34	−1.84	0.05	−0.28	0.85	0.98	2.03	1972–82
	(6.09)	(4.24)	(−5.88)	(0.86)	(−4.33)				
	13.37	1.22	−1.74		−0.26	0.86	0.96	2.20	1972–82
	(6.27)	(4.39)	(−6.16)		(−4.54)				
	15.04	0.83	−1.62		−0.33	0.78	1.18	1.84	1972–83^a
	(6.10)	(3.08)	(−4.74)		(−5.61)				

^{a} Preliminary data.
See table 7.A.1. $\dot{M}^{US}_{-6m}$ is annual percentage growth in American M1 lagged 6 months, and $\dot{M}^{US}_{-18m}$ is lagged 18 months. $\dot{E}$ is concurrent percentage change in dollar exchange rate, and $\dot{E}_{-1}$ is lagged one year (see bottom of figure 7.1).
Source: US GNP taken from IMF, International Financial Statistics. M1 data are taken from the Federal Reserve Bank of St Louis, 'International Economic Conditions', June and August 1983.

TABLE 7.A.3   PRICE INFLATION IN AMERICAN TRADABLE GOODS,
THE DOLLAR EXCHANGE RATE, AND GROWTH IN US AND WORLD MONEY
(OLS regression coefficients, t-statistics in parentheses)

$\dot{P}^{US}$	C	$\dot{M}^{US}$	$\dot{M}^{US}_{-1}$	$\dot{M}^{US}_{-2}$	$\dot{E}_{-1}$	$\dot{E}_{-2}$	$\bar{R}^2$	SE	DW	Period
	0.94	0.32	0.21	0.13			0.43	1.09	1.87	1958–69
	(−1.35)	(1.73)	(1.29)	(0.64)						
	−0.83	0.37	0.23				0.47	1.12	1.99	1958–69
	(−1.28)	(2.18)	(1.49)							
	−1.61	−1.80	2.06	1.43			0.50	3.73	1.72	1972–83
	(−0.19)	(−2.60)	(1.81)	(1.63)						
	0.36	−0.86	0.72	1.47	−0.45		0.80	2.37	2.29	1972–83
	(0.68)	(−1.70)	(0.91)	(2.68)	(−3.64)					
	−2.72		0.55	1.16	−0.43	−0.30	0.84	2.09	1.90	1972–83
	(−0.60)		(0.82)	(2.24)	(−3.82)	(−2.32)				

$\dot{P}^{US}$	C	$\dot{M}^{W}$	$\dot{M}^{W}_{-1}$	$\dot{M}^{W}_{-2}$	$\dot{E}_{-1}$	$\dot{E}_{-2}$	$\bar{R}^2$	SE	DW	Period
	−3.15	0.45	0.21	0.05			0.00	1.59	1.20	1958–69
	(−0.92)	(1.04)	(0.66)	(0.15)						
	−4.89	−1.10	1.12	1.44			0.86	1.97	2.60	1972–83
	(−1.25)	(−2.94)	(3.23)	(5.02)						
	3.81	−1.01	0.49	1.03	−0.32		0.93	1.41	1.75	1972–83
	(0.93)	(−3.70)	(1.49)	(4.11)	(−2.91)					
	0.433		−0.14	1.03	−0.34	−0.19	0.83	2.15	1.97	1972–83
	(0.07)		(−0.33)	(2.51)	(2.02)	(−1.38)				

$\dot{P}^{US}$ is percentage annual inflation in the US wholesale price index, which approximately reflects tradable goods prices. $\dot{M}^{US}$ is the percentage increase in the annual average US M1. $\dot{M}^{W}$ is the percentage annual increase in the average money supply (M1) of 11 major industrial countries including those from North America, Western Europe and Japan – aggregated by using fixed GNP weights as described in table 7.1. $\dot{E}$ is the annual percentage increase in the average-trade-weighted value of the dollar, measured against currencies of major US industrial trading partners by the International Monetary Fund. See figure 7.1. $\bar{R}^2$ is the percentage of variance explained adjusted for degrees of freedom. SE is the standard error of the regression. DW is the Durbin–Watson statistic. The period reflects the span of the dependent variable. Hence 1972–83 and 1958–69 each consist of 12 observations.

Sources: $\dot{P}^{US}$ and $\dot{E}$ data taken from IMF, *International Financial Statistics*, line 63 and line amx respectively. $\dot{M}^{US}$ data taken from the Federal Reserve Bank of St Louis, 'International Economic Conditions', 1984.

NOTES

1   See R. Meese and K. Rogoff, 'Empirical exchange-rate models of the 1970s: do they fit out of sample?, *Journal of International Economics*, vol. 14(12) (1983), pp. 3–24.
2   See Michael Mussa, 'Empirical regularities in the behaviour of exchange rates and theories of the foreign exchange market', *Carnegie–Rochester Conference Series on Public Policy*, vol. II (1979), pp. 9–58; and Jacob Frenkel, 'Flexible exchange rates, prices and the role of news: lessons from the 1970s', *Journal of Political Economy* (August 1981) pp. 665–705.

3   See Ronald I. McKinnon, *An International Standard for Monetary Stabilization* (Institute for International Economics, Washington, DC, 1984), ch. 3.

4   Ronald I. McKinnon, 'Currency substitution and instability in the world dollar standard', *American Economic Review*, vol. 72(30) (1982).

5   How such coordination could evolve in stages, so as to be both technically and politically feasible, is discussed in chapter 5 of McKinnon's book, *An International Standard for Monetary Stabilization*.

6   The average money stock is computed over each calendar year, and then annual percentage changes are taken in these averages and reported in table 7.1. If, instead, percentage changes were based on point estimates of the money stock on the last day of each year, the resulting statistical series of money growth would be much less stable.

7   In my econometric analysis, the signs of the *a* coefficients are not constrained to be positive. More conventionally, money growth is often measured by three- or four-year moving averages, or other similarly common statistical procedures designed to ensure that the *a*'s are always positive. Unfortunately, such standard smoothing techniques are not appropriate for measuring business cycles of between one and three years' duration. A natural, but disconcerting consequence of my using linear regression analysis to measure cyclical effects in GNP is the pattern of positive and negative signs on the money supply variables in the fitted equations shown in the appendix.

8   It remains true, of course, that countries such as Portugal and Italy, with high trend rates of growth in their money supplies, will have higher trend rates of price inflation than hard-currency countries such as the Federal Republic of Germany and Japan.

9   As explained in chapter 3 of McKinnon, *An International Standard for Monetary Stabilization*.

10 Using different lag structures for both M^{US} and $\dot{E}$, as shown in tables 7.A.1 and 7.A.2 in the statistical appendix, b_{-1} varies within a range of -0.26 to -0.33 for the regression based on the 1972–82 interval. The numerical values for b_{-1} become considerably higher, between -0.30 and -0.35, when the 1983 data are included.

11 As analysed in chapter 3 of McKinnon, *An International Standard for Monetary Stabilization*.

12 Eurocurrency deposits *per se* are omitted, because they are more like bonds than money, important though these interbank deposits may be for linking national capital markets and providing a channel for indirect currency substitution. Eurocurrency deposits are not checking accounts used by non-banks as a means of payment.

13 One could justifiably argue that US money growth decelerated more sharply because of financial innovation: the rapid growth in interest-bearing checking accounts in the latter period. This complication does not affect my main argument.

14 The annex to chapter 5 in McKinnon, *An International Standard for Monetary Stabilization*, shows how these institutional arrangements could be altered to yield a more symmetrical monetary adjustment between the United States and other hard-currency countries.

15 See Alexander K. Swoboda, 'Gold, dollars, Euro-dollars, and the World money stock under fixed exchange rates', *American Economic Review*, vol. 68, (1978).

16 For a complete algebraic development of how these demand-side and supply-side disturbances work themselves out under passive sterilization, see McKinnon, 'Currency substitution and instability'.

17 In single equation statistical regressions, changes in ROW money growth (unadjusted for exchange-rate fluctuations) turn out not to be directly useful in explain-

ing fluctuations in US nominal GNP. See the critical comment in Christopher Radcliffe, Arthur Warga and Thomas Willett, 'Currency substitution and instability in the world dollar standard: Comment', unpublished paper, Claremont University, California, Processed, March 1983, and the reply by Ronald I. McKinnon and Kong-Yam Tan, 'The dollar exchange rate as a monetary indicator: reply to Radcliffe, Warga and Willet', Stanford University, California, Processed, July 1983.

18 The same story can be told slightly differently. LDCs faced a decrease in the real – inflation-adjusted – rate when the dollar depreciated. Correspondingly, the 'real' interest rate on their outstanding debts increased sharply when the dollar appreciated in the early 1980s. See William R. Cline, *International Debt and the Stability of the World Economy* (Institute for International Economics, Washington, DC, 1983).

19 See Steven Ambler, 'On calculating net foreign asset position', unpublished paper, Stanford University, California, Processed, September 1983.

20 The preliminary evidence suggests that no qualitative change in my conclusions would emerge if the price of oil is somehow included as an additional 'exogenous' explanatory variable. See Radcliffe, Watga and Willet, 'Currency substitution and instability: comment'.

21 Other common price indices, as in the CPI, contain hard-to-measure non-tradable services such as medical costs or housing. They are less immediately sensitive to international monetary influences. Nevertheless, inflationary cycles in commodity prices (the WPI) typically lead inflation in other indices. There is a presumption that the central bank should focus on stabilizing some broad commodity price index. See Ronald I. McKinnon, *Money in International Exchange: The Convertible Currency System* (Oxford University Press, New York, 1979).

Comment 1

TOMMASO PADOA-SCHIOPPA

1) The paper presented by McKinnon develops along the lines of his long research on the possible ways to reform the international monetary system. Ten years ago, when McKinnon first proposed 'A New Tripartite Monetary Agreement' in an essay published in the Princeton series, it was widely believed that the newly started system of floating exchange rates would ensure a smooth adjustment of external imbalances and would restore independence to domestic economic policies. Today there seems to be broad consensus that floating has not lived up to expectations. Although it has contributed to the adjustment process and has helped to maintain an open payments system in face of large real shocks, it has also shown very high volatility with large swings of exchange rates that were not justified by the underlying economic conditions.

The search for greater stability has become evident in the multiplication of proposals of reform of the international monetary system. Most of these proposals have had little success and have not appealed to policy-makers, since they appeared too complicated or impractical. This may be a reason why the floating-rate regime has continued to be regarded as the only workable alternative.

McKinnon's recent work in this area represents perhaps the most concrete and systematic proposal of reform of the current regime. Starting from an overview of the major shortcomings of the floating-rate system, he advocates a simple rule to restore stability in foreign-exchange markets.

In a way, McKinnon's suggestion can be viewed as presenting certain analogies with the proposal, made at the domestic level, of setting nominal income as a target for economic policy. This proposal was advanced on the grounds that the instability of the demand for money would render the targeting of monetary aggregates counter-productive. Economic policy should therefore consider the exogenous changes in the income velocity of money and, to the extent that they are determined by portfolio shifts, accommodate them.

I have five comments on McKinnon's paper. Three are of a technical nature; two (the first and the last) are of a more general, or systemic character.

2)   My first general comment is very short. It is simply that McKinnon's work contains many of the elements that I consider to be necessary 'ingredients' of a better international monetary order.

Let me just list them briefly without elaborating. The framework he proposes is based on recognition that nation-states as we know them have become sub-optimal currency areas. The central and by now inevitable role of capital mobility and currency substitutability is fully recognized, thus moving beyond the Bretton Woods world. A strong link is established between exchange-rate policies and other policies, particularly monetary policy. The Weltanschaung is one of stable exchange rates, thus moving beyond the collective infatuation with floating that has dominated the last fifteen years. Certain positive elements of monetarism are incorporated in the analysis, thus recognizing the contribution that monetarism has made to the restoration of financial stability in many countries. Finally, it is a global and systemic proposal, one that refuses the more fashionable and allegedly realistic preference for piecemeal solutions.

For all these reasons McKinnon's approach goes in the desired direction of re-establishing greater international co-operation and should be appreciated for its ability to address the basic issues of the present international situation.

3)   Precisely because of my agreement with these basic features and the ultimate goals of McKinnon's ideas, I cannot underestimate the technical problems that the international community would have to face if it decided to follow this proposal. I shall mention three of them.

The first technical problem is one of *initial conditions*. McKinnon recognizes that the application of his proposal requires an initial situation of price stability and full financial equilibrium. If this is not the case, he suggests a gradual, two-stage approach. In stage one, the foreign-exchange intervention mechanism would be limited to a purchasing-power parity rule, which would maintain the *real* exchange rate around an appropriate level. In stage two (that is, once equilibrium has been restored), the *nominal* exchange rate would be fixed within a narrow band, and domestic financial policies would be more closely coordinated and geared towards world price stability.

The problem is that a country with inflation may not be able to restore price stability, if it abides by McKinnon's rule for stage one. The purchasing-power parity rule is actually a policy of monetary accommodation of inflation differentials, so that the targeting of the real exchange rate is incompatible with the use of monetary policy as an instrument to reduce the initial disequilibrium. Unless some other instrument, such as fiscal or incomes policy, is adopted, the country will not be able to adjust the initial imbalance. In general, the adequacy of the money-supply rule seems to postulate that fiscal and other policies of the countries in the agreement are conducted along mutually consistent paths.

Alternatively, a greater degree of flexibility should be allowed in the short-term adjustment of real exchange rates. In fact, I think that the reduction of the rate of inflation almost inevitably involves a (temporary) real appreciation of the exchange rate, and recent experience in several industrialized countries confirms this belief. In the five years from 1979 to 1983, the effective exchange rate appreciated in real terms by 27 per cent in the US, by 4.7 per cent in Canada, by 6.8 per cent in the UK and by 4.2 per cent in Italy. Only in Japan and the Federal Republic of Germany did the real effective exchange rate depreciate (by 4 per cent and 6 per cent respectively).

4)   The second technical problem, which may arise once the equilibrium situation has been reached, concerns the *relative size of the participating countries*, and, in particular, the ability of the Federal Republic of Germany and Japan, the two countries that would intervene in the foreign-exchange market, to stabilize both the (dollar) exchange rate and interest rates in US markets. Taking an interest elasticity of 10 per cent for the US demand for money, the stabilization of a 1 percentage point change around a 10 per cent US interest rate would involve a change of about 5 per cent in the German money supply and a corresponding 19 per cent change in its official reserves; in the case of Japan, the corresponding figures would be about 1.5 per cent for the money supply and about 21 per cent for official reserves. Given the recent interest-rate variability in the US financial markets, the potential changes in the German and Japanese monetary aggregates and official reserves could well be exceedingly large.

A possible solution to this problem would be to extend the system to other countries, for instance, those participating in the European Monetary System. This would also be justified because participation in the tripartite agreement could create some problems regarding Germany's EMS membership, since this involves foreign-exchange interventions that are potentially incompatible with the rule of stabilizing the world money supply; and also because the weight accorded to the FRG in the determination of the world money supply overestimates its importance relative to the US.[1]

5)   The third technical problem stems from the *nature of the disturbances* that the intervention mechanism is supposed to tackle. Portfolio substitution between the three major currencies is viewed as being the major factor of instability in the international financial system.

However, other types of disturbances may affect the economy of the three major countries. At least four can be mentioned: an unexpected increase (decrease) in output; a fiscal expansion (contraction); a financial innovation; an increase (decline) in the demand for the domestic currency by investors of the other countries that do not participate in the agreement.

Since all of the above events would cause, *ceteris paribus*, a change in domestic interest rates and exchange-rate pressures, the policy response suggested by the application of McKinnon's rule would be an increase (or decrease) in the domestic money supply, which would be compensated by a symmetric decrease (or increase) in the other two countries, even if in the latter the demand for money did not change. This would produce undesired deflationary (or inflationary) pressures in the countries that are not subjected to such shocks.

Can one discriminate between the various types of disturbances that affect the economy? It seems to me that the information lag will not allow a quick, clear-cut distinction. For instance, data on the real sector of the economy or on the effects of financial innovation are made available with a certain delay, whereas interest rates and exchange rates are immediately observable and react rather promptly to the changing conditions of market fundamentals.

In any case, even if the above distinctions were possible, the nice automatic properties of McKinnon's rule would be lost, owing to the need to take a decision on the nature of the disturbances before any action was taken. The problem would thus arise of establishing a procedure by which the three parties could agree on the nature of the shocks that may affect the foreign-exchange market, and hence on the appropriate action to be taken.

6)   These technical considerations lead me to my second general, or systemic, remark on McKinnon's approach. If the McKinnon proposal were to be adopted, it would have to be extended and enriched to enable it to deal with a wider range of problems. For the system to be workable, it would have to allow for a sufficient degree of pragmatism to cope with various types of disturbances. It would also have to allow

choices between a wide combination of policy instruments. A degree of flexibility and judgement would also be desirable regarding the co-ordination of national economic policies, as the unexpected changes in the underlying economic conditions may render the overall intervention mechanism sub-optimal.

The successful implementation of the rules that are supposed to maximize the welfare result of the co-operative solution therefore presupposes the use of discretion. This requires the existence of an institutional framework that guarantees a stable and efficient decision-making process.

The reform of the international monetary system proposed by McKinnon requires that an international institution should be given the task of overseeing the application of the rules and deciding the circumstances in which they should be applied.

Finally, the importance of this international institution is made evident by the need to guarantee the stability of the overall system over time, in spite of the economic and political changes that may occur in individual countries. The global credibility of the final objectives of the system would be guaranteed only by the existence of this factor of continuity.

To conclude, the framework proposed by McKinnon should be viewed as a major contribution to the 'new' international monetary system that could gradually emerge in the years to come. Although many crucial problems still have to be solved, McKinnon's work is a stimulating and constructive proposal that will deeply influence both the thinking of policy-makers and the research in this field.

NOTE

1   One should note that the exchange-rate target calculated by McKinnon of 2 DM per US dollar is incompatible with the setting of a world money supply target. In the presence of portfolio shifts, the world money supply remains constant if the rate of substitution between German and US currencies is 1.28, which is the ratio of the weights of the two currencies. A portfolio shift in favour of US dollars would, for instance, induce a reduction of the world money supply, since the rate at which the two currencies would be exchanged would be of 2. If, instead, the Federal Republic of Germany is substituted by the whole EMS area, the compatibility between the two objectives would be restored, as the exchange rate of the ECU (which, by the way, also includes the pound sterling) with respect to the US dollar is exactly 1.28.

Comment 2

PASCAL SALIN

I have read with great interest Ronald McKinnon's paper, together with a number of other pieces that he has written in this field, in particular *An International Standard for Monetary Stabilization*,[1] of which a part features in the paper under discussion here. His position can be summarized as follows: McKinnon starts from the idea that news continually arrives in the market and, by producing changes in the relative preferences for financial and monetary assets, is transformed into variations in interest and exchange rates. Suppose that the central country, the United States, uses a monetary rule, that is to say a rule for the orderly growth of the monetary base or the money stock. The arrival of news may be sufficient to alter the exchange rate. If, then, the central banks of the peripheral countries intervene to stabilize their exchange rates, this results in a certain variability in the growth of their money stock and thus instability in the world economy, which, in turn, manifests itself upon the United States.

I am in disagreement with Ronald McKinnon both on the description and on several points of the underlying analysis of this sequence of events which has just been sketched rapidly. I will underline three particular problems before turning my attention to what seems to be the key issue, the organization of the monetary systems.

1) McKinnon holds that there are continual changes in the relative portfolio preferences for assets and it is these that explain short-run economic variations. Let us suppose, in order to examine the problem, a simplified model with two countries, each with its own money or currency and one other financial asset; the demand for each of these is a

function of the interest rate of each of the two financial assets, the actual exchange rates, the expected exchange rates and a certain number of other variables.

Let A and B be the two countries, M_a and M_b be their respective quantities of money, and A_a and A_b be their respective quantities of financial assets. If a piece of information of news increases the attractiveness of A_b, normally the demand for A_b increases and the demand for the three substitutes (M_a, M_b and A_a) diminishes. However, while McKinnon supposes that portfolio holders sell A_a to go into A_b – which is indeed probable and leads to an increase in the interest rate in A and a fall in B – he also supposes that those holding money M_a prefer not to get out, but to hold A_a to gain from the now higher interest rate. This hypothesis is very strange precisely because the holders of A_a preferred to go into A_b, after taking account of the new information. McKinnon here is keeping to the traditional idea that there will be substitution between money and bonds in function of the rate of interest, but this idea, elaborated for the closed economy, is applied in an automatic manner in the analysis of an open economy. The situation that he supposes is thus very particular. It must suppose one or other of the following hypotheses:

a) There exists no substitutability between M_a and A_b while nevertheless M_a is convertible into A_a and A_a is convertible into A_b! It is thus necessary to suppose that only the inhabitants of country A hold currency A (M_a and that exchange-control measures prevent them from buying A_b or M_b, so that they only have a choice of holding A_a or M_a. Substitutions between A_a and A_b will thus only take place through foreigners not covered by exchange controls and consequently able to sell A_a to buy A_b. However, in this situation, instead of, as McKinnon does, advocating co-operation between the central banks, it would be better to advocate the abolition of the exchange controls, which are the real cause of the instability decried by him.

b) The speeds of adjustment are different in different markets for reasons that are not specified. Nevertheless, McKinnon's model is a particular type of model of overshooting, and it should be recalled that in general overshooting models suppose an initial variation in monetary conditions. However, there is no reason to suppose *a priori* that the sequence of events assumed by McKinnon necessarily take place. It is, nevertheless, these substitutions between moneys and assets which lead McKinnon to his conclusions about the exchange rate and to his proposals for exchange-rate policy. Thus, the abandonment of these specific assumptions permits one to contest his conclusions. For

the exchange rate to alter, these must be a change in the conditions of demand and supply of one money against another
money. However, that need not necessarily be the case. If one
accepts that it is new information or news which increases the
attractiveness of A_b and that there is substitutability between all
assets and moneys, then the relative rarity of the two moneys –
and thus their relative prices – is not necessarily affected, or not
necessarily in the sense indicated by McKinnon.

2)   According to McKinnon, the market is unable to predict correctly
the future exchange rate and he sees the proof of this in the fact that the
forward exchange rate has been a bad predictor of the spot exchange
rate. He concludes implicitly that stabilization measures, coordinated
by the principal countries, are necessary to compensate for the effects
of this supposed market 'imperfection'. However, the fact that the forward exchange rate is a poor predictor does not allow one to conclude
that there is a market imperfection, nor to suggest that as a consequence of it there should be a stabilization policy. As a matter of fact,
the evolution of the exchange rate is unforeseeable precisely because it
is affected by the very news which constitutes the basis of McKinnon's
reasoning. The 'erratic' character of exchange rates is only a reflection
of the erratic nature of economic, especially monetary, policies, which
produce so many large-scale exogenous shocks that no one is able to
forecast the exchange rate correctly. This is the manner in which the
authorities fail to provide, or at least not sufficiently in advance, the
market with the information or news that would permit it to function
correctly. Furthermore, it is important to know what exactly is the
nature of the information or news. This is not specified by McKinnon
and he is content to say that it can have monetary, political or
economic origins. On the other hand, he supposes that monetary policies are made unstable by exchange-rate variations, but an explanation
for the latter is always left in the dark. Would it not in fact be possible
to reverse the reasoning and say that it is the instability in monetary
policies which provokes the instability in exchange rates, so that instead
of trying to coordinate monetary and exchange-rate policies between
the principal countries, it would be better to start by bringing about
stable monetary policies in each country? With this in mind, one can
underline the fact that McKinnon assumes from the outset of his explanation that the United States does follow a stable monetary policy
under the guise of a monetary rule and that the instability is produced
by the shocks, called new information or news, which are left largely
unexplained and are perhaps *ad hoc* constructions which are not
justified. This also forgets the fact that the United States has not had a

stable monetary policy in recent years and it is the latter that can probably explain the instability in exchange rates.

3)   It could be that exchange-rate instability is equally linked with phenomena not connected with the demand for money or financial assets, but with the supply of money, in particular to the possible variability in the creation of dollars on the Euro-dollar market.

4)   The problem of the organization of the world monetary system seems to me to be the essential one. McKinnon seems to accept the idea that exchange rates are determined in the long run by purchasing-power parity and thus, basically, by relative growth rates of money creation in the different countries. His proposals actually consist of adopting a monetary rule for the zone as a whole, made up of, for example, the United States, Japan and Germany, but adding nuances to this with two other rules:

a)   in the short term, adjusting the respective growth rates of money creation in the countries concerned in such a manner as to stabilize the exchange rate and reduce the immediate instability;

b)   decentralizing decision-making since the 'world money stock' is produced by three centres of decision: the monetary authorities of the United States, Japan and Germany.

McKinnon advocates in this respect co-operation between monetary authorities. However, the market constitutes the best system of social co-operation. What McKinnon calls 'co-operation' is in fact the coordination of decisions between people – those self-same monetary authorities – *who are supposed to know better than other people* what will be the evolution of certain variables, for example exchange rates. One often finds a bias in favour of co-operation, but this is generally made necessary by the fact that one finds oneself in a system without rules or where the authorities act in a totally discretionary manner. In comparison with a system of monetary competition,[2] or with a system of monetary rules, co-operation is no more than a second-best solution.

I certainly realize that McKinnon tries to define some rules and not to return everything simply to the discretionary decisions of the authorities, but I think those rules are defined in such a way that they will nevertheless finally end up accepting discretionary decisions. First and foremost, the construction of the rules for coordinated money-supply growth encounters serious difficulties. It supposes that one has a perfect knowledge of the functioning of the international macroeconomic system in such a way as to be able to localize disequilibria and thus the need for intervention. However, the remarks made above show precisely that this knowledge is far from being satisfactory. Furthermore, McKinnon's proposals do not resolve several important practical problems, for example, how is it decided as to which country should intervene to stabilize the exchange rate? Past experience has shown clearly that under a fixed exchange-rate regime countries often pass the responsibility for intervention on to the others. Above all, there is the risk of ending up in a situation of contradiction, faced with, for example, the monetary rule that the United States sets itself and announces, and the divergence from this rule which requires future intervention in the exchange markets. This is because, and it is yet another example, we lack sufficient information on the actual functioning of monetary systems in the short run. It is impossible for us to define the rules that are capable of assuring an equilibrium exchange rate or interest rate in the short run.

All we can do is to adopt rules for the long run (for example, a rule for a monetary growth rate *or* a particular exchange rate). However, the difficulty, or even the impossibility, of reconciling a long-term objective with the wish to achieve a so-called stabilization in the short run is well recognized by McKinnon. Indeed, as he forcefully points out, it is not at all clear how to share out the growth of the total money stock among the three large countries; it is also unclear whether there is, or is not, an initial equilibrium. Thus, it is necessary to modify little by little the division of the respective responsibilities of the three countries from that decided at the start. Ronald McKinnon makes in this respect ingenious proposals that consist of modifying the part in world monetary growth allotted to each country in function of the tendency for its money to appreciate or depreciate. It is here that one finds the discretionary character of the system: one can easily imagine the discussions that would take place between the monetary authorities before accepting the frequent changes in monetary policy, and thus the abandonment of monetary rules, that the functioning of this system implies.

In conclusion, the major criticism I have of McKinnon's approach is the following: he tries to reconcile rules for the economic policy for short-run stabilization with the (monetary) rules applicable in the long run. These two types of rules risk being incompatible. More generally, automatic rules for short-run stabilization of the economy are bad because they rest on the implicit hypothesis that the functioning of the economic system is perfectly known, in this case it is the functioning of the whole international system. McKinnon assumes that overshooting exists, without explaining anything about the arrival of the news that is at the origin of the short-run instability, and considers as general a sequence of events that is only particular. To say that there is short-term instability which needs correcting is to say that the market is unstable and there is the need for a corrective policy. However, we do not even know how to analyse these supposed disequilibria. McKinnon supposes that it is possible to know how to vary several different rates of monetary creation in the short run without even knowing the causes of the presumed instability. In such conditions, it would be better to be satisfied with defining long-run rules (monetary or exchange rate) and keeping to them whatever happens to make them credible. This would allow the market to play a stabilizing role and precisely avoid the production of destabilizing news.

NOTES

1   Ronald McKinnon, *An International Standard for Monetary Stabilization* Washington, Institute for International Economics, Washington, DC, 1984; MIT Press, Cambridge, Mass., 1984).
2   See Friedrich Hayek, *Denationalisation of Money* (Institute of Economic Affairs, London, 1978); Pascal Salin (ed.), *Currency Competition and Monetary Union* (Martinus Nijhoff, The Hague, 1984).

Comment 3

ROLAND VAUBEL

Ronald McKinnon's paper contains an empirical analysis and a policy recommendation. I shall argue that his empirical analysis is somewhat inconclusive and probably not an optimal test of his hypothesis, and that his policy recommendation is not the best solution to the problem at hand.

McKinnon's hypothesis is that, in the 1970s, shifts in currency preferences led to large changes in money demand and that exchange rates, price levels and real growth rates had to fluctuate as a result. Currency preferences, as defined by him, change when the holders of money or of non-monetary financial assets shift their demand from assets denominated in one currency to assets denominated in another currency, because new information alters the relative attractiveness of currency denominations in terms of expected exchange-rate change and risks. Thus, he allows for two types of currency substitution: direct currency substitution between moneys and indirect currency substitution, which is due to the effects which demand shifts between bonds denominated in different currencies may have on the demand for money.

McKinnon tries to test his hypothesis by adding the exchange-rate change as an explanatory variable in regressions of the inflation rate or nominal GNP growth on monetary expansion (M1). Thus, he tries to use the exchange-rate change as a proxy for direct and indirect currency substitution. This is in line with a proposal which the German Economic Expert Council submitted in 1978 and which Langfeldt and Lehment subjected to econometric scrutiny in 1980.[1]

Shifts in currency preferences, it is true, will *ceteris paribus* affect the exchange rate. But there are many other reasons why the exchange rate may change. The exchange rate will vary in response to all demand and supply changes that alter the relative scarcity of the two currencies concerned. For example, a shift in demand between domestic money and domestic bonds *ceteris paribus* affects the exchange rate, even if the shift is not part of indirect currency substitution. Since the exchange-rate variable does not discriminate between currency substitution and other factors affecting the relative scarcity of currencies, theoretical considerations indicate that this part of the analysis is incapable of testing for currency substitution.

Are the results consistent with McKinnon's hypothesis? The reported estimates are somewhat difficult to interpret because many of them reveal significant first-order serial autocorrelation of the residuals and nothing is done to correct this. What is most disturbing, however, is the difference in the lags for monetary expansion and the exchange rate: the lag for the exchange rate is one year longer than the lag, if any, for monetary expansion in 7.A.1 and 7.A.2, and it is one year shorter in 7.A.3. Changes in the scarcity of money should have the same effects, regardless of whether the demand for, or the supply, of money has changed. Even if we assume that, for some reason, money-demand changes are more accurately anticipated than money-supply changes, this would only explain the shorter exchange-rate lag in 7.A.3; it would be inconsistent with 7.A.1 and 7.A.2.

Given the inconclusiveness and inconsistency of these results, one might improve the analysis by inserting the (real) exchange-rate variable into a full-fledged money-demand function as Langfeldt and Lehment have done.[2] Their results for the Federal Republic of Germany show that the real exchange rate does not take a significant coefficient and that the coefficient does not even have the hypothesized sign.

McKinnon's second piece of evidence is his finding that US wholesale price inflation is more closely correlated with 'world' monetary expansion that with US monetary expansion. This result is much more difficult to explain without resort to currency substitution. Indeed, McKinnon's story is quite plausible. However, as Spinelli has pointed out,[3] McKinnon's estimates are not at all robust. And even if they were, his approach is not helpful for central banks, which want to find out whether currency substitution is taking place; for the price level is a very late indicator.

It would be at the same time more convincing and more helpful to test for shifts in currency preferences by inserting an unambiguous indicator of the incentive for direct and indirect currency substitution into the money-demand function. Direct and indirect currency substitution is induced by changes in exchange-rate expectations and in relative currency-related risks. Both types of changes are captured by changes in the forward premium/discount. A forward premium indicates that the currency is expected to appreciate and/or is considered to be less risky; for low risk makes for low interest rates.

Several studies – including three of my own – have used the forward premium as the currency-substitution variable in the money-demand function or in transformations thereof. These studies reveal at best marginally significant currency substitution for the US dollar.[4] The evidence is more robust for the Deutsche mark, the Canadian dollar and the Danish kroner.[5]

McKinnon objects to the use of the forward premium or the interest-rate differential on the grounds that 'interest rates are not free to reflect accurately changing assessments of international riskiness unless the national money supply changes with international portfolio preferences'.[6] He believes that, say, an increase in the risk of domestic-currency bonds would not raise the domestic interest rate, because at the higher interest rate money demand would fall short of money supply. This need not be true. If only domestic-currency bonds become more risky, the increase in their interest rate does not reduce the demand for money; for the higher interest rate does not indicate that domestic-currency bonds have become more attractive relative to domestic money.

The situation is different, however, if risk increases for *both* domestic money *and* domestic-currency bonds. This is probably the case which McKinnon has in mind. In this case, it is true that the domestic interest rate need not change, for the relative attractiveness of domestic money and domestic-currency bonds need not be affected by the increase in risk. In this case, international portfolio equilibrium requires an increase in the expected rate of appreciation of the domestic currency to compensate for the higher risk. Since interest rates need not change, the forward premium/discount need not change. It is only the composition of the forward premium which changes: the relative risk premium on domestic-currency assets increases and their expected rate of appreciation rises. Thus, in this specific case, the only conclusive test of indirect currency substitution would be to estimate the relative risk premium in the forward premium/discount and to insert it into a full-fledged money-demand function.

So much for the empirical analysis. I now turn to McKinnon's policy proposal. McKinnon criticizes the Federal Reserve for not sufficiently 'ironing out the American business cycle', and he believes that international coordination of monetary policies would help in this respect. It is important to note that the 'ironing out' at which he aims is not Keynesian fine tuning of monetary policy. He does not want to use monetary shocks to offset fluctuations in employment, but to avoid monetary shocks by adjusting the growth of the money supply to the growth in real money demand. There is widespread agreement that such a policy would be desirable, if it were feasible. If we knew the extent of direct currency substitution, we might use non-sterilized foreign-exchange interventions to offset it. If we knew the extent of indirect currency substitution, we might use non-sterilized or sterilized foreign-exchange interventions to offset it. Unfortunately, we usually do not know it. We often do not even know between which currencies the substitution is taking place. The crucial question is whether we know enough in order to act or whether attempts to offset such shifts would make things worse. Moreover, there is the danger that currency substitution may serve as a pretext for Keynesian fine tuning: the deliberate generation of monetary shocks.

According to McKinnon:

> the central bank should continually adjust the domestic money supply to maintain the exchange equilibrium [exchange-rate constancy?] against 'hard' foreign currencies (that is, those which are convertible and whose own internal purchasing powers are known to be stable).

This statement ignores the diagnostic problem. In a world of currency substitution, it is difficult to tell which foreign central bank is pursuing the least inflationary monetary policy. The current inflation rate does not tell, and if current montary policy turns out to be inflationary, it is too late. The notion of a stable foreign reference currency is a *deus ex machina*, a fiction which assumes the problem away. Moreover, a constant price level abroad and exchange-rate fixity do not imply a constant price level at home, if real factors require real exchange-rate changes.

McKinnon suggests that the central banks of the major industrialized countries should agree on the rate of growth of their joint money supply in order to prevent substitution-induced foreign-exchange interventions from producing unintended inflation or disinflation (McKinnon: 'deflation').

The objective of McKinnon's proposal is worth supporting. The objective is to make sure that if currency substitution is correctly diagnosed and leads to foreign-exchange interventions, both central banks should refrain from sterilization. However, this objective can be attained without international monetary coordination and the implicit weakening of international currency competition. It would be perfectly sufficient to convince the individual central banks that it is not in their enlightened self-interest to sterilize in such cases. As my critique of McKinnon's empirical analysis indicates, it would be even better to convince the central banks that, at least at the present time, they do not know enough about the currency substitution that is taking place to intervene usefully at all.

NOTES

1   Enno Langfeldt and Harmen Lehment, 'Welche Bedeutung haben "Sonderfak-
    toren" für die Erklärung der Geldnachfrage in der Bundesrepublic Deutschland?',
    Weltwirtschaftliches Archiv, vol. 116 (1980), pp. 669–84.
2   ibid.
3   See Franco Spinelli, 'Currency substitution, flexible exchange rates, and the case
    for international monetary co-operation', *IMF Staff Papers* (1983), pp. 755–83.
4   José L. Gutierrez-Camara and Roland Vaubel, 'International shifts in the demand
    for money in a small monetarist model: some further evidence', *Kiel Working Papers*,
    no. 121 (Institut für Weltwirtschaft an der Universität Kiel, 1981).
5   For the Deutsche mark, see Roland Vaubel, 'International shifts in the demand for
    money, their effects on exchange rates and price levels, and their implications for
    the preannouncement of monetary expansion', *Weltwirtschaftliches Archiv*, vol. 116
    (1980), pp. 1–44; Hans-E. Loef, 'Geldnachfrage in einer offenen Volkswirtschaft:
    Bundesrepublik Deutschland 1970–1979', *Kredit und Kapital* (1982), pp. 517–38;
    and John T. Cuddington, 'Currency substitution, capital mobility and money
    demand', *Journal of International Money and Finance*, vol. 2 (1983), pp. 111–33. For the
    Canadian dollar, see Guttierez-Camara and Vaubel, 'International shifts in the
    demand for money in a small monetarist model'. For the Danish kroner, see
    Roland Vaubel 'Monetary divergences and exchange rate changes in the European
    Community: the 1970s', in M. T. Sumner and G. Zis (ed.), *European Monetary
    Union. Progress and Prospects* (Macmillan, London, 1982).
6   Ronald I. McKinnon, *An International Standard for Monetary Stabilization* (Institute for
    International Economics, Washington, DC, 1984).

8

Politics, Trade and Money

SUSAN STRANGE

Beneath the economic conflicts over trade protection, industrial and agricultural subsidies, taxation, exchange rates, interest rates and the rest lie two major political failures – one largely American, the other largely European. It is my contention that none of the distressing and troublesome economic conflicts can be properly understood unless both of these political failures are openly recognized and conscientiously analysed; and that none of them can be resolved unless the political failures are not only acknowledged, but acted upon. The key to the economic reconciliation therefore lies under a political mat. The cure for economic difficulties lies outside the realm of international economic relations, but inside the political systems of the United States and the member states of the European Community.

The first failure, I shall argue, is the failure of the United States to make sure that in an interdependent world economy the creation of credit continues to grow at a steady even pace, neither too profligate nor too parsimonious. The second is the failure of the Europeans to provide for their own defence and security, so as to modify in part, if not altogether, their dependence on the United States and its nuclear weapons systems. Each of these failures, I believe, stands in the way of any constructive dialogue on the management of trade in agriculture, manufactures or services and on the management of exchange rates and economic growth.

I propose therefore to attempt a brief explanation in each case of the nature of each of the political problems and how each affects the disagreements between Europeans and the Americans over economic policies, and to suggest the direction in which it might be useful to look for some solution, or progress towards one. For, in each case, it is possible already to discern the beginnings of a move in the right direction.

Before proceeding to the question of European defence policies – which is an issue of which at least a good many Americans are aware and are to some extent already agreed – let us see why the lack of any coherent system for regulating and monitoring the issue of private credit to the world economy should be directly relevant to some of the thorny questions responsible for the souring of transatlantic relations between the United States and the members of the European Community. Basically, the argument is that it is a failure of a rather particular and fundamental kind that is the reason for the distortion of markets for internationally traded goods and services. But it is not 'market failure' in the sense in which that term is normally used by economists. It is market failure in the sense that the market for credit is exceptionally unstable – partly because the laws of demand and supply do not work in a usual way. Supply is not at all constrained by the cost of production, and bankers, as Fred Hirsch observed, have an innate tendency to overbank[1] and thus to oversupply. Demand, meanwhile, does not always contract as price increases; some borrowers will actually increase their demand for credit when interest rates rise. They are so desperate not to fall into default that price becomes irrelevant to their decision. These are markets, therefore, as every government of a developed economy has discovered, which require active political intervention in the broader interests of the economic community at large in order to check their innate tendencies toward over-exuberant expansion followed by over-fearful contractions. Thus there is always a risk of 'market failure', if that intervention is absent or insufficient.

This simple truth has been more than amply demonstrated by the international financial history of the past decade. Ten years ago, as the first oil price rise hit the non-oil-producing developing countries (NOPECs), the resulting deficits in their balance of payments could have been met in one of three ways. Either they could, conceivably, have cut their imports of oil so drastically that they compensated for the fourfold increase in price – a solution that no one else wanted, neither the OPEC oil producers whose markets would have been undermined, nor the oil companies whose profits would have suffered, nor even the industrialized countries whose exports to the NOPECs would have immediately suffered when the latter's economies ground to a halt for lack of fuel for industry, agriculture and transport.

Or else the industrialized countries in control of multilateral development agencies could have devised a scheme far larger and more comprehensive than the Witteveen Facility cobbled together with some difficulty by the IMF in 1974/5 to ease the NOPECs over the oil price increase, while giving some incentive to conservation and the development of independent energy resources. This the industrialized countries – and, more particularly, the United States (as the Americans made clear at the Washington Conference in February 1974) – were reluctant to do, not so much for the ostensible economic reason that to do so would have been inflationary, as for the real political reason that to do so would have conceded at long last the rich countries' fundamental responsibility for the economic welfare of the poor countries. This was a responsibility they had strenuously denied for thirty years, but one still alleged both by the Marxists and by Third-World radicals persuaded by Prebisch and others of the inherent structural bias of the world market economy against the primary-producing developing countries and in favour of the industrialized developed countries.

Instead, as we all know, the third option was adopted – of leaving it to the banks to 're-cycle' the petrodollars deposited with them by the newly rich oil-producing states. The result was that private bank lending to the NOPECs grew at the phenomenal rate of almost 20 per cent per year in the decade 1970–80. It continued to grow in the last two years of the decade to take care of the NOPEC deficits arising from the second oil price rise of 1978/9, increasing from $26 to $41 billion, by 1980 to $49 billion, and in 1981 to $51 billion.[2] At that point, the system failed. Bank lending in 1982 fell by more than half to $25 billion. The share of NOPEC current-account deficits financed by net bank lending had been 47 per cent in 1981, but fell to 29 per cent in 1982.[3] In the meanwhile, instead of the OPEC countries continuing to deposit their oil revenues with the banks, they themselves became the largest net users of bank credit instead of the largest net suppliers, as they had been throughout the 1970s and even in 1980.

It was no accident that 1982 was the year in which the two biggest LDC borrowers, Mexico and Brazil, got into serious trouble over repayments of interest as well as capital on their bank loans and had to be bailed out through the direct intervention of the United States government. Washington put pressure on the commercial banks to lend more money so that, instead of defaulting, the debtors were able to negotiate rescheduling of their financial obligations both to governments and to the banks.

The banks had their arms twisted to come up with fresh funds to these two countries (and later to Argentina). They were all the more reluctant to keep up the flow of new lending in other directions. Going sharply into reverse gear, they drastically cut their lending to the East Europeans – the Polish debt crisis had come a bit earlier than Mexico's in March 1981 – and to other developing countries. In fact, even without some sort of crisis, the scale of bank lending to LDCs had been so vast that it probably could not have continued indefinitely. Third World and East European debtor countries had tripled their 1976 bank loans by 1982, when their total debt amounted to $626 billion. The result was predictable. Other countries unable to roll over past debt were obliged to ask for rescheduling – no less than 15 of them between the Mexican crisis in August 1982 and the following spring. The only remedy provided by the international financial system when commercial bank money was not to be had at any price was to go to the IMF. That body, in its role as watchdog and guardian of confidence in the system, had no levers to use against the creditors and could only apply the brutal tourniquet treatment of retrenchment, devaluation and deflation on the wretched debtors, making little distinction between those who through folly, profligacy and corruption had 'asked for it', and those who were the unfortunate victims of coincidence and guilt-by-association. In order to stop the spread of panic and in order to maintain some sort of confidence in the financial system, all had to be treated more or less alike.

But although the developing countries were the most visible debtors, they were not the only ones. And although they were the first and worst to suffer, the consequences of the credit squeeze which the banks applied to them did not stop there. Both points – though hardly new – are worth emphasizing in order to substantiate the argument that the major failure of policy-making that lay behind the world recession of the 1980s was in the United States and concerned not trade, but the management of money, and especially of the creation of credit.

It will be recalled that corporate borrowing from the banks had also expanded in the decade before 1982 at about the same rate as LDC borrowing. Even the oil companies, which had been accustomed to finance their costly exploration and development programmes from their own profits, went to the capital markets to borrow. Everywhere, continuing inflation had given rise to cashflow problems, and mergers and takeovers called for extensive financing, even though the financial results of concentration were often disappointing. Yet the corporations' demands on the financial system had been exceeeded by those of the governments of the industrialized countries. Henry Kaufman once reckoned that even excluding the Communist countries, the total amount of credit created in the ten years between 1971 and 1981 had gone from $3.6 trillion ($3,600 billion) to $14.3 trillion. A lot of spoons were dipping into the pot, and the moment inflation slowed down it was inevitable that competition would push up the price of borrowing.[4]

To say, therefore, that the LDCs were the victims of the rising budget deficit of successive US governments is obviously a simplification. US government borrowing was not solely responsible. It was just that the US government, borrowing in dollars and able to 'pay any price, bear any burden' (in John Kennedy's memorable words) to repay in dollars, was always leading the field. Because of the widespread use of the dollar in Eurocurrency markets and in international finance, only the United States could take the decision to stop using inflation to extend the amount of credit in the pot. Once it did so decide in November 1979, the inevitable consequence of rising real interest rates soon followed. It was the combination – not, obviously, entirely coincidental – of rising interest rates and drastically falling commodity prices that felled so many developing countries. According to the World Bank, commodity prices other than oil fell by 14.5 per cent in 1981 and by another 8 per cent in the first half of 1982. Interest payments, which had added $10 billion to LDCs' debt-servicing charges in 1981, continued to rise in real terms in 1982. With oil priced in dollars and the dollar appreciating against other currencies, the combination of adverse factors was overwhelming.[5] It is also worth noting that, under some systems, the inability of one country such as Mexico or Poland to pay its debts on time would have led to that country's loans or bonds being marked down in price, while increasing the price of any new borrowing by that country. That was what normally happened before 1914, when international lending was largely accomplished by the issue of bonds. Under that system, the result of sovereign risk did not spread – as it did in the early 1980s – like wildfire through the whole system, visiting Mexico's affliction on Brazil, Poland's on Hungary.

Nor was this the only way in which the system was vulnerable to some such combination of adverse factors. An important difference between the international credit system of the last century and that of recent years is that, in Victorian Britain, reasonably effective barriers separated the national commercial banking system from the activities of the British overseas banks, who were the major channel for international lending. It was still possible for an overseas operator like Barings to rock the City of London. But the 1890 crisis would surely have been a lot worse if Barings had also been financing British industry and depending on the confidence of High Street depositors. By contrast, the Americans allowed a system to develop in which, despite restrictions on interstate banking, financial power was concentrated in half a dozen very large banks,[6] in which most of the major corporations of the United States and the major employers of American labour were customers of these same half-dozen American banks; in which these banks had come to depend on foreign operations – especially syndicated Eurodollar loans – for a large and sometimes a major part of their income; and in which these foreign operations were inadequately supervised and regulated.

The major weaknesses of bank supervision have now been well documented.[7] Some of these studies, however, hardly mention the most important gap in the system. This is that though by the Basle

Concordats (of 1975, 1979, and 1983) the major central banks agreed
to oversee and, if necessary, support their own commercial banks, not
one of them individually nor all of them collectively had any control
over the total volume of international bank lending. It might expand
fast or slowly; it could even decline. The central banks do not have, nor
do they seek to take, any responsibility for the result. Other gaps are
more widely understood and admitted. The concordats cover only the
banks of the major industrialized countries which report to the Bank for
International Settlements in Basle. Arab, Asian and other banks are
beyond their reach. The restrictive rules drawn by some of them for
these commerical banks are too easily evaded – notably perhaps the US
rule that banks should not make more than 10 per cent of outstanding
loans to any one customer. This has been interpreted in the past to
mean that Pertamina was independent of the Indonesian government
or Petrobras of the Brazilian government. Even more important is the
extent of supervisory ignorance of transactions in the interbank
market, and consequently of the extent of any one bank's dependence
on very short-term support from other banks. Paradoxically, too, the
cross-default clauses introduced by American lawyers into bank-loan
contracts were designed to prevent non-repayment by increasing the
penalties to the defaulter. Yet its effect, when generalized in the system,
was that real default was disguised under the accountant's euphemism
'non-performing loans', thus excusing banks from making timely and
prudential provisions to safeguard both their profitability and their
capital/loans ratios.

That failure, in turn, meant that when an accumulating series of
near-misses (Penn Square, Drysdale and Continental Illinois, to go no
further back) had alerted the US Comptroller of the Currency's office
to the vulnerability of US banks to Third World and especially Latin
American debt, their response was to toughen up their demands. In a
properly-run financial system, regulation should have been tougher in
the earlier profligate moods of the banks, but easier and more encouraging when, for the sake of world trade and prosperity, the need was
to put backbone into the creditors lest in their panic-stricken timidity
they prematurely turned off the debtors' life-support system.

For non-US banks, the temptation in the years 1982–5 to cut back
severely on exposure to the risk of Third World default has been even
greater by reason of the strength of the US dollar. Not only did this add
to the LDCs' import bills including imports of oil, even when oil prices
were falling quite steeply, it also added to the risks in terms of local currencies for non-US banks of operating in a credit market in which
assets were predominantly denominated in dollars.

The hazards and uncertainties of the financial system, in short, have
undoubtedly been exacerbated by the increased uncertainty in the last

decade of the international monetary system – using that phrase in its narrow and conventional sense of the rules and customs governing the international relations of national currencies. The two are distinct, though necessarily related. It is therefore just worth noting in passing that the increased anarchy, uncertainty and volatility of the semi-managed floating exchange-rate system in the decade since 1973 has exacerbated in some measure these and other shortcomings of the international financial (i.e. credit-creating) system. Here, the prime responsibility of the United States as the only government with an irresistible veto over change – as demonstrated, for example, in the Committee of Twenty – and a virtual monopoly of initiative is even more obvious and more generally recognized.

For the result of going by stages from the gold exchange standard to the exclusively paper dollar standard has meant that other countries – and especially those in Europe most open to financial flows – have had to adjust first to the depreciation of the dollar that resulted from US inflation in the mid-1970s, and then to the deflation that came after 1979. Though that deflation was intended to be – and indeed was – a necessary corrective for the excesses of the American domestic economy, the absence of barriers between that and the world financial system meant that everyone else in that system felt the impact of high American interest rates. For many that impact was a good deal more painful than it was for the Americans. While the US economy suffered a check in growth rates and in non-construction investment, the rest of the world was thrown into a depression. On top of the diminished purchasing power in the Latin American debtor states came the reduced spending of the oil producers in the Middle East and elsewhere. Their demand even for LDC exports of manufactures sagged in 1982 from $11.40 billion the year before to $10.80 billion.

The moral of the tale, however, is more that the United States has abused its position of power in the international financial system than that it has lost that power. The difference is an important one. For the conventional wisdom among many international political economists, especially in the United States, is that the troubles of the world – including Third World debt, slow growth in the Western world, protectionism in trade and the precariousness of the banking system – all stem from the unfortunate loss of hegemonial power by the United States. The hegemony theory is familiar and has been extensively expounded by Kindleberger, Gilpin, Keohane and others.[8] Explicitly or implicitly, this theory likens the loss of leadership by the United States from the mid-1960s onwards to the loss of leadership by Britain after the First World War. Evidence is found in the increasing economic size and competitiveness of Japan and the Federal Republic of Germany, not to mention OPEC and the NICs (newly industrializing countries).

The alleged consequence is the impotence of the United States to manage an international reserve and transactions currency and, by this means, to maintain the world economy on an even keel.

What its exponents consistently overlook is that there was nothing *in the system* which obliged the United States to finance its foreign and defence policies by inflation, or which prevented its authorities from exercising some control over the extraterritorial activities of American banks. All these and many other aspects of US policy were matters of choice and not of destiny. Perhaps the accelerated advance towards economic 'interdependence' was so unexpected that the US and others were ill prepared for it. But though glad enough to profit from growing trade and expanding markets, there was no subsequent recognition of the choices that these changes presented, and more particularly the choices presented to the United States as the largest well-spring of international credit for trade and investment.

Briefly, there were three possibilities. In theory, it might have been possible to effect a separation between domestic and international bank activities, so that the banks would have been forewarned that there was no way that the monetary authorities would underwrite the risks they undertook in lending to dubious Third World governments. In view of the transnational character of their corporate clients, however, this would have been difficult, if not impossible. The second possibility was the Brandt Commission solution of endowing multilateral agencies with power and resources (including dollars, of course) adequate for Keynesian demand-management in the world economy. It was already clear, though, from the first oil price rise that the world's economic history in the late twentieth century could be subtitled (with apologies to Raoul Dahl) 'Tales of the Unexpected'. The World Bank and the International Monetary Fund, or some combination of the two, would have had to be able to compensate for the unexpected disappearance of the petrodollars or for a 20 per cent fall in commodity prices. Consistently and decisively, however, the United States had resisted any increase in the power of international economic agencies and any but the most symbolic use of their limited resources as levers on economic activity.

Thus the only remaining choice was for the United States itself to act as an international lender of last resort, not just for its own banks registered in the United States, but for any major bank taking deposits or making loans denominated in dollars. Unless it did this, its own banks could legitimately complain that they were being unfairly handicapped in competition with their foreign rivals. Had the United States chosen to do so, there is little doubt that the importance of New York as the leading international financial centre – especially after the introduction of International Banking Facilities (IBF) in 1980 – to any major

international bank, European or Japanese, gave it the necessary leverage, even without the co-operation of other central banks. In practice,
it seems probable that if the lead had come from the United States, other
governments, would have probably followed suit, making the regulatory authority look (as the IMF looks) more or less like an international
agency, while leaving the real decision-making power with the American government.[9]

The result of refusing any of these three possibilities has been (as we
are all only too well aware) a financial system perpetually on the brink
of collapse. As the late Jan Tumlir said, 'the key issue of the moment is
the precariousness of all financial structures . . . unless a comprehensive plan for the stabilisation of the world economy as a whole is
prepared within a few months the current efforts at salvage will collapse.'[10] Writing in the summer of 1983, Tumlir foresaw the fragility
of an economic recovery largely based on stimulation applied to the US
economy, but failing (like the other beers in the Heineken adver-
tisement) to reach other parts of the system. For that to happen, confidence had to be restored; the debtors had to find means to service their
debts, and the creditors had to maintain a flow of credit sufficient for
the continued growth of production and trade.

This is where the remedies prescribed by the IMF teams are inherently contradictory. The banks can only be persuaded by the IMF
– except in certain cases of special economic strategic interest to the
United States – to keep up this flow of credit, if they can see clear progress by the debtor towards a reduction of budgetary deficits in government spending and towards a surplus on the balance of payments. Yet to
bring this about in time to stop the banks from running away altogether,
the emetic has to be so drastic that the patient is brought to the point of
collapse. Only the prospect of being cut off altogether for years to come
from foreign capital and technology persuades these countries, in utter
desperation, to comply with the IMF's prescriptions.

Two implications follow from this analysis. One is that, as in the inter-
war period, the lack of purchasing power due to the shrinkage of credit is
the prime cause of economic depression. Those who become agitated
about the resort to protectionism in trade therefore are misdirecting their
attention to a symptom, while failing to attack the malady itself. The
symptom, moreover, is a pimple, not an abscess: the fall in world trade
has been of the order of 1–2 per cent at most, compared with over 25
per cent in the early 1930s. The reason, I believe, lies in the internationalization of production between the 1930s and the 1980s, and the
immunity of inter- and intra-corporate trading to the availability of
either credit or of foreign exchange. Bilateralism is not, as the last
GATT report alleged, something to be feared. In this larger sense, it is
to be welcomed as a support to the maintenance of world trade.[11]

The other implication is that the cure for slow growth is not to be found in economic summits, nor in other attempts to reach a better convergence of national economic policies. This has been most recently advocated by James Tobin, in an essay contributed to a Council of Foreign Relations publication.[12] But if a major contributory cause of economic depression lies outside the major industrializing economies in the reduced purchasing power of OPEC and the LDCs, coordinating the rich countries' economic policies – although it may conceivably be helpful – is only dealing with part of the problem. In each of these countries, the major corporations depend for their profitability on a world market. The proportion of sales to LDCs is less indicative of their importance than of their utility at the margin, where the difference is decided between profit and loss. The result of Micawberish indifference to the foreign-exchange positions of non-OECD countries has been that the major OECD countries from 1979 onwards were led to apply overkill to their own economies, thus producing a severe decline in growth and employment throughout the world.

Nor is the reason for the failure of macroeconomic policy coordination due only to the fact that it leaves untouched the stop-go response of the banking system to Third World borrowing. Most of all, perhaps, it is due to political factors and, in particular, to the impotence of European countries, dependent on the United States for their defence and security, to exercise any influence whatever on the United States' economic and monetary management. At four out of the nine summit conferences, European heads of states have pleaded strongly with the United States to take a lead in substantially lowering interest rates. All their speeches have been like water off a duck's back. And the reason is very clear. The United States could point to the burdens of its defence programme as an immovable obstacle to the reduction of the US government budget deficit. It was this which made it necessary to pay high interest rates to anyone, foreigner or native, who would lend money to Uncle Sam. So long as the Americans were spending twice as large a proportion of their national income on a defence programme which included not only an expensive nuclear weapons system, but the added extravagance of keeping large US forces permanently in Europe, the Europeans could hardly complain of the economic consequences of the *Pax Americana*.[13] The point was clearly made by Henry Kissinger in 1979[14] and by John Connally more than ten years ago. It has been repeated by American political scientists and political economists.[15] One of these even proposed that the United States withdraw its forces unilaterally as a means of bringing the Europeans to their senses.[16] As Marina Whitman recently observed, the original 'unspoken compact' was that the US would subordinate its short-run national interest to the general welfare of the world economy, while

Europe conceded special financial privileges to the United States 'as a concomitant of the special responsibilities it undertook for the military security and economic stability of the non-communist world'.[17] That bargain is breaking up under the pressures on the United States to give priority to its own national economic interests in the 1980s depression, and as a result of divided European opinion about the nature and planned use of American nuclear missiles for European defence. President Reagan's verbal bellicosity and apparent intransigence on arms-control issues adds to European unease. As Whitman says, what is needed is a new bargain in which the Europeans would more willingly share the responsibility for maintaining Western security, while the United States would modify its tendency towards 'global unilateralism'.

But for the moment, the absence of such a new bargain not only makes Washington deaf to European complaints – even more deaf than the Europeans are to American complaints against the CAP and European protection of service industries – but it obstructs the way ahead for the Community itself. Monetary co-operation, in particular, cannot progress much further unless the ECU is made attractive enough to offer a serious challenge to the dollar. This it cannot do so long as it is the US economy which leads economic recovery; and so long as the security issue inhibits the Europeans (and especially the Germans) from making such a provocative move. This is not to dismiss as unimportant any of the internal domestic political reasons behind the stalemate in Brussels, only to assert that these would seem less formidable if the major foreign and defence policy obstructions common to all were to disappear.

Yet some hopeful signs of change on the way can be detected on both the American and the European political horizons. On the long-term management of Third World debt, the omens are not quite so ominous as they were a year ago. The Reagan Administration succeeded in getting congressional support for the IMF quota increase and for the GAB extension to match Saudi Arabia's $3 billion, even though agreement is still lacking on supplementary funding for IDA. The restraint of the Latin American debtors in the past year and their rejection of any plan for collective default puts Mr William Clark's horror-story, *Cataclysm – the North–South confrontation of 1987* more firmly than ever into the realms of fancy. Perhaps most important, the shock of the Continental Illinois near-collapse has awakened much American financial opinion to the vulnerability of domestic financial stability to shock waves from the international environment. Faith in repeated rescheduling of the kind now going on with Poland, Mexico, Nigeria, Brazil, Argentina, etc. is faltering, and this is a necessary prerequisite for more fundamental rethinking of future long-term policies.

On the European side, too, there are some hopeful signs of change
on the way. The most important is probably the quiet high-level talks
on weapons procurement and forward planning that have been pursued in 1984 by the French and German governments. Developing
greater complementarity between the two major continental powers is
the necessary prerequisite for any broader-based move towards the
'Europeanization' of NATO. Another hopeful sign is the concession by
the German NATO commander of the necessity for some defence in
depth in the event of any threatened incursion from the East. The
pretence that all the available defence forces had to be equally distri-
duted along the entire frontier only exaggerated the disparity between
Western and Eastern ground forces, whereas any move toward a more
realistic assessment of the problem must contribute very substantially
to the confidence that Europeans can put in the third option, avoiding
both precarious dependence on the American nuclear umbrella and the
supine adoption of a non-nuclear 'neutrality'.

In the current situation, Britain, unfortunately, has not been very
helpful. Although contributing a higher percentage of GNP to defence
than any of its European partners, the British government has nevertheless contributed too little politically and morally. Things might be
changed, however, if, first, a response could be made to the Irish
government's appeal for serious joint efforts to resolve the Northern
Irish question, thus releasing British military resources for European
defence; and second, if Britain would make the significant gesture of
formally joining the European Monetary System and adding the potential of its financial power to that of the other governments. Both moves
would open up new possibilities of collaboration on security questions
between the major European states.

In short, the conclusion must be that the solution for transatlantic
economic conflict does not lie, as so many Americans believe, in the
recovery of US hegemony, but in a more even balance of power within
the Atlantic alliance. Only by this means will it be possible to achieve
both the better management of the global financial system (and therefore greater stability in the world market economy) and, in the long
term, a more stable balance of power between the Western and Soviet
alliance systems.

NOTES

1 F. Hirsch, *Money International* Allen Lane, London, 1967; J. K. Galbraith, *Money –
   whence it came and where it went* (Penguin, 1975); C. P. Kindleberger, *Panics, Manias
   and Crashes*, (Macmillan, 1978).
2 BIS and Fund staff estimates, *IMF Survey*, 22 August 1983. Actually the figures are
   an underestimate, since they are based on data supplied to banks in the BIS

reporting area only and take no account therefore of lending channelled through Asian, Middle Eastern and other non-BIS financial centres and banks.

3 'International capital markets – developments and prospects', *IMF Occasional Paper*, No. 23 (1983). As much as 60 per cent of the current-account deficits of LDCs from 1979 to 1981 was paid with commercial-bank borrowing.

4 Darrel Delamaide, *Debt Shock* (1984), p. 8, *Federal Reserve Bank of New York Quarterly Review* (Autumn 1982), p. 23.

5 International Bank for Reconstruction and Development, *Annual Report* (1982).

6 A. Sampson, *The Money Lenders* (1981).

7 B. Cohen, *Banks and the Balance of Payments: Private Lending and the International Adjustment Process* (1981); T. Killick, *Third World Debt* (ODI, 1983); M. S. Mendelssohn, *Commercial Banks and the Restructuring of Cross-Border Debt* (Group of Thirty, 1983); OECD, *External Debt of Developing Countries* (1982); E. Rothschild, 'Banks: the coming crisis' and 'Banks: the politics of debt', *New York Review of Books* (May and July 1976).

8 C. Kindleberger, *The World in Depression*.

9 For a fuller discussion of this, see M. Lipton and S. Griffith-Jones, 'International lenders of last resort: are changes required?, *Midland Bank, Occasional Paper* (Midland Bank, London, 1984); also J. Guttentag and R. Heming, 'The lender of last resort function in an international context', *Princeton Essay in International Finance*, no. 151 (1983); also S. Strange, 'The credit crisis', *SAIS Review* (Washington, DC, Summer 1983).

10 J. Tumlir, 'The world economy today: crisis or new beginning?', *National Westminster Bank Quarterly Review* (August 1983), p. 26.

11 For a development and explanation of this argument, see S. Strange 'Protectionism and world politics', *International Organization*, vol. 39, no. 2, (1985), and also 'GATT and the politics of North-South trade', *Australian Outlook* (August 1984).

12 J. Tobin 'Unemployment in the 1980s: macroeconomic diagnosis and prescription' in A. Pierre (ed.), *Unemployment and Growth in the Western Economies* (Council on Foreign Relations, New York, 1984).

13 Percentages of GNP spent on defence in 1980 averaged 4.4 per cent for all NATO countries: 5.6 per cent for the United States; 5.1 per cent for Britain; 4.1 per cent for the Federal Republic of Germany; 3.3 per cent for France; and 2.4 per cent for Italy.

14 H. Kissinger, *Time Magazine*, 5 March 1979.

15 D. Calleo, 'Inflation and security', *Foreign Affairs* (Winter 1982); M.V.N. Whitman, 'Persistent unemployment; economic policy perspectives in the United States and Western Europe', in A. Pierre (ed.), *Unemployment and Growth in the Western Economies*, (CFR, 1984).

16 Lawrence Radway, 'Toward the Europeanisation of NATO', ISA mimeo paper, Mexico City, April 1983. The narrowly-defeated Nunn Amendment put to the US Senate in 1984 also proposed progressive withdrawal of US troops unless European members of NATO increased their defence contributions.

17 Whitman, 'Persistent unemployment . . .'.

Comment 1

BENJAMIN J. COHEN

Susan Strange's paper is just the sort of contribution we have come to expect of her – interesting, provocative, and full of enlightening insights. But, being English, she will surely not take offence if I remind her of the oath taken by witnesses in Anglo-Saxon courts of law: I promise to tell the truth, the whole truth and nothing but the truth. Strange has told the truth – *some* truth – but not the whole truth, and certainly not nothing but the truth.

Let us begin with the truth. Strange's basic proposition is that international economic relations must be *managed*, in order to cure market difficulties and resolve policy conflicts; and that the key therefore lies, in her words, 'under a political mat'. Economic troubles are *political* failures, she says. And at this high level of generalization, I could scarcely agree more. Where I disagree is on the specifics, many of the more practical points of her analysis, which of course are by no means unimportant. In the comment that follows, I shall attempt to explain where my disagreement lies, and also to suggest some alternative insights on these issues, by addressing two key questions. First, *why* must international economic relations be managed? Second *how* may they be managed?

First, the *why*. There are two reasons. One, arising at the private level, is the risk of *market failures*, of which there are many examples to choose from. Strange emphasizes one such example – the failure in recent years of the private financial system, which first lent abundantly to deficit countries in East Europe and the Third World, and then, just when financing was most needed, went sharply into reverse gear, cutting debtors off without (in her words) a 'life-support system'. As she

says, a properly run financial system requires active political intervention to check tendencies toward both 'over-exuberant expansion'
and 'over-fearful contraction'. Niels Thygesen emphasized another
such example when he described the high degree of short-term volatility
and unprecedented medium-term misalignments of market-deter-
mined exchange rates in the floating currency world that we have been
living in for the last decade.

The second reason, arising at the government level, is the risk of
policy conflicts, which almost inevitably occur in the absence of conscious
efforts at communication and co-operation. That such a danger of conflict exists is one of the most fundamental insights of game theory; it is
also the basic point of the redundancy, or *n*th-country, dilemma as
originally expounded by Robert Mundell. The policies of individual
nations, so long as they are formulated and implemented independently, will only rarely turn out to be mutually consistent. Examples
are rampant in international economic relations, particularly in the
trade field, as illustrated in previous chapters in this book.

This brings us to the *how*. How may international economic relations
be managed? Like any well-run business enterprise or public agency,
we need some kind of effective 'management system' – what I have
elsewhere called an 'organizing principle'. In theory, there are four
possibilities: automaticity – a regime of automatic adherence to universally agreed norms and rules; supranationality – a regime run by a
world economic authority; hegemony – a regime managed by a single
dominant power; or pluralism – a regime conducted through formal
negotiation and bargaining. Of these four, the first two are manifestly
unrealistic in a world of jealous and competing national sovereignties.
In reality, the choice lies somewhere between the third and fourth,
hegemony and pluralism.

With respect to the former of these two, Strange mentions the so-
called theory of hegemonic stability as developed by a number of
scholars in the United States. In fact, the theory comes in two forms – a
weak form, in which hegemony simply tends to be *associated with* stability in the international economy; and a strong form, in which
hegemony is said to be *necessary* for such stability. Strange ridicules the
strong form of the theory, and I agree. There are indeed alternatives to
hegemony. But she also ridicules the weak form, arguing that the
United States has not lost its power, but rather abuses it. Here I take
issue.

The evidence of US abuse, presumably, is to be found in its recent
policy behaviour which, as many observers (including myself) agree,
has indeed tended to be destabilizing, owing to instability in America's
handling of its own economic and monetary affairs. According to
Strange, this represents a discontinuity of performance rather than of

power. America's hegemony, she argues, is as great as ever: Europe is still 'dependent' on the United States; the 'paper dollar standard' still exists, to which others must adjust; the 'lead' must still come from Washington. I disagree. In my opinion, Strange both overestimates US power and misunderstands US performance.

In fact, US power has declined far more than she suggests. One need only compare present monetary arrangements with the Bretton Woods system created some four decades ago, when the creation of international liquidity was essentially a function of domestic US economic policy. In more recent years, all that has changed, as commercial banks gradually took over the role of liquidity creation through their lending for balance-of-payments purposes. Liquidity creation became largely 'privatized'. As a result, America lost power not only relative to other governments, in Europe and Japan, but also to the *markets*. The United States may still be *primus inter pares* in the international system, but it is certainly no longer dominant enough to look after matters entirely on its own.

Suppose, however, that it could still do so. Strange feels that America should act, first and foremost, in the interest of systemic stability – an understandable attitude. Put differently, the US should identify its national interest fundamentally with the systemic interest, and therefore with Europe's interest. This reminds me of Henry Higgins's complaint in the musical comedy 'My Fair Lady': why can't a woman be more like a man? In other words, why can't the United States be more like Europe, and act on Europe's behalf? The answer is obvious – because America has its own goals and objectives, its own fish to fry. In fact, the US has always been torn between a drive to pursue its own national interests, narrowly defined, and a willingness to sacrifice some of those immediate interests for the sake of broader and longer-term systemic goals. There is no discontinuity of performance here. Throughout the twentieth century, American foreign policy has generally tended to swing between moods of co-operation and self-sacrifice (for example, the Marshall Plan) and moods of self-assertion and 'global unilateralism' (to quote Strange's phrase). In this respect, the US is just like everyone else – *self*-interested. If this is an abuse of power, then every country everywhere is guilty of the same charge.

This brings me to the principle of pluralism – the only remaining possibility. A pluralistic regime is by definition political. But let us try to be more specific. If all governments share an interest in the successful management of economic relations, what prevents them from achieving it? The shorthand answer is 'politics' – which is merely a simple way of referring to the very complex question of distributional gains and losses. As a political scientist might ask, whose ox is gored? Negotiation means that there will normally tend to be losers as well as winners as compromises are hammered out, not only between countries (the distributional issue Strange emphasizes), but, even more importantly, within countries. Here we approach the true heart of the matter.

Consider trade policy. If protectionist barriers cannot be reduced, it is more probably because someone benefits from them. It follows, therefore, that liberalization may be impossible unless the potential losers can somehow be compensated by the potential winners, for example, through adjustment assistance programmes and the like. Otherwise, those who gain from the status quo will simply resist any effective change. The same point holds for other areas of possible economic conflict as well. The key is compensation, within nations as well as between them – in game-theory terms, what are called side-payments; in plain language, bribes. Unless effective and convincing compensation mechanisms can be designed, coalitions will not be found to support desired outcomes, hence economic relations will not be successfully managed. That is what is meant by the shorthand answer 'politics'. I submit that this is the real issue underlying Strange's paper, and defines the essential problem toward which our thinking should now be directed.

Comment 2

MICHEL AGLIETTA

The great merit of Professor Strange's analysis is to propose an interpretation of the persistent difficulties in Euro-American relations, and, one might add, the internal divisions within the EC, which is placed in the context of the world economic crisis, together with East–West strategic rivalries and the arms race. It might appear that divergence on the management of public finance, aid for sectoral restructuring, trade protection, interest-rate levels, exchange-rate instability and the effects of international capital mobility, constitute distinct problems which can be treated separately. Strange, on the contrary, thinks and affirms with conviction that these problems arise and continually reappear because they result from conflicts which grow on fertile ground. This is above all due to the failure of international monetary regulation, which is itself a product of the grave disorders in the whole mechanism of credit.

This interpretation is seductive and should be examined with attention, because it has far-reaching implications. If it is correct, the transformation of the international monetary system by the provision of viable rules is the primary task, which could lead to the re-establishment of a certain degree of compatibility of differing national interests. The Strange thesis is concerned with some of the theoretical questions raised in giving priority to the analysis of the system of international credit; the political problems arising from the overlapping nature of monetary disorders and the constraints imposed by international indebtedness. In this brief comment, I would like to put forward several observations on these two types of problems.

WHY IS THE ANARCHY IN THE INTERNATIONAL CREDIT SYSTEM SO SEVERE?

Strange thinks that the rupture in the rhythm of international liquidity creation, the contraction of credit since 1981 after excessive indebtedness, especially in certain less developed countries, is the basic cause of the very deep world recession of 1981–3. Other theorists consider that Euro-bank credit, the major component of total international credit, has no global monetary incidence. It is only a more efficient method of financial intermediation which assures international capital mobility. Which of these two interpretations is correct is an important question and it seems to me that Strange's diagnosis is more pertinent.

Recent theoretical work on the nature of the risk of insolvency shows that credit does not have an equilibrium price that can be derived from a rational expectations framework. The borrowing–lending relationship is bilateral and information about the quality of the real assets which motivate the loans is both incomplete and asymmetrical. This relationship thus gives rise to conflicting strategies, where concealment is rational behaviour. Borrowers may have an interest in increasing their exposure to risk during economic booms (leading to overindebtedness) in order to force the hand of their creditors and to place the latter before a *fait accompli* when the economic downturn occurs. Lenders are incapable of perfect discrimination between their clients in terms of the actual risk each represents. They must therefore operate a rationing system so as to force the borrowers to declare these risks indirectly. The whole credit system is thus blemished by moral hazard, which can easily turn into cumulative movements oscillating between overlending and excessive restrictiveness. The existence of precise rules governing the activities of banks, together with a body in ultimate authority and a well-defined lender of last resort, are the essential conditions for credit regulation. It is clear that these are lacking in the case of international credit provided by the Eurobanks.

The international credit system, as with a domestic credit mechanism, is no more than a means of allocating a given quantity of savings. Nevertheless, a credit system is endowed with its own power of expansion, which creates liquid assets that stimulate effective demand and encourage savings equal to that part of effective demand generated by investment. Strange remarks that in the 1970s this power of expansion had increased in a disquieting manner, because of the integration of domestic and international credit mechanisms resulting from the universal usage of the dollar. This international credit system was indifferent to various exchange-rate regimes and thus did not change substantially before or after 1973. The essential characteristic of this system is that a credit expansion is demand-determined and creates a corresponding increase in liquidity, which avoids the strict controls placed on the domestic money supply (M1). The transmission of inflation by this mechanism can only be halted by the financial suffocation of the debtors, deliberately provoked by the US monetary authorities, thus transforming unbridled indebtedness into financial crisis.

The credit system has freed itself of monetary constraints by combining different mechanisms which developed progressively under the indifference, if not the active complicity, of the central banks, obsessed by the control of the stock of money. First, the dollar obligations of American banks became the universal form of international money. This is why the financing of a deficit anywhere in the world by American banks leads to a transfer of deposits, and thus creates a new possibility for the rest of the world to borrow, without American banks losing reserves. Nothing is altered if the foreign commercial banks request conversion of these deposits by their central banks, because the latter hold their exchange reserves in US Treasury bonds or other monetary assets, or else they supply redeposit in the Eurobanks, but do not deposit with the Federal banks.

The expansion of credit has no endogenous constraint, because it creates an increase in liquidity for the rest of the world without an offsetting reduction in liquidity in the United States. This asymmetry, which characterizes the international credit system, is the origin of the power of expansion which is capable of monetizing international deficits and thereby suppressing the progressive constraints to their absorption. The expansionary power of credit is multiplied by the way banks manage their liabilities and by bank policies in favour of large-scale loans to support the increase in their credits. This is the fundamental reason for the financial innovations that integrated the money markets and that caused liabilities that are outside the conventionally controlled monetary aggregates to appear as the counterpart of these credits. This is why bank credit has grown faster than the strictly defined world money stock, its counterpart being found in the explosive growth of liabilities of banks and other financial institutions that have been considered as non-monetary. The Eurodollar is only a continuation of these mechanisms, the net effect being a credit expansion which could be accompanied or not, depending on how the corresponding deposits were held, by an increase in the money stock inside the United States or abroad. In all cases, the flexibility of the supply of credit and its negation of reserve requirements is the fuel for inflation.

WHY IS THE DEBT PROBLEM AT THE SAME TIME BOTH MONETARY AND FINANCIAL?

In a credit system which has lost its internal regulators, one can only stop the inflationary path to over-indebtedness by an action that is both brutal and extremely short-sighted, consisting of the stifling of demand for credit by raising financial charges to dizzying heights. This places the whole burden of the past disorder on those who are the weakest debtors, both private agents and states. The unexpected reduction in the value of the stock of debt also has repercussions on the most fragile parties within the credit system. These are the Eurobanks, which are now vulnerable to withdrawals of funds either provoked by losses of confidence or by the needs of the previous creditors who have now become borrowers (OPEC). As long-term borrowers have a pressing need for new distress loans, whilst the banks are trying to reduce the supply of credit to rebuild their own liquidity position, the international credit system becomes very vulnerable to interest rates in the American money market. Furthermore, the existing structures do not allow monetary policy to exercise strict control over the Eurobanks. This is because they are under-capitalized, lacking in reserves and without any obligation to hold reserves in any case, as well as lacking direct access to an institutionally responsible lender of last resort. Debt financing is the only way open to them. This is how deficiencies in monetary regulation have made the stability of the whole credit system come to depend upon the consolidation of the financial structure of the principal debtors, because the debt is highly concentrated among a few countries.

In this respect the situation is more than just worrying. Simulations with financial constraints imposed on these countries for the future – that is, a balanced current account excluding interest repayments – suggest that for the majority of the countries in question growth rates will be less than is necessary to prevent a fall in real income per head. If one includes the additional constraint deriving from past borrowing, the debtor countries would have to produce a current-account surplus in order to at least repay the interest on past borrowing. In this situation the increase in net indebtedness would stabilize and solvency ratios would progressively improve. However, such a financial adjustment poses a dilemma. If it is rapid, it entails a collapse of production that is socially unsustainable and economically disastrous. If it is spread out over time, which seems more likely following recent agreements, total debt will continue to grow at least temporarily and the cumulative external surplus needed will be even larger than in the case of brutal adjustment. In such a case, the economic loss for a country will become even greater.

Such structural adjustment is totally unreasonable if interest rates do not fall and are not subsequently stabilized (at low levels) in the long run. This, however, would imply that the whole system of credit would have to become again the subject of strict and continuous monetary control, in order to avoid periods of indebtedness which feed on each other in real vicious circles. This reform of the whole credit structure cannot be achieved without overcoming a major intellectual obstacle: the abandonment of monetarist theories in which credit is passive (it has a counterpart in a liability) and is thus without significance or importance.

Comment 3

JONATHAN STORY

Professor Strange's thesis may be briefly summarized in the form of two propositions: the United States fails to live up to its responsibilities as a world banker; the states of Western Europe will achieve greater autonomy from United States dollar policies on condition that they reduce their dependence on the United States in matters of defence. Are these propositions challengeable, and does the conclusion follow that the solution to permanent transatlantic economic conflicts lies in a more even balance of power in the Atlantic alliance?

Before getting argumentative for the sake of debate, it may be worth while sketching in the wide areas of agreement between myself and what I take to be Strange's position. The arena of international finance is not identifiable with the asceptic market-place, beloved of the economics fraternity, but is endogenous to international relations between states. Financial markets are therefore fashioned by the domestic policies of states, and by their rivalry and co-operation. Their behaviour indicates awareness on the part of market participants that one of the permanent features of international politics is the inequality between sovereign states. As Thucydides remarked, the strong take what they may and the weak suffer what they must.

It is therefore within the same terms of reference of Strange's paper that my remarks fall. First, the privilege of acting as a world banker has been acquired over a long period of time and is supported by a dense network of vested interests ranging from Treasury officials, bankers, international corporations, oil sheiks or Moscow Norodny. The international role of the dollar serves to finance American outlays at home and abroad, whether those be private or public. It is sustained by the country's huge capital markets, and by the various uses to which it is put in international trade by states and corporations. It gives the American economy a flexibility in policy available to no other state, as President Mitterrand discovered belatedly on coming to power in 1981, only a few months after Reagan's inauguration. Both France and the United States pursued reflationary policies, but in the conditions of the 1980s only the United States was able to finance ever larger deficits.

Such flexibility in policy deriving from the privileged role of the dollar in international financial relations is not an asset that American policy makers are likely to abandon lightly. The argument that became current in Washington following the decision of President Nixon in 1971 to end the convertibility of the dollar into gold was that the world responsibilities falling on American shoulders exempted the United States from the usual stabilization policies associated with profligate governments. Other central banks would have to adapt either by absorbing dollars into reserves, or by allowing the markets supplied with dollars to set relative currency prices. As Strange points out, the same argument is used in modified form in the 1980s, when European heads of state or government ask Washington to reduce the budget deficit, but to no avail at all. It is not just that the administration can cite the Soviet threat and the cost of defending Western Europe; more importantly, perhaps, the transformations in domestic American politics since 1973–4 are such as to make agreement on anything else but a deficit budget an impossibility. One may conclude that American domestic political cohesion has come to depend on the external policy flexibility related to the dollar.

This points to a simple modification to the conclusion that the solution for transatlantic economic conflict lies in a more even balance of power in the Atlantic alliance: United States officials in charge of international monetary relations are unlikely to duplicate the State Department's enthusiasm for European integration in the 1950s, by encouraging the emergence in Europe of a rival to the dollar, sustained by a European Monetary Fund. On the contrary, the concern expressed in the Treasury over the initial scope of the Giscard–Schmidt proposals of 1978 leading to the constitution of the EMS in March 1979 indicate that further moves to a European monetary identity could just as well aggravate transatlantic economic conflicts.

What, then, of the second proposition, to the effect that the states of Western Europe will only achieve greater autonomy from the United States dollar policy if they reduce their dependence in matters of defence? Three comments may be made. First, the United States has achieved the general objective of securing the dollar's primacy in all major post-war negotiations, even if there have been occasions when the Europeans and Japanese have affected the outcome to some degree.

Thus, de Gaulle's challenge to the dollar in 1965–8 was followed by the explosion of central bank reserves, and the rapid expansion of the Eurocurrency markets; the Europeans failed to stem the tide towards floating exchange rates in the early 1970s; in 1979, the EMS was set up to establish more stable exchange rates, and at the same time Washington was becoming less enamoured of floating; under Reagan, the dollar's supremacy was unchallenged.

Second, the Western Europeans have been divided over monetary matters on non-security grounds. De Gaulle's ambiguous proposal of February 1965 to return to a gold standard, or to its equivalent, ran against the intellectual climate favouring greater discretionary powers to public officials. Even in the French government, there were considerable differences as to how the international monetary system could be best reformed. By the early 1970s, the gap between words and deeds in Western Europe was widening. The talk was about keeping to stable exchange rates, but domestic monetary policies – including the French – could not have been better designed to promote the shift to floating exchange rates. During the discussions on the creation of the EMS, one of the principal bones of contention was the burden to be borne by surplus as against deficit countries – duplicating the discussions earlier in the 1970s in the EC, and indeed those between the United States and other Western European countries, on the one hand, and the Federal Republic of Germany on the other. Finally, the dollar policies of the Reagan Administration have served the domestic strategies of particular groups across Western Europe. Thus tighter economic conditions in the 1980s undermined the reigning conservative parties in France, Italy, Greece and Spain, but their continuation equally has reassured conservatives that strict limits are set to social reforms. World recessions, in short, have their advantages.

Third, there is precious little sign of any will to greater autonomy in Western Europe. On the contrary, the present condition of Western Europe may be likened to eighteenth-century Germany, which fell back after the Treaty of Westphalia into a comfortable provincialism, where each prince had his opera house, mini-Versailles and court retainers. The states accommodated the ambitions of the great powers of the period – France, Austria or Prussia. They did not seek to combine with a view to altering the European balance of power. Similarly, the Western European states seem to have come to terms with their dependence. Their opinion is held in thrall by periodic reminders of Soviet military power, and therefore of American protection; their national currencies are tied into the dollar standard; the size and openness of their economies is such that each state is drawn inwards in efforts to manage a delicate reconciliation between national cohesion and competitiveness; foreign and defence policies are often more the expression of party political struggles and positioning, and seldom form consistent priorities to which all significant domestic actors accommodate. Switzerland, Finland and France are examples which come to mind, but all pursue some form of neutrality policy.

American preponderance, the divisions among Western Europeans and their lack of any will to greater autonomy hardly point to any early move in Western Europe to redress the balance in the Atlantic alliance. If that is so, then Strange's argument would lead to the conclusion that economic conflicts in the alliance can only sharpen. My position, on the other hand, is that the Europeans fear the inevitable conflict with the United States, which must accompany any further move to union, most especially in the fields of monetary and defence policies. But because the United States requires the flexibility deriving from the dollar privileges to maintain national cohesion, then acquiescence by Western Europeans in their fate may earn them the gratitude of American policy-makers intent on sustaining a financial order increasingly biased to the American national interest; but such acquiescence is increasingly at the cost of their own national and regional cohesion.

Why is it that the Western Europeans have become so notably introverted over the last fifteen to twenty years? One answer is that 'rigidities' have been allowed to accumulate nationally and regionally, which impede the further development of European markets. The first task, then, of the Western European states is to create domestic economic and social conditions that are more compatible with progress towards a market of continental dimensions. Each state has enough on its hands for the next few years to get its own house in order, as a contribution to the wider European scheme of things, not to venture into any foreign policy revisionism. The context of domestic Western European politics is set by the Atlantic alliance, where all states recognize the leadership of the United States. The most that the Western European states can do in the area of foreign policy is to ensure that the EPC (European Political Cooperation) mechanism is coordinated with Washington, and that communications between Washington and the European capitals are as intense as possible. A coordinated and effective European defence effort in conventional defence and in arms procurement would encourage the United States in its continued commitment to the security of Europe.

An opposite answer is that the internal 'rigidities' of Western Europe are the accumulated result of defensive social reactions to disturbances arising from determined efforts to cling on to American coat tails, long after the Atlantic alliance has passed its prime. Thus, as the United States in the 1960s began to export inflation, and reverse the terms of the original deal with Western Europe on defence and finance, Western European states accepted higher domestic inflation rates than would have been necessary, but at the cost of increasingly conflictual labour relations; they then accepted more volatile exchange rates, despite the implications for mounting protectionist pressures. Most of the growth in government revenues in the last fifteen years or so is due to inflation; much of European protectionism lies in the field of non-tariff barriers and procurement. It follows that a more vigorous European policy requires a combination of internal and foreign policy measures: internal measures aiming to facilitate the creation of more efficient markets, and foreign policy measures designed to reduce the disturbances from without. This means the move to a European Federal Reserve Board system, and the organization of a confederal defence.

The European Community and those states closely associated with it in Western Europe account for more than 30 per cent of world GNP, compared to less than 30 per cent for the United States and about 10 per cent for the Soviet Union. Western Europe is the heart of the world trading system. Its potential is vast – disproportionate to the talents of its present political leaders. They would do well to consult Thucydides, that the weak suffer what they must and the strong take what they can. There is much to take, but also much to defend in Europe.

Index